Chasing Freedom

The Philippines' Long Journey
to Democratic Ambivalence

THE SUSSEX LIBRARY OF

Series Editor: Prof. Mina Roces, School of Humanities and Languages, The University of New South Wales

This Sussex Library series publishes original scholarly work in various disciplines (including interdisciplinary and transnational approaches) under the rubric of Asian and Asian American studies.

China's Rising Profile: The Great Power Tradition, Harsh V. Pant, King's College London.

Chinese Identity in Post-Suharto Indonesia: Culture, Media, Religion and Language, Chang-Yau Hoon, Singapore University.

Dancing the Feminine: Gender & Identity Performances by Indonesian Migrant Women, Monika Swasti Winarnita, University of Victoria, BC, Canada.

Family Ambiguity and Domestic Violence in Asia: Concept, Law and Process, edited by Maznah Mohamad, National University of Singapore, and Saskia E. Wieringa, University of Amsterdam.

Han Shan, Chan Buddhism and Gary Snyder's Ecopoetic Way, Joan Qionglin Tan, Hunan University, China and University of Wales, Lampeter.

Heteronormativity, Passionate Aesthetics and Symbolic Subversion in Asia, Saskia E. Wieringa, University of Amsterdam, with Abha Bhaiya and Nursyahbani Katjasungkana.

The Independence of East Timor: Multi-Dimensional Perspectives – Occupation, Resistance, and International Political Activism, Clinton Fernandes, University of New South Wales.

In Women's Words: Violence and Everyday Life during the Indonesian Occupation of East Timor, 1975–1999, Hannah Loney.

Negotiating Malay Identities in Singapore: The Role of Modern Islam, Rizwana Abdul Azeez, Institute of Southeast Asian Studies.

Media Events in Web 2.0 China: Interventions of Online Activism, Jian Xu, University of New South Wales, Australia.

The Politics of Dress in Asia and the Americas, edited by Mina Roces and Louise Edwards, University of New South Wales, Sydney and University of Technology, Sydney.

Pool of Life: The Autobiography of a Punjabi Agony Aunt, Kailash Puri (co-author of *The Myth of UK Integration*), and Eleanor Nesbitt, University of Warwick.

Southeast Asian Migration: People on the Move in Search of Work, Marriage and Refuge, edited by Khatharya Um, University of California, Berkeley, and Sofia Gaspar, ISCSP-ULisboa, Portugal.

Women and Politics in Southeast Asia: Navigating a Man's World, Theresa W. Devasahayam, Singapore University.

The South China Sea Arbitration: Understanding the Awards and Debating with China, Alfredo C. Robles, Jr., De La Salle University, Manila.*

Chasing Freedom: The Philippines' Long Journey to Democratic Ambivalence, Adele Webb, Griffith University, Brisbane, Australia.

Victims, Perpetrators and Professionals: The Representation of Women in Chinese Crime Films, Tingting Hu, Wuhan University, China.

Governance of Islam in Pakistan: An Institutional Study of the Council of Islamic Ideology, Sarah Holz, National Institute of Pakistan Studies, Quaid-i-Azam University Islamabad, Pakistan.

Thinking Beyond the State: Migration, Integration, and Citizenship in Japan and the Philippines, Johanna O. Zulueta, Soka University, Tokyo, Japan.*

* Published in association with De La Salle University, Manila.

For my parents

Adele Webb

Chasing Freedom

The Philippines' Long Journey to Democratic Ambivalence

Brighton • Chicago • Toronto

Copyright © Adele Webb, 2022.

The right of Adele Webb to be identified as Author of this work has been asserted in accordance with the Copyright, Designs and Patents Act 1988.

First published in 2022 by
SUSSEX ACADEMIC PRESS
PO Box 139
Eastbourne BN24 9BP

Distributed in North America by
SUSSEX ACADEMIC PRESS
Independent Publishers Group
814 N. Franklin Street
Chicago, IL 60610

All rights reserved. Except for the quotation of short passages for the purposes of criticism and review, no part of this publication may be reproduced,stored in a retrieval system or transmitted in any form or by any means, electronic, mechanical, photocopying, recording orotherwise, without the prior permission of the publisher.

British Library Cataloguing in Publication Data
A CIP catalogue record for this book is available from the British Library.

Library of Congress Cataloging-in-Publication Data
To be appplied for.

Hardcover ISBN 978-1-78976-043-9

Typeset and designed by Sussex Academic Press, Brighton & Eastbourne.
Printed and bound by CPI Group (UK) Ltd, Croydon, CR0 4YY

Contents

Preface by Series Editor Mina Roces — viii
Author's Preface — ix
List of Tables and Figures — xv
List of Abbreviations — xvi
The Cover Illustrations — xvii

Introduction
The Problem with Democratic Freedom — 1

Democracy and Conquest
1 Bridling the Rise of Asia to Make Way for America's "Democratic" Empire — 33

Democracy and Duress
2 The Colonizer Outside: Living Democratically in a Paradox — 73

3 The Colonizer Within: Imperial Recursions in Imaginings of Democracy — 104

Democracy and Ambivalence
4 Searching for a Revolutionary Break with the Past — 145

5 "People Power", Populism and Ambivalence — 164

Conclusion
The Case for Democratic Ambivalence — 190

Notes — 199
References — 209
Index — 225

Series Editor's Preface

The Sussex Library of Asian and Asian American Studies Series publishes original scholarly work in various disciplines (including interdisciplinary and transnational approaches) under the rubric of Asian and Asian American studies – particularly Economics, Education, Religion, History, Politics, Gender, Comparative Studies with the West, and Regional Studies in Asia. The Series is keen to publish in emerging topics that demand attention in the Asian context—from the politics of dress to the representation of women in Chinese crime films for example. Seminal works and approaches will find a home here. The Series also welcomes single-country studies or anthologies that explore one important theme across a number of Asian contexts. We expect the Series to contribute to scholarly debates on topical issues, highlighting the importance of the region.

Adele Webb's *Chasing Freedom: The Philippines' Long Journey to Democratic Ambivalence* proposes a theory of democratic ambivalence using the lens of the middle classes and a case study of the Philippines in 'The Long Twentieth Century'. Webb traces the genealogy of the democratic experiment in the Philippines from the American-imposed 'democratic tutelage' that legitimized their colonial rule, to the various eras in the post-war period – from the first years of the independent republic through to the 1986 People Power Revolution that restored democratic institutions, until the present regime of President Rodrigo Duterte. *Chasing Freedom* presents us with a highly convincing narrative documenting both the inconsistencies between American colonial rulers' democratic discourses and their coercive rule and the intriguing responses of the Filipino middle class to the ideals of democratic government. Webb makes an original contribution to the field by offering a nuanced analysis of Filipino middle-class responses to democracy and linking this to the period of 'democratic tutelage' under American colonial rule. In presenting her work she fills a vacuum in the field where there are few studies of the middle class, especially in the period before the 1980s. Webb has given us an original and nuanced analysis, and her proposed theory of democratic ambivalence will have an impact beyond the field of Philippine studies.

Author's Preface

Around 10 a.m. on Friday 12 June 2015, Independence Day, a large crowd had gathered in Manila's upmarket business district of Makati, blocking the street outside the Chinese Embassy, and holding coloured signs printed on A4 paper reading "Hands Off PH." The Independence Day Rally was organized by Bayan (New Patriotic Alliance), a leftist, middle-class-led bloc of sectoral organizations founded in the last year of the Marcos dictatorship, with a similar program to the underground National Democratic Front (Communist Party of the Philippines). Representative to Congress Neri Javier Colmenares, from Bayan's party-list group known as Bayan Muna, climbed onto the makeshift stage on the back of a truck, and through perspiration from the June heat, he told the crowd they must "fight for freedom."

Friends with whom I was attending the rally took me around the back of the truck once the congressman had left the stage, and amongst the bustling television crews with large microphones, I was introduced as a researcher from Australia. After some small talk, I asked the congressman what he had meant by "freedom." What was the freedom he was calling the crowd to fight for? "We are building a national movement for sovereignty and independence", he replied. "Freedom is not just the semblance. It is lack of imposition by any foreign power." Soon we were interrupted by a television crew with a microphone. The congressman continued his message in front of the cameras: "We cannot claim to be genuinely sovereign today if a country like China controls part of our territory."

Meanwhile, the MC on the makeshift stage continued to rally the crowd, recalling the victory of 16 September 1991, when 12 senators voted to block the continuation of United States military bases in the Philippines. As the various guest speakers and performers were welcomed onto the stage, calls for freedom or "*kalayaan*", independence, sovereignty, and democracy continued. "We need to rely on our own strength, not rely on the United States; we must strengthen our capacity to defend our national sovereignty and democracy", Bayan Muna Secretary General Renato Reyes Jr told the crowd. "We do not have freedom if our stomachs are empty", said the speaker from

Pamalakaya-Pilipinas, the National Federation of Small Fisherfolk Organizations.

This was the first year the Independence Day rally organized by Bayan Muna had convened outside the Chinese Embassy in Makati. The crowds were then packed into rented jeepneys and the protest moved to its usual location close to the United States Embassy on Roxas Boulevarde, Manila Bay, although by the time we arrived, the police had formed a barrier to keep the crowd at a distance.

On the street under the intense midday sun, one of the people I was introduced to was a medical doctor who teaches at the nearby University of the Philippines college of medicine. He belonged to a Bayan member organization, HEAD (Health Alliance for Democracy), a group founded just before the 1986 EDSA revolution by a group of medical professionals opposed to the violence of the Marcos dictatorship. "It was intended not just as an anti-Marcos thing", he explained to me, "it was anti-US, anti-capitalist, anti-neocolonialism, since Marcos was considered a US puppet. It was against the concept of the Philippines not being free."

"The reason we [are] in the Independence Day rally is because HEAD believes that America has a big role to play in [why] we are still like this after so many decades [...] We declared independence of the Philippines under the auspices of the US, so it's not really our independence. [This] is a way of telling the US to get out."

At around 3 p.m., we made our way back to one of the waiting jeepneys, squashing inside alongside members from the urban poor association also heading back to Quezon City, next to refreshments, banners and rally equipment.

Just two days later, on the afternoon of Sunday 14 June, I gathered along with a group of around 70 people, mostly men, inside the exclusive venue of Club Filipino in Greenhills, the symbolic site of Corazon Aquino's victory speech on 25 February 1986, at the height of the People Power Revolution. Passing the security guards, the mural commemorating Cory's "yellow" victory, and the members-only swimming pool, we congregated in a meeting room to the side. The attendees represented moderate and for the most part religiously affiliated civil society groups and associations based in Metro Manila.

The theme of the meeting, displayed on the opening PowerPoint slide, was "You Shall Not Steal." One of the co-organizers from reformist alliance the Movement for Good Governance, formed in 2009, rose first to address the room. Asking "Why are we here?" he presented a slideshow entitled "Our Philippines Dream", presenting a vision of society very different from the present: "We dream of a country", the PowerPoint read, "where the government is truly of the people, by the people, and for the people; a country where all are equal before its laws, where the government strengthens the weakest and controls the excesses of the might, where our elected officials do not come from political dynasties or traditional politics." The final slide read, "This is the Philippine dream, for all Filipinos! This is the country we shall strive to build. We vow to offer the best of ourselves." The text was superimposed on an image of Benigno Aquino, deceased and lying face down on the airport tarmac following his 1983 assassination – the event that would spark an uprising big enough to end the Marcos dictatorship.

Next to speak was a highly respected lawyer, businessman and author, who had run unsuccessfully for the Senate in 2010 under the Liberal Party Coalition of Benigno "Noynoy" Aquino III. He had been invited by a group of ten Jesuits who were searching for a way to make the 2016 election transformative. "Our leaders are our problem"; "That's why we're here today", he told the room, "to explore the idea of a People's Primary." He explained the plan, to pool the convening power of their organizations, with their estimated 7–10 million members, to support the election of upright candidates for President and Vice President.[1]

A second meeting was held two weeks later, again at Club Filipino, to discuss the priorities of the reform agenda for this new coalition. Only 12 attendees were present this time, of whom I was the only woman. What followed was a two-hour discussion on a wide range of possible reform measures, from healthcare to agriculture to freedom of information and anti-dynasty legislation, things that seemed to me to lack a cohesive ideology, but which were deemed possible with the right leadership.

These stories from one of my periods of residence in Metro Manila during 2015 reflect the two pronounced languages of democracy that I found animating the middle-class civic sphere. Both speak in metamorphic terms, of a vision of transformation for the nation, born of a dissatisfaction with the present and in the search for a state of democracy and government not yet reached. One looks to the past, and in the name of the "unfinished revolution" calls for the heavy weight of more than a century of history to be lifted off the nation's shoulders. Refusing to accept the indignity of subjugation, it rejects the imperial forces that still constrain the nation and make for a democratic pantomime. The other, in contrast, looks introspectively for the sources of struggle and transformation. Though also speaking of a democratic impasse, it believes that both the current obstructions and the catalytic potential to overcome them centre on the correct democratic agency of the Filipino people themselves, including the moral reconstruction of the Filipino character led by the middle class, and the appointment of anointed leaders who will be the vanguard of national redemption.

Scholars have identified these two positions with the ideological polarization of establishment and anti-establishment factions within middle-class civil society. As Michael Pinches (2010) observes, one is the "national democratic" movement associated with the Communist Party of the Philippines (CPP), which under middle-class leadership rejects the legitimacy of the neo-colonial state and aims to destabilize government and business and to build a mass movement to overturn the current democratic regime. The second position is voiced by a more moderate and conservative segment of the middle class, which in response to the realities of endemic corruption, poverty, and a general lack of social progress, sees its role as one of moral leadership, memorialized in the image of the peaceful yet decisive street demonstrations of 1986, and the rise of a "civil" middle class imbued with the spirit of "people power" – a shared determination to do what was right, in the face of Marcos's moral corruption.

While such a split is an undeniable feature of the Philippines' civil society landscape (see Shiraishi 2008), during my research I began to realize that these two seemingly opposing impulses – one defiant and rebellious, the other sober and submissive – reflected more than siloed ideological responses to the ongoing political, economic and social challenges facing the nation. Actually, the political currents in these contemporary middle-class narratives bear a relationship to a dualism that has long inhabited the Philippines' democratic story, and the search for freedom – a "double-sided response" (Maggay 2011a: xv) to democracy that has been carried within the language of freedom. What I came to perceive was that the demand for democracy holds within it an indignation that rejects the infantilization and humiliation implicit in the nation's colonial past, and the denigration of sovereignty effected by external expectations and imposed constraints. This fuels the imperative to continually chase freedom and to realize a more authentic democracy. At the same time, the demand for democracy is haunted by anxiety about living beyond the restraints of hierarchy and plagued by self-scrutiny and self-doubt over the innate capacity of the nation and the people to correctly manage the freedom that democracy provides. Two forces at odds with each other, pulling in opposite directions, yet sustained, nurtured and reproduced by a collective democratic imaginary.

Chasing Freedom tries to illuminate the historical rootedness and contingency of the Philippine middle-class's inconsistent relationship to democracy; in particular, to demonstrate the way the emergence of a middle-class democratic imaginary was shaped, and constrained, by the collective experience of colonial democracy. Just as the Spanish three centuries earlier had brought Catholicism to the islands of the Philippine Archipelago under conditions of imperialism, the legacy of which remains evident in everyday religious practice (Cornelio 2016), the Americans brought to the Philippines ideas and practices of democracy that were entangled with hierarchy, violent coercion and subjugation. It is the relationship of these historical conditions, and the concomitant abuse of power, to middle-class knowledge of democracy and the construction of themselves as political subjects, that this book attempts to unpack.

The United States sailed into Manila Bay in 1898, carrying a gun in one hand and the textbook of American democracy in the other. That the Americans came to the Pacific to teach Filipinos about political independence and democratic freedom, but did so by war, conquest and external rule, is precisely what philosopher John Dewey meant when he said that to force individuals to be free in the name of democracy is a form of intellectual hypocrisy which leads to anti-democratic results (Pappas 2008: 271). If, as Dewey believed, the ends of freedom and individuality for all can only be attained by means that accord to those ends, then America's forced intervention in and occupation of the Philippines fundamentally offended the democratic ideal. It was also, as I argue, the starting point of the Philippines' long journey to democratic ambivalence.

If it were not for the time I spent in the Philippines during 2010 and 2011, this research would not have begun. For inviting me into the ISACC family and being my initial guide into the captivating contradictions of Philippine history, society and culture, I owe Dr Melba Maggay (Ate Melba) the deepest gratitude. This book was born out of a doctoral dissertation, begun in 2013 under the guidance of John Keane. To say that it would not have happened without John is a mountainous understatement. From a distance, the scale and imaginative depth of his writing on democracy inspired me to embark on my own intellectual journey. Pinching myself to end up at the Sydney Democracy Network under his mentorship, his sense of wonder, his intellectual generosity, along with the gentle inspiring and unwavering support he offered were of inestimable value to me. From Amsterdam, Rosanne Rutten's sagacious input into the project, especially in its early phase, along with the grace and patience she extended during the somewhat sinuous process, were also invaluable.

The opportunity to undertake this research and to engage in the field work it required was made possible by postgraduate research grants from the Australian government and the University of Sydney.

I also received invaluable assistance from a number of fellowship grants. First, from the Institute of Philippine Culture (IPC) to attend the 2014 doctoral researchers summer school at the Ateneo de Manila University. I'm particularly indebted to Leloy Claudio, Jojo Abinales and Ramon Guillermo for their tips, guidance, feedback and advice. The following year, in 2015, I returned to the IPC as a Visiting Research Associate while undertaking field work. Thanks to the kind team at IPC whose intellectual input and logistical support made my time there more productive. I was awarded a second fellowship in 2016 through a University of Sydney/Berlin Social Sciences Center (WZB) initiative and wrote critical parts of the book at the Democracy and Democratization Research Unit with the support of Wolfgang Merkel.

Along the way, I was profoundly lucky to enjoy the support and friendship of faculty members from the University of Sydney, especially Ariadne Vromen, Stewart Jackson, Anika Gauja, Diarmuid Maguire, Gerard Goggin and Kim Weatherall. I owe a debt of gratitude to Nicole Curato, who has gone out of her way to encourage this research and help it to reach a wider audience, especially in the Philippines. Thanks also to Trevor Hogan for comments on early drafts. In Manila, I am deeply indebted to Rei Lemuel Crizaldo, Emil Jonathan Soriano, Bryan Paler, Ima Ariate, Sarah Raymundo, Rachel Hauser, Lidy Nacpil, Claudette Arboleda and Gerry Arances. Others who need thanks include Gianni Wise, Christine Winter, Judy Betts, Jenny Mason, Sandra Urquiza-Calderon, Lindy Baker and Janice Zhang.

I completed the dissertation draft of this research at the end of 2018, just four short weeks before the arrival of our twin boys. The three-year journey between those multiple births and the publication of this book has been a radical one, and at times seemingly impossible. A number of things made it happen. First, the endorsement and enthusiasm of the Asian & Asian American Studies series editor, Mina Roces, who made the pathway to publication as smooth and expedient as one could hope. Second, the support of family both in Australia and Germany, especially when we found ourselves straddled between the two worlds in the midst of a global pandemic. Third, the expert editing skills of Daniela Di Piramo. And last but not least, I cannot envisage how any of this would have come about without the material, intellectual and emotional sustenance and companionship of Max. He has patiently walked with me through the whole adventure, and together with Leo and Otto, made the challenge worth it.

List of Tables and Figures

Tables
0.1 Preferred system of governing the country among middle class (per cent).
3.1 *Philippines Free Press* 1946–1950, Inventory of texts analysed.
3.2 *Philippines Free Press*, Predicates from staff-authored cover stories, 1946–1950.
3.3 *Philippines Free Press*, Predicates from public-authored texts, 1946–1950.
3.4 Analysis of *Philippine Free Press* entries relating to the Hukbalahap, the National Peasants Union or the Democratic Alliance.

Figures
3.1 Izon, Esmeraldo. "The One Year Old." Cartoon. *Philippines Free Press*, 28 June 1947.
3.2 Izon, Esmeraldo. "New Gulliver." Cartoon. *Philippines Free Press*, 7 August 1948.
3.3 Izon, Esmeraldo. "Democracy Gone Mad." Cartoon. *Philippines Free Press*, 14 November 1953.
3.4 Izon, Esmeraldo. "Execution." Cartoon. *Philippines Free Press*, 15 October 1949.
3.5 Izon, Esmeraldo. "Hocus Pokus!" Cartoon. *Philippines Free Press*, 5 April 1947, p.1 7.
3.6 "Huk Captured." *Philippines Free Press*, 9 July 1949, p. 44.

List of Abbreviations

CPP	Communist Party of the Philippines
DA	Democratic Alliance
EDSA	Epifanio de los Santos Avenue
GDP	Gross Domestic Product
HEAD	Health Alliance for Democracy
HUK	Hukbalahap
PKM	Pambansang Kaisahan ng mga Magbubukid (National Peasant Union)
MAN	Movement for the Advancement of Nationalism
NATDEMS	National Democrats
NGO	Non-government organization
NPA	New People's Army
SOCDEMS	Social Democrats
SWS	Social Weather Station
TRD	Today's Revolution: Democracy
US	United States
USAFFE	United States Army Forces in the Far East

The Cover Illustrations

FRONT – Supporters of former Davao City Mayor Rodrigo Duterte cheer as they attend his 'Miting de Avance' prior to the presidential elections at Luneta Park in Manila, Philippines. May 7, 2016 (copyright © Basilio Sepe). BACK – Demonstrators close down part of the busy Epifanio de los Santos Avenue (EDSA) highway in Quezon City, Manila to mark International Workers' Day, May 1, 2010 (copyright © Ima Ariate). Illustrations reproduced with permission from the copyright holder.

Introduction

This book tells the story of the love/hate relationship of the Philippine middle class with democratic politics. Middle classes, from the time of Aristotle, have been viewed as the harbingers of democratic progress and as insurance against political instability. A global middle class, the predominant modernist narrative imagines, is the foundation stone for widespread economic prosperity, political stability and social development (Birdsall 2016). In recent times, however, rather than democracy's safeguards, middle classes globally have found themselves at the centre of debates about "democratic backsliding", with a widespread disenchantment with the performance of existing democracies registering perhaps most strikingly in the success of authoritarian populist figures: the likes of Trump in the US, Orbán in Hungary, Kaczyński in Poland, and Bolsonaro in Brazil. All of whom, it appears, captured the allegiance of substantial segments of the middle class despite, or perhaps because of, the threat they pose to democratic institutions and processes of governance. This success has seen the current political science scholarship on the middle class reach an impasse, providing fewer insights into increasingly complex instances of middle-class behaviour in both established and emerging democracies.

Few middle classes have failed to emulate the predications of modernization theory as dramatically as in the Philippines. They seem, as Kurlantzick has argued in his book on democratic backsliding in the developing world, the prime example of a middle class in revolt against democratic rule (2013: 77). Since the days of intense optimism following the 1986 "people power" overthrow of Ferdinand Marcos, the rollercoaster of middle-class support for democracy is testimony, to Kurlantzick and others, that the Philippine middle class can no longer be taken for granted as a force for democratic change. The May 2016 election of self-professing "strong man" Rodrigo Duterte, with the highest levels of support amongst the middle and upper classes (SWS 2016), appeared lucid evidence that the middle class, themselves steeply disillusioned by the pace of change, had turned their backs on the democratic ideal. Yet the reality is not so simple. A closer look will tell you that, despite the fact it was the middle class who voted overwhelmingly to elect Duterte's disciplinarian government, these voters are neither wholly for democracy, nor wholly against it.

When I began conversations with middle-class respondents ten months before Duterte's watershed election, it wasn't the absence of democratic aspiration or an abandonment of the ideal I found. To the contrary, all of my interviewees expressed a strong attachment to democracy. Almost without exception, my respondents located the value of democracy in the idea of freedom – "freedom of expression", "freedom to live", "freedom to exercise your liberty" was part of a reoccurring narrative of the Philippines as a freedom-loving country. Nothing defined the positive sentiment of democracy as freedom more powerfully than the vivid memory of the 1986 People Power uprising against former leader and dictator Marcos. Removing Marcos was an act of "claiming and enforcing our freedom", said Victor.[1] It was a demonstration, a performance of the Filipino love of freedom – "this is who we are, the Filipinos are peace-loving, Filipinos are a democratic country", said Nathan.

Yet in these open discussions of the challenges facing democracy in the Philippines, the idea was repeatedly put to me that freedom had become a problem. The post-1986 period had become one defined by "abuse" of the freedom that was restored. Now there's "too much freedom", chuckled one of my interviewees, a lawyer and human rights advocate in her mid-30s, in a throwaway remark. "We forgot that democracy was more than [freedom]", said Victor. "It's not just a case of changing the leader, we ourselves have to change – as an individual, as a community. It starts from within . . . democracy is about exercising restraint also." "Sad to say", Nathan told me, "we don't have that moral compass yet, we don't have that strict freedom in our hearts."

Too much freedom? During the various extended periods I had spent living in Metro Manila, I had become accustomed to hearing the sentiment that "Filipinos are undisciplined" and "Filipinos don't follow the rules." It seemed especially common when driving. Entangled for hours in chaotic traffic jams where the only rule that seemingly applies is "every car for itself", I could sympathize with the frustration I understood as underlying the opinion. But as I began to interview participants for this study, most of whom were to some extent politically engaged, I didn't expect to hear this same sentiment expressed; nor did I expect that the notion of "needing discipline" would be part of a recurring middle-class narrative of how democracy "works" in the Philippines. Repeatedly, at the heart of beliefs expressed about democracy, was a contradictory adage: the

Philippines is a freedom-loving country; but in the Philippines, freedom needs restraint. Or to paraphrase the sentiment another way: democracy is good, but too much democracy can be dangerous in the Philippines. Freedom may well be the ideal value of democracy, my respondents seemed to be saying, but being free doesn't yet work in the Philippines. If the country is going to transform itself, socially and politically, freedom needs to be restrained, or at least closely supervised, until the population, both ordinary citizens and the political class, learn how it should be responsibly discharged.

This book is the fruit of a pursuit to both understand and explain this attitude to democracy. Located within a small group of ethnographically-inspired historical studies of middle classes in developing and postcolonial societies,[2] it supports a modest but growing concern within the democracy scholarship about the need to analyse relationships to democracy through a more complex frame. In particular, it takes issue with the simplistic dichotomous model through which middle class political positions are evaluated as either for democracy or against it.

At the heart of this book is the claim that democracy in the Philippines has been, and continues to be, lived by the middle class in an *ambivalent* way – that a sustained and synchronous saying of "yes" and "no" to democratic politics is one of the defining features of the middle class's democratic journey. Carried within a middle-class demand for democracy has been a co-existing desire for equality and freedom on the one hand, and an inclination towards hierarchy and restraint on the other. It is a double-sided response to democracy, a simultaneous embrace and distrust, that manifests in a paradoxical yet grounded reasoning – that an exercise of authority that infringes on people's democratic rights may, in some circumstances, not only be legitimate but central to democratic renewal.

Rodrigo Duterte was little mentioned in national public discourse when I began a second phase of field work in June 2015. But as the months continued and the prospect of his candidacy for President became more likely, it was increasingly common to hear discussions considering the credentials of this local politician, his track record in Davao, and what a Duterte presidency might mean for the nation's future. "Many people [at the moment] are abusing their freedom and doing things which are not good", said Garrett, one of my interviewees. "[B]ut we have this one politician, Duterte, [whose] type of leadership is like Marcos. And many people like that. And if you see Davao right now, it is one of the safest places in the Philippines. For me, if that type of leadership is implemented again, I think it's much better." "Honestly, to tell you bluntly", said Nathan, a lawyer in his early 40s, "I'm leaning toward Duterte . . . you might not agree with his methods, but when you come to listen to his discussion of why he's doing it, you have to give it to him . . . he refuses to be a tool."

These sentiments cannot adequately be explained as a contemporary turn towards authoritarianism following the 1986 transition to democracy. Nor do they simply reflect a lingering "authoritarian nostalgia" (Chang, Zhu, and Park 2007) left over from the Marcos period, for they predate this era. As far back as the 1940s, a perceived need for discipline was shaping middle-class perceptions of what was a legitimate exercise of democratic power – in particular, the type of leadership that was deemed necessary. In the late 1950s, when Harvard scholar Carl H. Lande[3] was conducting his own doctoral dissertation research amongst a nationwide sample of (male) respondents, one in five agreed with the statement that there was "too much democracy" and that "a little less democracy would be better for the country." Asked to explain why, they mentioned the fact democratic freedoms were being abused, whether in the form of libellous attacks against public figures by post-war tabloids, the anomalies committed by government and elected officials, or as Lande summarized, "what was felt to be a general increase in the rate of crime and disorder since the end of the war" (Lande 1959: 9). By the early 1970s, when Marcos declared the resuscitation of Philippine democracy as only possible through his strong, autocratic leadership, a newspaper columnist at the time summed up a prevailing mood: "For lack of discipline the nation plunged into the depths. It was exactly what the President did – he put a stop to a total lack of discipline" (Valencia 1973: 7).

How can this sustained and contradictory stance towards democracy be explained? The argument in this book is that ambivalence can be traced back to the conditions of duress under which "colonial democracy" was introduced to the nation at the turn of the last century – that a protracted and deep-seated ambivalence towards democracy is a striking, yet to date unacknowledged legacy of the American colonial period of "democratic tutelage" in the Philippines.

While more than three centuries of Spanish colonialism had left indelible marks on Philippine populations and society, the legacies of the Spanish period cannot explain recent Philippine political history (Hedman and Sidel 2000: 7–8). For this, we need to look at the American colonial era, and in particular to the legacy of the defamations of Filipino personhood used to justify democratic ideals. The American imperial state that emerged from the events at the turn of the twentieth century was arguably more complex than imperial powers of the past. This is not because, as is commonly argued, it was a modern version of empire with tempered excesses. The American imperial state encountered by the Philippine was characterized by a complex of democratic idealism and brutalizing means (Suri 2009). It unleashed for the first time in Asia the paradox of "democratic empire."

All empires claim exceptionalism (Said 1979). What is more, historiographies across the globe attest to the founding of empires on modes of governance that include ambiguous zones, partial sovereignty, temporary suspension of basic rights, provisional states of emergency, technologies of surveillance, differentiation between subjects and citizens, and deferred or contingent independence (Stoler 2016). Yet it is the fundamentally contradictory nature of this polysemic empire of American intervention, and the cacophony of rhetorical alibis used to justify its Philippine intervention, that this study brings to the fore. Profound inconsistencies underlay the American colonial project: love and violence, freedom and conquest, benevolence and discipline. It is the Janus face of America's "democratic imperialism", the book argues, that is the source of perhaps its most insidious legacy: a lucid awareness of democracy's corruptibility intertwined with an unquenchable hope in its transformative potential. The result is an ambivalence about democracy that continues to be manifest in the politics of today.

On Democratic Ambivalence

What does it mean to be ambivalent? Despite recent popular and scholarly use of the term, there remains considerable confusion about what it means to be ambivalent. We often equate ambivalence with disinterest, apathy, or indifference, all of which imply inaction or lack of concern, but ambivalence is a more complex and spirited term. Its Latin stem, '*ambi*', means "both", and it reflects our capacity to say "yes" and "no" about a person or an object at the same time.

When it comes to politics, we often hold conflicting, even mutually exclusive visions of the type of society we want to live in. What the political psychology literature terms as "conflictive values or feelings" (Nai 2013), and "competing considerations" (Lavine 2001: 915) are found to be both prevalent and non-trivial in people's political opinions and evaluations of political objects. Yet the term has a psychoanalytic dimension that is underplayed in these treatments. Ambivalence does not simply connote fluctuating attitudes but refers to the maintenance of these oppositional attitudes or feelings; it suggests that such oppositional attitudes are not only simultaneous and inseparable, but also durable, rather than a dialectical opposition that will eventually be transcended (Laplanche and Pontalis 1973: 26–8).

The concept of democratic ambivalence developed in this book is defined as the simultaneous and sustained holding of oppositional feelings about democracy. It describes the situation where individuals, or indeed publics, are neither singularly committed to democracy, nor singularly in favour of non-democratic politics. Democratic ambivalence captures the way that democratic dispositions, rather than overcoming contradictory inner tensions that may exist, can be (and often are) durably inhabited by forces that simultaneously work with and against democracy, an empirical reality for which existing political science research offers few insights.

Indeed, the notion of ambivalence in relation to democracy is contentious. Most of the existing research relies on the normative assumption that citizens, and middle-class citizens in particular, take a journey towards unequivocal commitment to democracy. Inconsistencies or irregularities in political beliefs (such as the case when people favour democracy yet fail to denounce authoritarian governance) are derided as ignorant and confused, a danger to themselves and others, their views considered a subversion of democracy's founding legitimacy.[4]

Here, the relationship between ambivalence and democracy is entirely reframed. The conceptualization of democratic ambivalence developed in the book makes the case that ambivalence is not a pathology of democracy, but rather a product of people living democratically. It is an immanent feature of democratic life that needs to be accommodated into our descriptive and normative accounts of how democracy works.

Ambivalence has a double source in democracy, the book claims. On the one hand, ambivalence is produced by the fact the lived reality of democracy never meets the grand ideal. Ambivalence is rooted in negotiations of the messy realities of democracy in practice. The disappointments, frustrations and unmet aspirations that nurture ambivalence are not only possible in democratic life, they are an inevitable part of it. The "democratic deficit" model of Pippa Norris implies the gap between public support for democratic ideals and their satisfaction with the government's performance of democracy is a temporary phenomenon, not devoid of usefulness through its arousal of "critical citizens" but destined to be overcome through a Habermasian-type process of "enlightened" engagement (Norris 2011). The claim is at odds with this approach. Democracy promises something it can never fully deliver. The presence of a rift between the ideal and the lived experience is not a temporary flaw, it is an inescapable reality. Through ambivalence, citizens are able to deal with unmet desires, disgruntlement and despondency without withdrawing altogether. It is a down-to-earth, pragmatic approach to a situation in which democracy is both a venerated ideal and a misused rhetoric.

The other source of democracy's ambivalence lies within the grand ideal itself. The principle of democracy rests on the premise that although paradise on earth is never realized, efforts to correct, improve and innovate are always possible. Democracy as a political form is defined by its acknowledgement of failure, distinguished from monarchy or dictatorship by the permanent possibility of change. The ability to question power makes democracy peculiarly vulnerable not only to charges of hypocrisy and imperfection, but to feelings of disappointment and disgruntlement (Keane 2008). Representative democracy contains provisions for the expression of such disappointments. Elections, most obviously, allow for periodic judgements of the performance of power, and for the expression of dissenting minority views. They are disciplinary mechanisms, designed to accommodate for the fact that representatives are not always virtuous, competent and impartial, and from time to time need to be thrown out. Democracy heightens the awareness of citizens that power relations are not fixed in stone. It keeps open the possibility of radical transformation and nurtures imaginings and hopes of alternative visions, in so doing awakening an ambivalence with the present.

One doesn't need to look far to locate the presence of a stable ambivalence towards democracy in the Philippines. In the most recent wave of the World Values Survey (2019),[5] in relation to the question about what form of political system is preferable for governing the country, 66 per cent of university educated respondents expressed their simultaneous support for both a democratic political system as preferable, and "a strong leader who does not have to bother with Congress and elections." As Table 0.1 shows, over the past quarter of a century, since the World Values Survey began collecting data in the Philippines, more than 50 per cent of university educated Filipinos have expressed ambivalent views when it comes to democratic governance. While this level of ambivalence holds across all social classes in the Philippines, the fact that it is strongly present in the subset of highly educated respondents runs counter to what orthodox democratization theory would expect us to find – that the higher someone's socioeconomic status, the more likely they are to adopt emancipatory values, which in turn translates into an uncompromised demand for democracy.

An earlier, more targeted survey involving 800 Metro Manila middle-class households found the same trend. A majority "[...]

Table 0.1 Preferred system of governing the country among middle class (per cent).

		"A strong leader who does not have to bother with Congress and elections"							
		1996		2001		2012		2019	
		No	Yes	No	Yes	No	Yes	No	Yes
"A Democratic Political System"	No	4	8	7	8	11	14	4	11
	Yes	32	56	35	50	34	41	19	66

(Simultaneous support for democracy and autocracy. Notes: N = 1270. Based on WVS time-series dataset, variables E117 and E114. Subset for education at least some university (variables X025>7 and X025A2>6). Support for democracy and autocracy = Yes if response "Fairly good" or "Very good"; No = "Fairly bad" or "Very bad."

perceive the Philippines as a democratic country and recognize that a democratic form of government is suitable for the development of Philippine society." Simultaneously, however, the survey found "a significant majority (seven out of 10) are not averse to accepting any form of government, democratic or not, as long as it does a good job for the country" (Velasco 1997: 80).

Why do middle class Filipinos, in large numbers, attach high value to democracy, while at the same time failing to denounce all forms of authoritarian governance?

The contemporary democratization literature has failed to make sense of equivocal or contradictory democratic attitudes in late-industrializing countries like the Philippines beyond pejorative assessments of civic ineptitude, with insinuations about the persistence of "premodern" political cultures, poor levels of political comprehension, and even cognitive unsophistication in the ways of democracy (Huntington 1996; Pye 1985; Shin 2006). All such explanations contain a more or less hidden teleology. They intimate a failed agency on the part of middle-class citizens – that by failing to emulate the middle-class-led modernization narrative of the "West", they have not only let down the nation for which they were supposed to be the democratizing force, they also have brought their own capacity to understand the value of democracy into question. It is even suggested, in the case of the Philippines, that there is a kind of pathological naivety on the part of Filipino citizens – that the failure to embrace democracy is a "Filipino" problem, or as one author described it, a lack of cognitive capacity to distinguish "limited democratic rule from complete or full democracy" (Shin 2006: 17).

Such interpretations, I argue, are a product of the theoretical and methodological constraints in the study of democratic attitudes, more than they are a reflection on the empirical reality. On the question of methodology, answering this question using survey data alone, as the quantitatively inclined democratization literature tends to do, is not only insufficient, but produces misleading results. The very nature of statistical survey data means the contradictions, complexities and connections within an individual's answers are compartmentalized and flattened (Schaffer 2014) rather than identified and explored as data in themselves. Furthermore, the non-narrative nature of survey responses does not allow researchers to locate these responses within time and context, or as a continuation of past narratives. While these limitations fit neatly into a dichotomist rational choice model of success or failure, right or wrong, they discourage sociological investigation of citizens' evaluative frameworks, and fail to take seriously the historical, structural and cultural contexts of political preferences.

In the Philippine studies literature, on the other hand, notwithstanding the increasingly frequent mentions of the middle class in contemporary studies, the historical inconsistency of its democratic orientation has remained under-theorised. So, too, has the gap between the largely conservative political attitudes found in survey responses on the one hand, and instances of middle-class radicalisation at key historical junctures on the other (Rivera 2001, Turner 1995). Most scholars ultimately concede that the political character of the middle class is, as Velasco described it, "quite uncertain" (Velasco 1997: 80). Having said that, there is a prevailing and perhaps default assumption, that fluctuations in middle-class behaviour (and "misbehaviour") can be explained as the outcome of ideological hegemony. Such accounts reduce Philippine political history to a narrative of the power and agency of the elite, and whether intended or not, paint a picture of the middle class as passive and naïve, being duped in and out of democratic politics by a chicane political oligarchy.[6] This framing of the middle class as politically unsophisticated is consistent with another largely unquestioned presumption still prominent in the literature – that until the late 1970s and early 1980s the middle class remained immersed in clientelistic networks, and that a distinct and coherent middle class political consciousness did not exist (Kimura 2003, Kusaka 2017).[7]

The scholarly reticence to making the middle class itself a focus for enquiry and explanation (Turner 1995) can partly be explained by the fact that, in contrast to its East Asian and Southeast Asian neighbours, the middle class in the Philippines has remained a smaller proportion of the population.[8] Nor was it deliberately underwritten by modernity projects of the state, like that which occurred in Singapore and Malaysia (Rivera 2001: 254). Yet perhaps more consequential in explaining the missing middle element in studies of Philippine politics has been the "Great Divide" in Philippine historiography – the way in which American colonial writers constructed Philippine society at the end of the nineteenth century as a divide between oppressed people and a tyrannical elite; and the way nationalist scholars, from the late 1950s, sought to recast the Filipino "masses" as "the true subjects of Filipino history" (Hau 2000: 123–5). The assertion that the political past could be defined by a two-class dynamic had a profound effect on how social scientists, historians, and practitioners have represented Philippine society. In particular, the role of a middle element in the events at the turn of the twentieth century has been one of the most conspicuous silences in Philippine historiography. Only in the last two decades have new historical works confirmed the central agitative role of a middle element in the revolutionary events of the late nineteenth century (Mojares 2006; Cullinane 2014; Richardson 2013).[9] Emerging from the critical social, economic, and cultural transformations in the second half of the nineteenth century, a nascent Philippine middle class was integral to the formation of the ideational and discursive apparatus of an independent nation state on the eve of the twentieth century. Such a finding not only disrupts orthodox historiographical accounts of the period; it suggests that the starting point for studying the political beliefs and behaviours of the middle class lies much earlier than the current literature posits. It raises new questions, which this book explores, about the nature of the middle-class democratic imaginary prior to the imposition of American rule in 1901, and the effects on this imaginary of a paradoxical policy of subjugation in the name of "democratic tutelage."

In summary, the ambivalence thesis in this book stands at odds with existing interpretations of the middle class's oscillations towards and away from democratic politics – instead, it is an attempt to return much needed volition and agency to middle-class actors who have too often been subsumed into disempowering narratives of false consciousness, political promiscuity or failed democratic practice.

Rethinking Normative Theories of the Democratic Middle Class

Stretching all the way back to Aristotle, there has existed an almost ubiquitous belief about the symbiotic relationship between middle classes and democracy. It is not only the causal belief that without a middle class, a stable democracy will not survive; the presence of a progressive middle class has become a barometer for a nation's democratic health. This pervasive view is built on a set of assumptions of how middle-class citizens value democracy and what they expect it to look like – assumptions that provide the scaffolding for a normative middle-class political subjectivity that portrays middle classes, wherever and in whatever circumstances they may find themselves, to be innately in favour of democracy and as champions of its principles, procedures and institutions.

The tenacity of the belief in an innately pro-democratic middle class owes much to the ubiquity of the modernization paradigm. Despite serious challenges to its political normativity in the work of postmodern and postcolonial thinkers, modernization thinking continues to influence contemporary democratization debates, and to frame the way that middle class political subjectivities are diagnosed and discussed. Codified into democratization theory by Seymour Martin Lipset's "the more well-to-do a nation, the greater the chances that it will sustain democracy" (Lipset 1959: 75), modernization theory encompasses the belief that economic growth, achieved through capitalist development, leads to liberal enlightenment and thus the spread of democratic ideals. Adherents to the modernization paradigm view the emergence of the middle class as the chief casual mechanism in this transformation. Societal-wide socioeconomic development causes political systems to transition towards democracy, via the cognitive changes that occur within individuals as they attain higher levels of education and occupational skills.[10]

Yet the certitude of this proposition that is central to theories of democracy and democratization needs to be reviewed. The starting point for this is not yet more statistical data on the political values of middle classes – it is laying bare the imperial roots of the epistemology underlying the dominant claims about middle-class-led modernity. The tacit assumption underpinning the modernist theory of middle-class values is that there exists an ideal, objective definition of middle classness that allows our knowledge of a middle-class citizen in one time and place to be substituted by another. Being drawn towards democracy is a basic middle-class experience. If a person identifying as middle class cannot transcend their local conditions and context to reach this universal state of being, they are presumed flawed. This is a form of knowledge that takes the subjective experience of one group of people, namely those in the US and Europe, and generalizes these experiences and norms into an ideal model (Code 1992). Attributes and experiences that don't align are then rendered as "otherness", with little to no appetite shown for understanding the cultural and structural dynamics that influence divergent political preferences.

The normative proposition that the subjective experience of middle classes in Europe and the US should become the universal experience of middle classes everywhere is an imperialistic claim. It serves to protect the fantasy that the specific processes of change that occurred in Britain and the US (and to a lesser extent Western Europe) during the nineteenth century represent the ideal democratic experience – a universal democratic path premised on the North Atlantic model that all other nations in the world should try to emulate. It makes the model of democratization ahistorical and ethnocentric, and propagates the implausible premise that change in one society will mirror that which occurred in a different society at a different time.

More than that, the lack of history that has accompanied the development of liberal democratic theory over the last half century has obscured its complicated roots in empire. More particularly, it has reified a global hierarchy of "democratized" versus "democratizing" countries (Slater 2006) as a natural "state-of-affairs", while erasing what Spivak labelled its "epistemic violence" (1988: 280–1): the centrality to Western epistemology of the construction of a non-democratic "Other."

Up until the end of the Second World War, the social world was constituted by imperial relations. As such, ideas of mass citizenship and liberal political economy emerged in the context of the world's leading colonial empires of Britain and France. This was not simply a coincidence of the ideas of freedom and empire; there was a co-determination which cannot be overlooked. The colonial control of the nineteenth century, Stovall writes, was liberal democracy's "handmaiden" (2013: 69). Put simply, not only did the ideology of liberal democracy serve to transform the rationale for empire as a "civilizing" process, it also brought about the biggest expansion of colonialism in history (Stovall 2013: 72).

This co-determination between imperialism and democracy wasn't reserved to the realm of realpolitik. As sociology was becoming institutionalized in the last decade of the nineteenth century, the contrast between the metropole and the colonial Other became the centrepiece of the system of knowledge about "origins" and "progress" (Connell 1997: 1520). As Connell's work explains, the "grand ethnography" of sociology's comparative method helped to resolve democratic imperialism's internal contradiction: colonial subjects were defined by their primitiveness, and the exclusion of whole peoples from basic liberal rights was deemed legitimate by the science of evolutionary biology (1997: 1531).

Without doubt, imperial histories are inherently bound up in the dynamics of middle-class formations, both on the side of the colonizers and the colonized. The emergence of middle classes and of bourgeois cultural milieus in European societies of the nineteenth century was intrinsically tied to the emergence of an imperialist global economy, built on the exploitation of colonial labour to produce commodities for consumption such as coffee, tea, sugar, cocoa and silk (Dejung, Motadel, and Osterhammel 2019: 18). At the same time, the very features often considered democratic flaws in late-developing countries, including the failure to develop a large, strong and independent middle class, are more often than not a legacy of these silenced colonial histories.

Highlighting the relevance of temporal and geopolitical dimensions in the process of class formation drives home the point that class consciousness is complex – integrated and entangled in transnational processes of history. And yet, the middle class has been the subject of relatively little historical analysis. The predominance of time-bound empiricism in political science has meant there has been little interest in qualitatively interrogating the history and nature of middle-class political beliefs. Even by class historians, who see the elites and working classes as having recognizable structural locations and shared interests, the middle classes are often deemed too heterogeneous for their formation to be carefully chronicled. Whether because the concept has been considered too fuzzy or too precise, it has seemed, as Lopez and Weinstein describe, to "preclude, rather than provoke historical interpretation" (Lopez and Weinstein 2012: 20).

There are exceptions, of course. Some of the most seminal works on democracy and class politics pertaining to the role of the middle class include those by Barrington Moore (1967), Rueschemeyer, Stephens and Stephens (1992), and Eva Bellin (2000). In contrast to the positivist comparative literature, all three formative works emphasize the historical contingency of middle-class political beliefs, and importantly, contextualize democratization within global conditions of possibility. However, they still fail to adequately capture the constructed nature of class subjectivity. Though rejecting the postulate of a direct causal link between economic development and commitment to democracy, these works still belong to a structuralist perspective that sees class consciousness as determined by the organization of economic relations of production. Not too dissimilar to the liberal model, middle classness is reduced to the instantiation of certain structural laws of history. It is one's access to economic resources and opportunities that determines their inclusion or exclusion from power, while non-material dynamics such as discursive power are ignored, as are the role of ideas and narratives in shaping the political consciousness of classes over time.

Moving away from over-arching structuralist theories which imply class as a given, the attempt in this book is to situate the Philippine middle class, and to examine the way it has been produced and produced itself in the context of specific structures of power, discursive conditions and lived experiences. Contemporary dispositions towards democracy are denaturalized through a long historical lens – one that pays attention to the way actors over time have attempted to negotiate the terms of democracy, and sheds light on how the experience of the actual practices of power has shaped and constrained the way that democracy and democratic agency are collectively imagined. Indeed, a central premise of the study is that variations in middle-class commitment to democracy, rather than being eschewed as a failure of democratic agency, are an invitation to understand the dynamics and social logics that underlie such indeterminacy (Koo 1991).

The Approach of the Book

While there is a predominant sense in political science that the researcher who deviates from orthodox methods and models risks over-complicating explanations or sacrificing parsimony (Mahoney and Snyder 1999), new insights require new frames through which to view complex dynamics, especially dynamics that have become obscured by excessive determinism. Taking an interdisciplinary approach, with scaffolding borrowed from historical sociology, critical theory, critical international relations and philosophy, this study develops an original research design intended to address the complexity of postcolonial middle-class political subjectivity. The book undertakes to write a broadly temporal genealogical narrative of Philippine middle-class ambivalence. It traces the development of a stable ambivalent disposition by paying attention to both text and context over the twentieth century, generating original data for analysis while also cross-referencing a broad range of secondary materials from history, anthropology, sociology and political science.

Key Analytical Concepts

A situated conception of middle classness requires an interrogation of both who middle class subjects imagine themselves to be, and how they in turn collectively imagine democracy. It follows that, in addition to democratic ambivalence, the analytical concepts central to the book's research are *middle class*, *political subjectivity* and *democratic imaginary*.

Middle class. The idea of a particular stratum of people sharing a common political orientation dates back to Marx, yet the question of how the layers of social classes in a society should be defined remains an arena of dispute. In particular, the concept of the middle class has faced unique challenges. Despite its ubiquity in discussions of democracy and globalization, debates about the use and usefulness of the term abound. It is the cacophony of voices using the term in often contradictory ways that has contributed to confusion over its meaning and has put the concept at risk of losing effectiveness (Southall 2016: xix).

In the development economics and much of political science literature, middle class is conceptualized as a socio-economic category. People who earn within a specified income range, for example, are deemed to be middle class. Though empirically useful, such static, objective categorizations of class are unable to capture the socio-cultural diversity to which Bourdieu was referring in his concept of *milieu*.[11] What is more, how do we account for the fact that the political, cultural and social attitudes of the middle classes – and the meanings and subjectivities that signify middle classness – are neither static nor universal and will inevitably vary across different time periods and diverse contexts.

The approach in this book proposes to move the concept of middle class as an a priori supposition to a working social and historical construct. Rather than presuming what it means to be middle class, the book tries to locate *middle classness* within specific historical experiences. It draws heavily on the conceptualization of middle class offered by Lopez and Weinstein, as "a working social concept, a material experience, a political project, and a cultural practice – all of which acquire meaning only within specific historical experiences and discursive conditions" (2012: 21).

Exploring middle classness through a more constructivist lens requires the analysis of values, ideals, and discourses as key data. A middle-class consciousness is not an imputed outcome of one's socioeconomic position, or a position in relation to the means of production, but a dynamic outcome of social change, embedded in time, place and culture. Nor are the questions of inclusion and exclusion from power confined to matters of material resources, as Marx and Weber assumed. I consider how discursive representations within the political public sphere shape or confine access to power (Calhoun 2012). Moreover, as mentioned earlier, the formation of modern middle classes has been a transnational process, with the meanings of what it is to be middle class, and the subjectivities and practices associated with being middle class having been "mutually – and coevally – constituted across the globe" (Lopez and Weinstein 2012: 12). As such, histories of colonialism, gender disparities, racial differentiations and religious projects are not tangential to the study of the middle class. They are constitutive of the transnational historical experiences that form both class structures and political consciousness.

In the current study, the focus has been on tracing the production, circulation, and revision of middle-class ideas and norms relating to democracy, and identifying the discourses and practices that have contributed to the construction of a shared middle-class imaginary. The aim is to illuminate the processes by which middle-class agents have been both created by and conveyers of meanings and subjectivities that have become embedded in shared political narratives.

Political subjectivity. The concept of political subjectivity is also central to this book's analysis. Talking about political subjectivities is a way of denaturalizing people's political positions. It draws attention to the historical conditions and practices – practices of inclusion and exclusion, as well as longings and desires – through which the positions of the political subject come into being (Krause and Schramm 2011: 118). The usefulness of subjectivity as a concept is in its encompassing of domains that are more often than not analysed distinctly – the personal, the political and the moral (Werbner 2002: 3). It includes not only how subjects should be conceived, but also how they conceive of themselves as agents. Political subjectivity allows us to think through the emotional attachment of subjects to formal authority, and the way this attachment does or doesn't give the subject voice and recognition and agency. At the same time, it considers the processes of subjectification by the authority itself.

Michel Foucault wrote about the processes of subjectification in relation to political projects – about the way the subject both makes itself and is made through the configuration of power relations. For Foucault, it was about showing how "the body" or "the subject" becomes an object of deployments of implicit power. In *Discipline and Punish* (1979), he argued that modern penal systems do not just punish people by depriving them of freedom; by categorizing inmates as dangerous subjects of a criminal nature, new and more insidious forms of domination are possible. Again, in the *History of Sexuality* (1978), control becomes internalized: "individuals internalize the norms laid down by the sciences of sexuality and monitor themselves in an effort to conform to these norms. Thus, they are controlled not only as objects of discipline but also as self-scrutinizing and self-forming subjects" (Gutting and Oksala 2018). Judith Butler later built on Foucault's work, along with Louis Althusser's concept of interpellation, to argue that "the subject does not exist before it enters into the relationship with an authority, but emerges by desiring to be addressed by that authority and by attempting to master a skilful response" (cited in Krause and Schramm 2011: 128).

In the current study, an analytical focus on subjectivity allows the political orientations and beliefs of the present to be denaturalized. Instead of the political character of the Philippine middle class being defined by its comparison to an imputed "universal" norm, the attempt here is to situate the formation of the middle-class subject in time, place and lived experience, paying attention to the processes of inclusion and exclusion that have shaped, and constrained its sense of its own democratic agency and the underlying collective logic of how democracy works.

The democratic imaginary. With the global spread of democracy during the second half of the twentieth century to diverse nations and across different global regions and contexts, quantitatively inclined students of democracy have striven to pinpoint the causal sequences and measurable variables involved in this tide of political change. As such, despite the lip-service often paid to democracy as an abstract and highly contested concept, the contemporary literature on democratization has become strongly biased towards studies that conceptualize democracy as a set of concrete and fixed procedures, institutions and norms.

However, seminal anthropological studies of democratization (Schaffer 1998; Paley 2002) have demonstrated the empirical blunders committed when a static, positivist conceptualization of democracy is imposed on citizens everywhere. Such studies, in contrast, illustrate why the "indigenization" of democracy demands more attention, including the dialectical processes by which collective democratic norms are produced, adapted and revised. To understand the way that citizens evaluate democracy, we need to reorient the lens from a focus on normative questions of how publics *should* value democracy, and the meanings they *should* attach to it, to more exploratory questions of how they *do* value democracy, and from where such evaluative frames derive. Questions need to be asked, such as in Frederick Schaffer's pioneering study *Democracy in Translation: Understanding Politics in an Unfamiliar Culture*: does it necessarily follow that just because people participate in the same formal institutions of democracy, they attach to these institutions the same purpose and meaning (1998: 8)?

In order to pay heed to these questions, democracy in this study is operationalized as an imaginary. Yaron Ezrahi defined the political imaginary as the "fictions, metaphors, ideas, images or conceptions that acquire the power to regulate and shape political behaviour and institutions in a particular society' (2012: 3). Unlike the study of ideology, which tends to denote the negative ideas of misrecognition or mystification, the study of imaginaries does not purport to unveil the "truth" about "reality", but rather to "bring into question those practices and institutions that are regularly allowed to pass inspection" (Grant 2014: 7). Given that our political imaginaries tend to be rooted in, and produced by, processes of exclusion and inclusion (Calhoun 2012), their study can give acuity to otherwise occluded practices of power.

The case for the "imaginary" having a central place in the study of democracy was best made by theorist Cornelius Castoriadis (2007, 1997, 1987). Rather than having to choose between normative and theoretical approaches to democracy, or historical and descriptive approaches, Castoriadis preferred to speak of democracy in terms an "imaginary", a big story that people construct and narrate to themselves, that gives them bearings, and lends meaning to their lives. Such an imagined story of meaning serves as the structuring link, Castoriadis argued, between "[...] the representations, the affects, and the intentions dominant in a society" (2007: 231). It was the restitution and analysis of these processes that precede the embodiment of democracy in the form of practices and institutions that Castoriadis implored social and historical research to make its ultimate objective (Castoriadis 1993: 102).

To the question of how an abstract concept such as the democratic imaginary can be observed, both Benedict Anderson's work (1983) and the more recent work of Craig Calhoun have demonstrated the way that social and political imaginaries can be detected in text and context, taking form in the shape of discourses animating the public sphere (Calhoun 2012), which in turn become the basis for political discussions and disputes over how a society should look, in what direction it should head, and where the boundaries of "legitimate" political behaviour are located. Competing narratives develop discursive logic, Laurence Whitehead (2002) further argues, through an open-ended and dynamic process of constructing, absorbing and revising political narratives and "necessary fictions" (Ezrahi 2012: 3), as past legacies are adapted to new political ideas.

There is another reason the concept of the imaginary is productive in a study such as this one. The idea of the imaginary brings to the fore the collective subjectivity inherent in democracy. In the same way that Benedict Anderson argued "the nation" only exists through the agency of individual and collective actors in absorbing, revising, and reproducing the imagining of their state as "community" (Anderson 1983), democracy cannot be sustained by institutional "bricks and mortar" alone. Political parties, elections, independent courts and legislatures are not enough. Democracy must be "imagined and performed by multiple actors in order to exist" (Ezrahi 2012: 1). Like the nation, democracy requires both an individual and a collective subjectivity. "Imagining democracy", as Craig Calhoun suggests, requires thinking of "'the people' as active and coherent and oneself as both a member and an agent" (Calhoun 2012: 151).

Further to this, the concept of the imaginary also elucidates how critical and entangled imaginings of the nation – a collective identity based on shared government, territory, traditions, languages and memories – are to people's understandings of democracy. While in the modern era nations formed the basis for the discursive formation of democracies, they have largely been dismissed from theories of democracy in the post-war period. This was no doubt made easier by the instances over the last century where nationalism has been mobilized to legitimate violent anti-democratic projects, as well as the increasingly multinational character of states and spread of multicultural ideals. Whatever the cause, the neglect of the role of the nation has left dominant theories of democracy lacking in their capacity to theorize the governing system not only as a mechanism for distributing power, but also as "the active creation of ways of living together", and as a form of social solidarity and political participation that is situated in culture and history. Nations create the "mediating structures" between globalization and conceptions of humanity as a whole, on the one hand, and on the other hand, the everyday interpersonal relations that create social cohesion and form the legitimating basis for social institutions (Calhoun 2007: 152–3).

The relationship between imaginings of the nation and of democracy are especially critical in postcolonial societies like the Philippines, where the processes of democratization have been intimately tied to the writing (and re-writing) of national histories and nationalist discourses. When writing about the nation as an imagined community, Anderson (1983) reminded us that nations do not exist in abstract: nations are a kind of written and spoken narrative, a psychological construct that makes for a potent political force and an object of strategic manipulation. This certainly resonates in the Philippines, where imaginaries of the nation have been and remain a potent political force, with interpellations of the Filipino "nation" and "people" providing fertile terrain for political actors seeking to legitimize and maximize their authority by emphasizing their service to the interests of the "nation." The result is a situation in which imaginings of democracy and of the nation are often indistinguishable. While such a fusion of the concepts might be problematic in theory, the reality of the efficacy of the notion of national sovereignty in democratic narratives is one that cannot be dismissed.

A (Post)colonial History of the Present

In discussions of the problems hindering the Philippines' consolidation of democracy, the political attitudes of contemporary Filipinos have become a focal point. The intermittent swings over the last three decades, from calls for democracy to the endorsement of autocratic forms of governance, have principally been assumed in the democratization literature to be the relic of an outdated political culture. In attempting to denaturalize the political attitudes of the present, one of the cornerstones of this study is the focus on exogenous factors that have shaped, and constrained, the formation of political identities, meanings and values, especially those relating to the idea of democracy. In the case of America's imperial rule in the Philippines during the first half of the twentieth century, the embedding of the rhetorical construction of a "self" and "other", even within the colonized subjects' perception of their own democratic agency, suggests the American colonization of the Philippines has left a political legacy that needs to be better understood. After all, the impacts of such colonial representational practices cannot be presumed to have ended with the era of decolonization and the global spread of democracy. While imperial discourses of the past cannot be assumed to have produced fixed ways of thinking, we can reasonably expect that they did shape and constrain political imaginings in ways that have material impact. The task of this study is to interrogate the "imperial durabilities" (Stoler 2016) of American colonial rule in contemporary democratic identities and formations of the middle class.

The location of lingering colonial constraints in the present has long been the preoccupation of postcolonial studies. Central to the writing of postcolonial histories is a conceptualization of implicit power: the way structures of power are built through a process of internalization and maintained through legitimating speech acts that reproduce and reinforce a complex of images upon which implicit power is based. Such implicit power processes are easily obscured from the researcher's view, since they are located in "everyday discourses and practices" which become the "commonsense categorization" people use in everyday life (Stobbe 2005: 107).

Bringing together Foucault's concept of discourse with Gramsci's concept of hegemony, Said's 1978 *Orientalism* exposed the power of imperial knowledge, specifically the asymmetrical power relations between the observer and the observed (2003), and the "epistemic violence" it entailed (Spivak 1988). He urged us to frame colonialism not strictly in terms of political or economic dimensions, but as having a more insidious legacy in the continuing legitimacy of signs, metaphors and narratives, which constituted a reality that protected the colonialists' power and privilege by sustaining the boundary between "us" and "them" (Gregory 2004: 255).

For scholars of democracy, this means not only questioning how a Eurocentric theory of democracy gained strength and legitimacy by setting itself off against a non-European, non-democratic "other." It also involves examining the effects colonial discourses of difference and political inferiority continued to have on the colonized subjects, even after the physical presence of the colonizer had been removed. To what degree has the "imperial gaze" of Eurocentric epistemologies altered the non-western others' perception of themselves (Singh and Schmidt 2000: 16–18)? Moreover, as Chen's illuminative study on China reminds us, how has Orientalism been accompanied by instances of discursive Occidentalism, by which subjects of the Western Other, both the local elite and those beyond, have "participated[d] actively and with indigenous creativity in the process of self-appropriation"? How have constructed, essentialized discourses of oppression been turned into constructed, essentialized discourses of liberation (Chen 2002: 5)? These questions serve to interrupt the teleological narratives of "the West"; they seek to expose the "continuing impositions and exactions of colonialism" and the trespassing into the present of imperial symbols, identities, imaginings, and meanings rationalized as constituting progress and development (Gregory 2004: 9).

Such a non-rationalist approach to the analysis of imperial histories has not easily found a home in the social sciences. Indeed, compared to the humanities and cultural studies, the social sciences have been slow to take up the post-colonial challenge (Go 2009; Connell 1997). Yet as part of the constructivist turn in international relations during the 1990s, Roxanne Lyn Doty's (Doty 1993, 1996) work became pathbreaking as it sought to reveal the constructed nature of a global hierarchy of "democratic" states which conventional approaches continued to reify and take for granted. In reframing the analytical lens for studying foreign policy from a "why" question, to asking "how" a certain policy, action, or practice becomes possible, Doty's work opened up questions of how ideas and identities came to be considered as natural rather than as purposeful constructions.[12]

Doty's approach to the study of language as power, and her method of discursive analysis is drawn on heavily in this book. Not only the content of discourse, Doty argues, but the rules of discursive production are central to the creation of meanings, identities and logics by which policies and practices otherwise deemed illegitimate can be claimed as legitimate and possible. In her 1996 book *Imperial Encounters*, Doty considers the United States foreign policy towards the Philippines, both during the colonial period and continuing after independence, as an exemplary case of the "politics of representation." Her analysis draws attention to the way the United States, through the discourse of politicians and early colonial officials, represented itself in a particular way in order to legitimize the US–Philippine encounter. Moreover, central to her argument is the way the American colonial project produced "knowledge" about the Philippines and the Filipino "native", that was "disseminated, and put to use to justify US conquest, violence, and subsequent control" (1996: 37) – used to create a consensus for annexation and control of the Philippines that made the action not only possible and legitimate, but a moral imperative for the United States.

While Doty's work examined the way US colonial discourse constructed a Filipino subject in such a way that legitimated a violent policy of domination in the name of democracy, by her own admission this work on the US–Philippines relationship left unexamined the interaction of US colonial discourse with local Filipino discourses, and the way these imperial ideas and practices delivered in the name of democracy were modified and merged with local cultures, norms and discourses. This is precisely the empirical challenge taken up in this book: to trace public dialectical deliberations on the reasoning of politics, through talk and text, in order to bring to light the way dominance, inequality and abuse of power have been enacted, legitimated, reproduced and resisted. The aim is to seek to understand how the encounter at the turn of the twentieth century set in motion certain social logics and constructed subjectivities that have been carried within the middle-class democratic consciousness, and what the history of imperial democracy has to do with contemporary ambivalence.

Genealogy as Method

Postcolonial scholars have raised questions about the analytical tools used to study the imperial past, and the false demarcations that are too often drawn between what is "colonial" and what is "postcolonial"; temporal frames of "before" and "after", and the language of historical "traces", which only serve to represent colonial remnants as "a faint scent of the past" (Stoler 2016: 6). Such distinctions, it is argued, obscure much more than they reveal. On the other hand, totalizing narratives of continuity fail to capture the way that imperial logics of power manifest themselves in ambiguous spaces rather than clearly identifiable forms. As such, a key challenge of this study is to find a methodological framework that might serve to write a history rendering visibility to forces and conditions that have shaped the political subjectivity of the Philippine middle class – effects otherwise occluded by existing frames. The principal method drawn upon in the book is genealogy.

Though often invoked as an abstract, theoretical frame, or as a fashionable euphemism for critical history, genealogy is taken here to be a "grounded, enabling political methodology" that offers acuities to displaced histories, underscores contingency, and avoids assumptions of coherent and singular historical trajectories (Stoler 2016: 23). The principal work of a genealogy is to make visible the "web of determinants that 'make' subjects" (Saar 2008: 302), hinging on the explication of effects of historical processes "on the construction and self-construction of human actors" (Saar 2008: 301). Against teleological narratives, or narratives that reduce present phenomena to preceding forms, genealogy brings to the fore the point that subjectivities are not only historically embedded, but fluid and discontinuous. Genealogical narratives are "activist" in the sense that they are meant to motivate reflection and revision, to "stir up resistance against already established judgements, institutions and practices" (Saar 2008: 313), and to disrupt assertions of naturalness when it comes to subjectivities. At the same time, genealogical narratives grant agency to the subjects of history by paying attention to competing conceptions of subjectivities, to differential histories and battles lost and won, to "unachieved visions and interrupted imaginaries" (Stoler 2016: 23), in order to underscore the contingent quality of historical transformations.

Although the colonial context was absent from the work of its two principal pioneers, Nietzsche[13] and Foucault,[14] the genealogical method has a critical role to play in studying colonial histories. Ann Laura Stoler has skilfully demonstrated the way colonial genealogies draw attention to the question of imperial duress – a condition of constraint that manifests in insistent, often non-verbal, "defamations of personhood" (2016: 8); they also trace imperial effects in what she calls "colonial entailment" – those obscured, often intangible but lasting logics that tenaciously cling to contemporary problems, defying temporalities and even spatial boundaries, and manifesting in seemingly inexplicable acts or beliefs. Colonial entailments, Stoler conceptualizes, are molten in form, adhering to underlying logics of governance, and fixing themselves to "the less tangible emotional economies of humiliation, indignities, and resentments that may manifest in bold acts of refusal to abide" (2016: 4).

Adopting this framework, the task set by this book is to write a genealogy of middle-class democratic ambivalence – to trace the roots of ambivalence's two opposing faces: an unresolved anxiety about the capacity for democratic agency, and a desire for radical transformation. It is the task of the book to demonstrate the way that middle-class orientations to democracy are complex, contingent and non-singular responses, situated in dissensions, unrealized possibilities and failed experiments.

Sources of Data

The data used in the book's analysis comes from a variety of sources. Research was undertaken at archive collections including the American Historical Collection and Filipiana Section at the Ateneo de Manila's Rizal Liberty, the Philippine Congressional Library, and the

Lopez Museum and Library. Primary historical texts, including official colonial documents, periodicals and speeches, were read with an eye to constructions of Filipino and American subjects, as well as meanings attributed to democracy within the texts. Such historical sources, far from being benign accounts, are a key site of social and political contest. Paying attention to conspicuous silences in particular not only serves to interrupt grand historical narratives, it brings into view dynamics of inclusion and exclusion and the struggle between dominance and resistance, which is part of the process of constructing democratic meanings and identities.

I undertake a close reading, including coding and analysis, of the most popular middle-class English language news magazine, *Philippines Free Press*, between 1946 and 1950. Considered the leading national weekly in the decades immediately following independence, the *Free Press* was an important space for discussion of national politics, and a reference point for debates about the nation's democracy. Attention is paid to the way middle-class actors participated in producing, reproducing, adapting and revising a complex of images, identities and norms upon which a shared democratic imaginary is based.

I also conducted 22 long unstructured interviews with middle-class actors in Metro Manila and Cebu City, the purpose of which was not to answer specific questions, but to critically engage with their constructed narratives of historical memories, of how democracy works in practice, and of the rationality of rule. While respondents were classified as "Class C" (middle class) in the Social Weather Station (SWS) stratification methodology, it wasn't on criteria such as income or education status that my sample of respondents was based. Rather, through snowball sampling I sought to include participants who varied in age (the oldest participant was born in the 1930s and the youngest in the 1990s) and gender (13 male, 9 female). I spoke with respondents across a spectrum of political orientations and affiliations, including members of left-wing revolutionary movements, human rights-based groups, business-led political reform programs, and conservative church-based initiatives. All interviews were conducted in person by the author. Each interview was electronically recorded, with permission of the participants, and then later transcribed by the author. Interviews lasted on average between one and two hours.

Along with the original empirical evidence included in the book, the study incorporates material from a broad scope of the existing literature on the Philippine's political history by both historians and social scientists. It is in the synthesis and reinterpretation of these diverse writings that new insights on middle class views have been drawn.

Organization of the Book

The chapters in the book are organized into three parts. The first part, *Democracy and Conquest* begins in the last decades of the nineteenth century, when the economic, social and technological innovations underway in the late Spanish Philippines had precipitated not only structural changes, including new inter-societal cleavages based on class, but a period of civic flourishing. Central to these transformations, and to the ensuing Philippine Revolution, were a new middle-class intelligentsia known as the *ilustrados*, and an embryonic petty-bourgeoisie, both positioned between the arbitrary authority of the Spanish and the worst exploitation of the masses. Though the Philippine authorities issued a Declaration of Independence in June 1898, the movement was interrupted and ultimately quashed by the entry of American forces, beginning a new era of colonialism that lasted until the end of the Second World War.

Building on existing critical American studies (Harris 2011; Kaplan and Pease 1993; Stoler 2006; Kaplan 2002; McCoy and Scarano 2009), this first part of the book brings to light the nature of the US–Philippine encounter beyond a territorial intervention and colonial occupation, as an exercise of implicit domination and subjugation in the name of democracy. Looking at the period of American rule in the Philippines through a constructivist lens, it seeks to problematize a history still dominated by a US diplomatic narrative of "American exceptionalism", "benevolent empire", and "white man's burden", by demonstrating the enabling myths upon which the United States constructed these narratives as a basis for intervention.

Chapter 1 details the way the violence and subjugation that underwrote US colonial policy was sustained by a deeply contradictory logic by which American officials claimed that the protection of Filipino liberties necessitated the indefinite denial of liberty. Compliance with colonial structures of power, however subjugating and violent, became equated with the behaviour required of the good student of democracy; to demonstrate a readiness for self-government was to accept discipline and domination. Daring to question the situation, or advocating independence, subjected Filipinos to accusations of being anything from mischievous, obnoxious, and ungrateful, to bandits, rebels, and conspirators, or simply too ignorant to comprehend what was in their best interests.

Having set out the implicit forms of power embedded within the American imperial architecture, the second part of the book, *Democracy and Duress*, turns to the Philippines' experience of the colonial democracy paradox, from the late nineteenth century to the early 1950s. Rather than subsume decades of history into a simple narrative of middle-class integration and collaboration with the American colonial regime, Chapter 2 demonstrates the way the middle class's response, first to US colonial officials and then to the Philippine's own political class, was far from a straightforward story of passive reception and mimetic reproduction of elite frames. It amplifies the voices of middle-class actors as early as 1910, in what can only be described as open and candid middle-class rejections of the United States' sanctimonious posturing in professing to teach Filipinos about democracy. Far from simple quiescence, these "bourgeois" actors asserted strong criticism of specific policies being introduced under the auspices of "democratic tutelage."

Middle-class actors confronted the complexities of living democratically under such colonial policies and responded in ways that were specific to the conditions of possibility within which they found themselves. As the decades passed, the underlying sentiment of indignation became entangled in a process of recursion, in which middle-class actors attempted to work within the constraints of the colonial order in order to overcome it. The response to the abuses of power by local political elites reveals the complex position in which middle-class citizens found themselves – constrained by the very colonial order that nourished their democratic aspirations.

Chapter 3 focuses on the early independence period, analysing the discourse in the post-war civic sphere to demonstrate the way the postcolonial Philippine society continued to negotiate the moral and political entanglements of the colonial era. Using a close reading of the discourse of the *Philippines Free Press* news magazine, the chapter uncovers an internalization of the constraints of the colonial order, not only through the reification of an asymmetrical relationship between the United States and the Philippines, but through the anxiety and self-doubt that such a construction of the Filipino subject nurtured. It is the most striking evidence to date of an ambivalence embedded within the postcolonial middle-class democratic imaginary – that alongside the deep-rooted and visceral desire for democracy lay an acknowledgment of hypocrisy and disappointment, which nurtured feelings of contrition, anxiety and self-doubt. Radical aspirations for freedom and independence became entangled with wariness about the innate democratic capacity of the Filipino subject. This ambivalent disposition towards democracy amongst the middle class manifested itself in an acquiescence to imperial forms of governance, including the legitimation of anti-democratic politics as a way of saving democracy and the welcoming back of direct American intervention in Philippine affairs.

The final part of the book, ***Democracy and Ambivalence***, seeks to reframe the events of the contemporary Philippines, from the 1960s until the present, through the contradictions of the past. It argues that the ambivalence over democracy deeply embedded within and carried by the middle-class democratic imaginary helps to make sense of a period marked by striking paradoxes and fluctuations. Chapter 4 explores the way the pursuit of freedom and a fulfilment of democratic promises in the postcolonial context made imperative the need for a revolutionary break with the past. Yet this desire for metamorphosis carried within it opposing impulses – an anti-imperialism that demanded dignity and autonomy, along with continuing anxiety and self-doubt about both the capacity of the Filipino subject to undertake the transformation that was required, and the capacity of democracy itself to address local problems. The underlying ambivalence about democracy culminated in broad middle-class support for Marcos's authoritarian regime. It was the same ambivalence, however, that just over a decade later would see the middle class as the key protagonist in a movement demanding an end to Marcos's oppression and tyranny.

Chapter 5 discusses the arrival on the political landscape of the discourse of "people power", following the pivotal anti-Marcos uprising of 1986. Although signifying a political emboldening of the middle class, rather than overcoming the ambivalence of the past, the chapter argues that the "people power" narrative carries ambivalence within it. Much meaning was imputed to the mobilization of February 1986. Democratization discourses from outside heralded it as a tangible expression of the "third wave" sweeping the developing world. In the language of regime transition this was the moment the Philippines moved from an authoritarian system of governance to a democratic one. Yet these teleological discourses failed to understand the complexity of the moment. The EDSA[15] revolution, and the "people power" trope that emerged from it, had (and continue to have) such resonance and political efficacy, not because they signalled the overcoming of democratic ambivalence, but because they accommodated it. The opposing tension – between a refusal to submit to oppressive power, and a sober reflection on the need for self-restraint and moral transformation – rather than being resolved, remained incendiary. The complexities within the "people power" idea culminated perhaps most clearly in the events of 2001, and the middle-class-led ousting of a democratically elected president, Joseph

Estrada, against the will of a majority of voters. Finally, in applying the democratic ambivalence thesis to the Duterte Presidency, sense can be made of the middle-class support for Duterte and his masterful rhetoric that framed an anti-democratic politics, including the denial of individual liberties, as a redemption of the nation – in its imbuing of the Philippine nation and "the people" with dignity and esteem, in its acknowledgement of the failure of democratic politics to transform society, and in its imposition of a strong hand intended to keep the wayward Filipino subject on the straight and narrow.

Summary

The idea of democratic ambivalence is decidedly abstract. It is a theoretical proposition that requires thinking, at a philosophical level, with and against the logics intrinsic to democracy. To convey the texture of the concept requires narrative and storytelling. As James Scott said in his seminal *Weapons of the Weak*, it requires "the flesh and blood of detailed instances to take on substance" (1985: xviii).

For that reason, this book tells a local story, of the indigenization of democratic ambivalence in the Philippines. Even then, it captures only the ideas, languages and negotiations of a relatively vocal segment of the middle class. Conspicuously absent are the ideas and languages of the lower classes. Issues such as ethnic conflict, geographical diversity and religion, which have almost certainly played a role in political events, are largely bracketed. So too, due to space constraints, is an integrated analysis of more than three centuries of Spanish colonialism. The trade-off for such limitations is the study's effort to bring to the fore those parts of Philippine history that show how rich and complex the development of democratic imaginaries can be; to demonstrate what can be learned from a study of democracy that is not centred principally on formal institutions, political behaviour, or on official discourses alone.

My hope is that telling the Philippine story will serve as a bridge to broader considerations about the relevance of the democratic ambivalence thesis in other parts of the world. For ambivalence about democracy in the Philippines may be perspicuous, even extreme at times, but it is not exceptional. In an age when a vast global disenchantment with democracy has been linked almost everywhere to eroding political freedoms, deepening authoritarianism and incidents of democratic breakdowns, the Philippines' journey to democratic ambivalence teaches us lessons of global importance. Ambivalence, this book contends, is not a pathology of democracy, but rather a product of people living democratically. It is the way that people mediate between promises and ideals on the one hand, and the actual reality of the exercise of democratic power on the other. It serves as a warning sign, not that citizens are failing to understand how democracy works, but that all is not well in the existing democratic regime. To disparage ambivalence as a failure of democratic agency, and in its place to make attempts at bringing rationality into democratic politics, is in the words of Nadia Urbinati, to "disfigure" democracy (Urbinati 2014). For not only does this remove from people the agency and volition enshrined in democratic politics, it denies the fact that democracy is, and will always be, both an aspirational ideal and a messy reality that inevitably triggers dissatisfaction and disappointments as much as it triggers trust, belief and hope.

Democracy & Conquest

Dewey could have gone about his affairs elsewhere, and left the competent Filipino army to starve out the little Spanish garrison and send it home, and the Filipino citizens to set up the form of government they might prefer, and deal with the friars and their doubtful acquisitions according to Filipino ideas of fairness and justice – ideas which have since been tested and found to be of as high an order as any that prevail in Europe or America. . . .

The more we examine the mistake, the more clearly we perceive that it is going to be bad for the Business. The Person Sitting in Darkness is almost sure to say: 'There is something curious about this – curious and unaccountable. There must be two Americas: one that sets the captive free, and one that takes a once-captive's new freedom away from him, and picks a quarrel with him with nothing to found it on; then kills him to get his land.'

> (Excerpt from Mark Twain's "To the Person Sitting in Darkness" essay, published in the North American Review in February 1901: 170)

CHAPTER

1

Bridling the Rise of Asia to Make Way for America's "Democratic" Empire

When the American eagle landed in Manila Bay in May 1898, there could scarcely have been a more significant time in history for the formation of the Philippine nation. It was, as Kramer described it, "an emerging 'civilization' finally capable of expressing itself as an independent state" (2006: 173). The winds of change sweeping through the Islands had unleashed a restlessness with the racism and suppression of Spain's colonial apparatus, and an intolerance for the hypocrisy and arbitrariness of clerical authority. When the late nineteenth- century struggle against Spain began in earnest, a revolutionary praxis was birthed, based on discourses of "nationhood" and "the people", that resonated throughout the broader region, leading influential Chinese intellectual at the time Ou Jujia to say the Philippine revolution signalled the "rise of Asia" (Karl 2002).

While the Philippine nation was struggling into existence, the United States was a nation on the brink of imperial dominance. The United States was looking to acquire influence in East Asia. In the crossroads that followed, rather than being emancipated from colonial rule by the American arrival, the Philippine nation would become embroiled in America's attempts to define itself as a benevolent empire and to defend its global pursuits. The encounter between the United States and the Philippines would not only define Philippine modern history; it would become one of the least acknowledged, yet most formative events in the development of American foreign policy.

Ultimately, the Americans would never recognize the first Philippine Republic. On the contrary, the United States was exhaustive in putting an end to the late nineteenth-century period of civic flourishing, aware that acknowledging the vibrant democratic mood would undermine the policy underpinning its takeover. On the ground,

American forces demanded that Filipinos acting under General Aguinaldo give up possession of government posts and withdraw – a dictate accompanied by threats, intimidation, torture, and violence. The ensuing two-and-a-half-year Philippine–American War would become a "forgotten" episode in US military and political history.[1] While American troops hunted Filipino insurgents like animals, in the lofty halls of Washington, Philippine diplomatic demands that their independent status be respected went entirely ignored; as fast as President McKinley and his supporters could close the question of recognizing Filipino independence, the population was converted into passive subjects of the United States.

Through the discourse of politicians and early colonial officials, the United States produced "knowledge" about itself, and about the Filipino "native", that was disseminated and "put to use to justify US conquest, violence, and subsequent control" (Doty 1996: 37). Colonial representations rendering Filipinos "in need of guidance, tutoring, and uplifting" legitimized the denial of Filipino agency. At the same time, this very denial of agency presupposed America's mandate to act. It made it possible, even necessary, to ignore, silence or forcefully repress Filipino attempts to exercise agency, and framed all such policy decisions and practices, not as conquests or exploitations, but as benevolent acts of deliverance and salvation (Doty 1996: 39–44).

"Pregnant with Possibilities": Democratic Discourses of the Late Nineteenth Century

Centuries before the Americans ever imagined annexing the Philippine Islands, the populations of the archipelago were well acquainted with the colonial experience. In 1521, explorer Ferdinand Magellan claimed the Islands for Spain, and over the next three and a half centuries, Las Islas Filipinas provided the Pacific anchor for the imperial trade routes of what was then a European empire. Despite Spain's Reformation Catholicism spreading to the vast majority of the population, the actual Spanish presence and royal control of the Philippine islands remained minimal in comparison to the Spanish Americas. Historians have thoroughly documented the ways that, rather than acquiescing, the populations learned to negotiate colonial power and manipulate colonial relations during the entire period of Spanish rule (Mojares 2006: 395). Catholicism in particular, despite being imposed by Spanish missionaries, was a key arena for subversion. For the largely rural and uneducated lower classes especially, Catholicism creatively evolved into a brand of folk mythology. It provided lowland Philippine society "with a language for articulating its own values, ideals, and even hopes of liberation", and became the basis for a language of anti-colonialism (Ileto 1979: 11–12). The epic of the *pasyon*, for example, was an adaption of the life of Jesus, his birth, death, and resurrection, into a form of pre-Hispanic indigenous poetry which, "far from promoting docility and acceptance of the status quo, actually probed the limits of prevailing social values and relationships"; in a society without legitimate channels of protest, Ileto explains, it provided "the masses" with "a language for venting ill feelings against oppressive friars, principales, and agents of the state" (1979: 15–16).

By the late nineteenth century, new political imaginaries were emerging in the Philippines. The Suez Canal had transformed not only the Islands' integration in commercial trade with Europe; it became an arterial for political ideas and aspirations, and for a new democratic vocabulary to arrive in the Spanish Philippines from the Continent at a time of great political change in Europe itself. The economic, social and technological innovations underway in the Spanish Philippines precipitated a period of civic flourishing. Indeed, this was a time aptly described by Mojares as "pregnant with possibilities" (2006: 474).

Churches, school, printshops and guilds were produced by, and themselves produced, new ways of thinking. It was social demand that drove the expansion of education in the colony rather than the progressiveness or altruism of colonial authorities (Mojares 2006: 420). Higher-level training was also taking place, with local competencies being developed in disciplines including history, anthropology, linguistics and political science, and Filipinos were engaging in research, producing theory, and writing for scientific journals, as well as participating in civic and professional bodies both in the Philippines and Europe (Mojares 2006: 427, 471). In addition, the population within and beyond Manila was becoming increasingly connected and mobile. A cable telegraph service connected Manila to the provinces (1873) and then to the outside world (1880), and within a few years the city would have "the beginnings of a telephone system (1890), electricity (1893), and a railroad service" (Mojares 2006: 434). Infrastructural developments, newspapers and education, along with changes to the systems of production and commerce, became the basis for the development of new class relations within the Islands populations. Printers, lithographers, woodcarvers and carpenters were amongst the workers who formed guilds as early as the 1870s (Mojares 2006: 434).

Structural changes were also accompanied by transformations in social relations, and in the way an increasingly stratified Philippine society viewed both the world at large and the colonial condition in particular. As was already occurring elsewhere in the industrializing world, the transition towards a capitalist economy intensified economic exploitation and social inequality, and on top of the existing asymmetry of colonial relationships, laid the ground for deep inter-societal cleavages on the basis of class (Mojares 2006: 406–7). This included the emergence of an embryonic middle-class intelligentsia, known as *ilustrados*, who were positioned between the arbitrary authority of the Spanish and the exploitation of the masses.

Wealthy *ilustrados* were leaving the Philippines for Europe to pursue their studies, where they joined emerging global networks of middle classes brought together by the realms of scientific knowledge. But rather than passively adopting European ideas and concepts, on the whole the Filipino intelligentsia adapted them, merging them with local culture and conditions. The cosmopolitan attitudes and the quest for individual and social development became intertwined with the articulation and invention of new social identities under conditions of imperial control. Ideals of democracy, equality and justice were discussed and developed alongside the presence of characteristics of empire, including racial discrimination and imperial arrogance (Dejung, Motadel, and Osterhammel 2019: 19).

Filipino intellectual José Rizal's writing was the most significant illustration of this. Addressing a banquet dinner in Madrid in 1884, Rizal made this evocative pronouncement:

> The patriarchal era of the Philippines is passing; the illustrious deeds of her sons are no longer wasted away at home; the oriental chrysalis is leaving the cocoon; the dawn of a long day ahead is heralded in brilliant shades and rose-colored dawns; and that ethnic race, fallen into lethargy during the historic night while the sun shone on other continents, again awakens, moved by the electric impact produced by contact with the people of the West, and begs for light, life and the civilization that once might have been its heritage, thus conforming to the eternal laws of constant evolution, transformation, recurring phenomenon and progress.[2]

Rizal's first novel, *Noli Me Tangere*, was published in the Philippines just before the author's return to his home country in August 1887. A portrayal of corruption and abuse by the colonial government and the Catholic Church, Rizal's book, as San Juan has argued, was "radically seditious in having been written by a native in a manner that actualises in Europe's own distinctive form, the capacity of the Filipino to comprehend, represent, and hence direct his own society" (2011: 62). Even in his choice of the novel, Rizal's writing provided for its readers the sensory experience of rupturing and unravelling colonial epistemologies about the Filipino subject, and undermining "the economy of colonial symbolic power" (San Juan 2011: 62). In doing so, Rizal constituted space for the Other – the repressed identity of the colonial subject – and allowed this new subjectivity to speak; not only to speak in the novel, but to secure independence, and to do so in such a way as to repel other European invaders from even trying to subjugate the nation.

Despite his own privileged social position, Rizal's anti-colonial ideas and propaganda resonated widely, helping to catalyse popular support for the revolution against Spain, and the military resistance against the United States that would follow. Far into the twentieth century, Rizal's name "was on the lips of many a peasant rebel" in the continued struggle against American subjugation (Ileto 1998: 70). His popularity wasn't confined to the Philippines. Given the prevailing international conditions at the time, Rizal became a hero for other oppressed people, and his novels inspired nationalist intellectuals in other parts of Southeast Asia.[3] For these thinkers, Rizal's life symbolized an alternative model of modernization, a path for non-European populations to become nations without having to be conquered.

From Europe, Rizal and compatriots had formed the Propaganda Movement to push for reform. These cosmopolitan intellectuals believed the Philippines could become a province of Spain, if only Spain would agree to certain reforms that included political and legal equality between the Spaniards and Filipinos, representation in the Spanish Cortes, freedom of religion, and freedom of the press. While they had high hopes the Propaganda Movement's campaign would succeed in Spain, when they realized it was failing they turned their attention back to their native country, convinced they could still effect the reforms if they waged their struggle from home.

The propagandists set up *La Solidaridad* in 1889, a political organization with a companion publication, *Solidaridad*, as a vehicle to air the *ilustrado*'s liberal thought, principally addressing the colonial power of Spain in the language of democracy and progress, and to raise the level of political consciousness amongst their fellow Filipinos. By 1895, however, the newspaper publication had stopped. Not that restlessness in the Islands had subsided. To the contrary. Apolinario Mabini, who would become Prime Minister of the revolutionary government, wrote to one of the Propaganda Movement's leaders based in Hong Kong: under constant repression from Spanish authorities the people had lost hope in the paper and had "transferred it wholly in another direction." The subtext was, as Mojares writes, that "the mood had turned insurrectionary" (2006: 464).

The turn away from the Reform Movement, with its assimilationist aspirations and conservative strategies, had begun three years earlier. In July 1892, Spanish authorities arrested Rizal on the charge of rebellion and deported him to Dapitan, on the southern island of Mindanao, his writing having been declared to be "heretical, antipatriotic, and subversive" (Mojares 2006: 448). In that same month the Katipunan was founded, a secret revolutionary society whose early members purchased an old hand press for 650 pesos from a Manila bazaar and began printing its own organ, *Kalayaan*, from January 1896. Within a year, membership of the Katipunan was estimated at 20,000 (Mojares 2006: 464).

The "Brains of the Katipunan", as he became known, was Emilio Jacinto.[4] Jacinto's family were lower-middle class. Unlike wealthier intellectuals such as Rizal, who had travelled to Europe to study, Jacinto completed his education in the Philippines, studying law at the University of Santo Tomas. It was during this time that he joined the Revolutionary Society. It was the negative phenomenological experience of debasement and indignity that shaped Jacinto's worldview, and that of those around him. Like the propagandists, Jacinto was heavily influenced by non-indigenous Western intellectual thought, including the language and concepts of the French Revolution, the Enlightenment's sense of progress, social contract theorists, and the tradition of Christianity long embraced by many Filipinos. He used this knowledge, as philosopher William L. McBride described it, to articulate "the stark, even brutal, contradiction between the ideals that had first been conveyed to the Philippine Islands by the early Spanish colonizers and that continued to be espoused in theory by their successors, on the one hand, and their inhumane, enslaving practices, on the other" (see Gripaldo 2001: xxi).

Critical to Jacinto's role in the revolution against Spain, and other leaders of the Katipunan like him, was the way their discourse connected the cosmopolitan ideas of the wealthier *ilustrados* with the anti-colonial impulses on the ground. Jacinto wrote in Tagalog, rather than Spanish, for a start. What is more, the proclamations, manifestos, songs and plays the Katipuneros used to spread the revolutionary message challenged some of the republican ideas of the *ilustrados*. "If man is essentially human", Jacinto wrote, "he would surely be equally at par with his fellow human beings on the ground of their basic humanity." Flowing from this human equality, there must be "equality in social treatment such that no man ought to enslave or dominate others by reason of race, colour, religion, economic status, etc." (in Gripaldo 2001: 46).

It was in the indigenization of new political ideas that was occurring during the last decades of the nineteenth century, that obvious hybridizations and even discursive contradictions began to emerge. Nowhere was this clearer than in the complexity of language around the notion of "freedom." Prior to the 1880s, neither the concepts of "political freedom" and "liberty", nor the concept of "independence" existed in the Tagalog lexicography. In 1882, when he was approving the translation of his work by fellow propagandist Marcelo H. Del Pilar, Rizal wrote that Del Pilar's coining of the term *kalayaan* was a legitimate equivalent for the Spanish *libertad*. In the ensuing years, the association of the Tagalog term *kalayaan* with the notion of freedom began to "seep down to the consciousness" of all Filipinos (Gripaldo 2001: 10). How people imagined the concept, however, was not straightforward. To nationalist *ilustrados* like Rizal and Del Pilar, whose principal language was Spanish, the Tagalog *kalayaan* was a direct translation of the Enlightenment notion of political independence and autonomous government, of which they saw themselves as the natural leaders (Rafael 2000: 11). To those for whom Tagalog was the vernacular, however, the word invoked a much more complex idea. The root word from which it was derived, *layaw*, referred to "the carefree state associated with childhood when all of one's needs are taken care of by one's parents." Middle-class leaders of the Katipunan Revolutionary Society, like Jacinto, used *kalayaan* not only in the call to end colonial domination, but in a broader moral critique of oppressive conditions under the social hierarchy, including the neglect of those below by those who dominated. But at the grass-roots level, *kalayaan* was a signifier for a kind of "idealized hierarchy", a "state of sublime dependency" (Rafael 2000: 12–13), and of utopian longings for a state of perfect dependency under a redemptive and benevolent patron (Ileto 1979). In other words, as Rafael explains, amongst Tagalog speakers there was a double connotation of freedom – one that undermined hierarchy and one that idealized it (2000: 12–13).[5]

It was precisely in the negotiation of worlds, between abstract and imported ideas, local realities of colonial subjugation, and the adaptation of religious beliefs and popular folk mythologies, that complex expectations and imaginaries of freedom were born in the archipelago in the late nineteenth century. The forcible introduction of American colonialism to the Philippines at this critical juncture not only exacerbated these complexities, but also ensured they became embedded in the imaginary of "democracy."

"Westward the Star of Empire Takes its Way": The Roots of America's Far East Policy

The colonialism of the late nineteenth century is most commonly associated with the "scramble for Africa", from the Berlin Conference of 1884 to the beginning of the First World War. Less commonly addressed is the violent history of invasion and occupation by Western powers in East and Southeast Asia. It wasn't until the Second World War that Asia became central to the discourse of colonialism and imperialism. But in fact, the closing years of the nineteenth century had witnessed "a tremendous unleashing of imperialism in East Asia"; by 1900 the great imperialistic powers had reached the conclusion "that their future strength and security would be determined in some major degree by their influence in or their control over areas in East Asia" (Clyde and Beers 1991: 247).

From the early 1890s, a Far Eastern policy had been taking shape in the minds of pro-expansionists in the United States. In realpolitik, the Philippines represented the establishment of a US command post in the Western Pacific, and a commercial port near China, signalling they meant business in global relations. But while the Philippines was not America's first foray into territorial acquisition,[6] the geographical distance of the Philippines and the scale of its acquisition saw domestic debates over the relationship between democracy and empire rise to previously unseen heights.

Proponents of territorial expansion argued that the United States had "come of age": that "it could no longer be held within the old continental borders; that the commerce of the world was beckoning to American enterprise; and that benighted areas and backward people were calling to the beneficent forces in American civilization" (Clyde and Beers 1991: 218). This last basis, they knew, appealed to something ingrained in the American psyche: the sense of themselves as a "blessed" people, with an obligation to export their "exceptional" culture and way of life to the rest of world. "Westward the Star of Empire takes its Way", Senator Albert J. Beveridge proclaimed in a famous 1900 speech: "Not the star of kingly power, for kingdoms are everywhere dissolving in the increasing rights of men; not the star of autocratic oppression, for civilization is brightening and the liberties of the people are broadening under every flag." It was a prophetic voice, Beveridge claimed, that was calling America to take its "star of empire" to the world – "the star of the empire of liberty and law, of commerce and communication, of social order and the Gospel of our Lord – the star of the empire of civilization of the world [...] And to-day it illuminates our path of duty across the Pacific into the islands and lands where Providence has called us" (in Frohnen 2009: 496).

The debates within United States over what to do with the former Spanish colony of the Philippines, along with the territories of Cuba and Puerto Rico, brought to light the contradictions in America's own national story, within nineteenth-century constructions of who American citizens were, and what their government's relationship with other nations should be (Harris 2011: 5). In the context of white American preoccupations with race, class and empire in the late nineteenth century, the prospect of becoming a colonizing power was in fact an opportunity to reaffirm the United States' own national identity, and to crystallize, as McCoy, Scarano and Johnson write, a "U.S. national consensus about the centrality of race to nationhood" (2009: 19).

Ideological Foundations of America's "Manifest Destiny"

The notion of "exceptionalism" has been and remains the political ideology around which the United States is organized. In 1831, when French aristocrat Alexis de Tocqueville first coined the phrase "American exceptionalism", he put his finger on a palpable ethos and spirit of equality with liberty, talking of the "American way of life" as "a great democratic revolution" sweeping the world (Tocqueville [1835] 2007: 9). Since then, the works describing America's innate assent to notions of democracy, liberty, individualism, and egalitarianism have been voluminous.

Nowhere is America's "exceptionalism" better demonstrated, so the narrative goes, than in relation to the century of American internationalism. Divorced from the histories of continental Europe, the United States' historiographic tradition has viewed American nation-building as materially different. "[O]ne of the central themes of American historiography", wrote William Appleman Williams in 1955, "is that there is no American empire" (1955: 379), a belief that was widely held until the late 1980s. This helps to explain why studies of colonialism and empire, until very recently, almost entirely omitted the role of the United States: an omission that has served only to reinforce the notion of "American exceptionalism" (Kaplan and Pease 1993: 17).

At the time of his visit to the new continent, Tocqueville was favourably comparing what he saw as the emerging democratic order in the "New World" with the "old" aristocratic politics of his home nation of France, yet he also took pains to point out in his writing the disturbing paradoxes and perils that threatened American democracy.

First was the contradiction that "civil society" excluded America's black population. In fact, for the French observer, American slavery presented the biggest and most immediate danger to representative democracy.

As in seventeenth and eighteenth-century Europe, the development of a democratic ethos in the United States was closely connected to the white supremacist character of the polity (Baum and Harris 2009: 3). American freedom, especially revolutionary republicanism, emerged in tandem with the belief in racial essentialism (Morgan 1975). Even as the Declaration of Independence (1776) asserted, "All men are created equal", it warned of the "merciless Indian savages", and was entirely silent about slavery (Baum and Harris 2009: 11).

The racism within domestic politics came to justify the United States' expansionary vision. First stated in the 1840s, the idea of an American Manifest Destiny was grounded in the "race science" of scholars such as Samuel George Morton, whose 1839 book *Crania Americana* made the biological case for white supremacy (Baum and Harris 2009: 12). This culminated as early as 1846–1848 in the Mexican-American War, in which the US government annexed the Mexican territories. It was followed by near annihilation of Plains Indians in the "US Indian Wars" between 1865 and 1890 (Hoganson 2017: 5). By the time of the Spanish–American War at the end of the century, the way was paved for global racial politics that would establish the United States as an imperial power.

The second half of the nineteenth century would justify another of Tocqueville's gloomy predictions about the fate of "American exceptionalism" – the corrupting force of money in politics. The "Gilded Age", as it became known, saw the rise of a new "aristocracy" to threaten democracy in the form of big business and big government. By the end of the century, democracy and dollars had American politics and its government system in a tight grip. The concentration of wealth in the hands of a new class of industrialists and financiers such as J D Rockefeller and Andrew Carnegie had transformed American social life. Elections became big business, as victory ensured access to contracts and funds, and a political patronage system saw voters enticed by party bosses and machines with the promise of jobs (Keane 2009: 338).

While American society created such wealth as the world had never seen, it was experiencing an unprecedented revival of Christianity. The millions of dollars accrued to Rockefeller's oil fortune were matched by evangelist Dwight Moody's one million converted souls. Another anomaly within the American imaginary of democracy was exposed – not only did commercialism and democracy go hand in hand, but the synthesis of religion with commerce and politics was an underlying conviction. As Melba Maggay aptly reflects, "the image of the Puritan fleeing the decayed monarchies and religious intolerance of Europe seems to have fused with the rugged pioneer pushing out into the vast expanse of frontier existence and the carpetbagger blowing into town with a fast deal" (2011a: 2).

Two tenets of the late nineteenth-century Protestant Church in particular were conducive to the sanctioning of the rapid social changes of industrialization. The first was the separation of the realm of economic activity from moral considerations. "Labor is a commodity", wrote the author of a religious journal in 1874, "and, like all other commodities, its condition is governed by the imperishable laws of demand and supply. It is all right to talk and declaim about the dignity of labor . . . But when all has been said of it, what is labor but a matter of barter and sale?" (in Brauer 1966: 236). Second was the equating of poverty with sin. "The number of the poor to be sympathized with is very small", wrote one clergyman at the time. "To sympathize with a man whom God has punished for his sins, thus to help him when God will still continue a just punishment, is to do wrong, no doubt about it" (in Gutman 1966: 76 n8). If the poor were offered any advice at all from the Church, it was to work hard, become rich, then give liberally of their wealth. While the premillennial evangelists of the American "spiritual revival" taking place at the same time lent a shallow sympathy, they saw no basis on which to offer redress since they believed that none of the basic problems of the world could be solved until Christ's return (Gutman 1966).

As with the issue of race, these ideas were applied to the question of citizenship: the capacity for citizenship and self-government became associated with particular behavioural practices and economic/social values (Harris 2011: 44). The linkage between values and behaviours on the one hand, and political agency on the other, was very important. The "performance of values" was the outward sign that a person had "internalized his or her culture's values." Judgements about the capacity for citizenship and the understanding of republicanism were based on how well people could embody the "American" identity (Harris 2011: 44). The goal of American educators was to teach nineteenth-century American schoolchildren not only numeracy and literacy, but also the basic values of American citizenship – honesty, self-control, orderliness, thrift – and "to help children understand the centrality of behavior [...] to their standing in the community" (Harris 2011: 50).

What is more, social and political questions of the day were interpreted through a religious frame, and as "battles between God and the devil so that compromise [was] virtually unthinkable" (Lipset 1988:

40). Maggay again points out the oddity that "the first country to formalise the separation of church and state as a constitutional principle should so wed religion and politics that its national sense of purpose and self-identity is framed within a system of meaning that is essentially religious in its underpinnings" (2011a: 7).

Together, these ideals and practices – commercial, religious, and racial – were deployed in the construction of the American identity and the national idea of "self"; they were the ground upon which the social meanings of democracy, freedom and citizenship were established. What is more, the racially, religiously and commercially charged "Manifest Destiny" narrative of the nineteenth century developed into a broader foreign policy. Over the next century, the expanding commercial and military footprint of the United States would be matched, and in fact supported, by the desire to make its cultural and religious presence a "force for good" in the world (Hoganson 2017: 9)

The Oriental Prize

Beginning in 1895, the developments in American foreign policy coincided with debates on whether the United States should intervene in Spain's brutal campaigns to repress the uprisings in its colonies (Hilfrich 2012: 14).

It was no coincidence that on the eve of the US entry into global politics with the Spanish–American War, domestic politics was a bubbling cauldron. Notions of egalitarianism clashed with the growing public awareness of unprecedented wealth disparities. The period of rapid transformation from an agricultural society into an urbanized, industrialized nation of bustling factories produced a poor and exploited proletariat, who formed the basis of a trade union movement pushing back against the injustices of the new industrial economy. An unprecedented number of workers rose up in protest against the abuses of the capitalist elite. Racial tensions had also reached boiling point, with fierce debates over who qualified as an American "citizen." The prospect of becoming a global power presented an opportunity to reaffirm and reinvigorate the narrative of the "exceptional" American national identity.

President William McKinley, previously reluctant, moved to favour war. In April 1898, he asked Congress's permission to intervene, arguing for the need to "put an end to the barbarities, bloodshed, starvation, and horrible miseries now existing" in Cuba (McKinley 1898). It was the claim that Americans were obliged to "liberate" the Cubans from Spanish oppression that had proved the most compelling factor.

Before long, the same justifications for the Spanish–American War came to be applied to the Philippines. From their anchor off Hong Kong, President McKinley ordered Commodore George Dewey and his squadron to head south to Manila Bay. On 1 May 1898, five American cruisers and a gunboat entered in single file during the night and within hours had sunk the Spanish fleet, forcing the Spanish to fully surrender (Cotterell 2010: 147). When news of Dewey's naval victory reached the United States, the country went wild with excitement. Streets were renamed after the new Admiral, and "Dewey" cocktails were sipped, despite the fact there was still no concrete policy on what to do with this "Oriental" prize. Nevertheless, President McKinley expressed to Congress that "[a]t this unsurpassed achievement the great heart of our nation throbs, not with boasting or with greed of conquest, but with deep gratitude that this triumph has come to a just cause […]' (Clyde and Beers 1991: 219–20).

At the time of the arrival in Manila Bay of Admiral Dewey and a US fleet, the Philippines revolutionary army under General Emilio Aguinaldo already controlled a majority of the archipelago. Spanish authorities were left defending little more than Manila and its immediate surrounds. At the inaugural session of the government of the first Philippine Republic, held at the Barasoain Catholic Church in Malolos, Bulacan on 15 September 1898, Aguinaldo as leader of the Malolos Congress addressed those gathered:

> I am deeply grateful to you for coming to this Congress. I can say that with the establishment of this Congress, our battle for freedom is at an end. Let all nations take notice that we have an Army, a Congress, and a Government, three things needed to replace the Spanish rule in our beloved Philippines. All progressive nations, like America, France and England, also 'availed of these three things to attain liberty, wisdom, and wealth.' (Guevara 1972: 210)

Revolutionary leaders at the time had written about the tenuous balance of power around the Philippines at the turn of the century, but the United States was not included in the list of potential threats. Most other intellectuals and political thinkers in the Philippines knew American political history well, and given the primacy of liberty and self-rule that underpin the founding documents of the once encumbered colony, they had no reason to suspect the United States would be anything other than a sympathizer and ally to Filipino aspirations of the same.[7] After all, as Aguinaldo would later reminisce, "we were in our own country upholding to the death the sound and sacred

Jeffersonian principle that government should be with the consent of the governed" (Abueva 1976: 118). US President William McKinley, what is more, had stated the American position on the Islands' independence in unambiguous terms: that "forcible annexation . . . cannot be thought of, [and] by our code . . . would be criminal aggression" (in Abueva 1976: 118).

During the first six months of the American presence in the Islands, the US military envoy sent reports back to Washington about the civilized and educated population of the Philippines (Van Meter 1900). By the following February, however, American soldiers had turned their guns on the local population. In November 1899, President McKinley held an interview with a delegation of Methodist ministers in Washington, during which he explained that after sleepless nights and fervent prayer, he had decided to acquire all of the Philippines "to educate the Filipinos, and uplift and civilize and Christianize them, and by God's grace to do the very best we could by them, as our fellowmen for whom Christ died." After which, he told those gathered, he went to bed and slept soundly, the next morning sending for the War Department's Chief Engineer and instructing him to put the Philippines on the United States map (Apilado 1999). From this moment, the two histories – one of the Philippine's struggle for independence, the other the emergence of America as an imperial world power – became irreversibly intertwined.

The "Imperialism Debate"

Although remaining largely submerged in American studies and diplomatic history, the policy of acquisition of the Philippine Islands in particular faced fierce opposition at home. Between the signing of the Treaty of Paris with Spain in December 1898,[8] and the US presidential election of November 1900, dramatic debates on the normative boundaries of America's democratic ideal occurred inside the US Senate, as well as in the press and on various public platforms. At its heart, the debate revolved around the question of how to evaluate the interaction between America's imperial and military pursuits on the one hand, and its democratic idealism on the other. The people of the Philippines were placed, unwittingly, at the centre of what became known as America's "imperialism debate" (Hilfrich 2012: 1).[9] At stake for the US was the chance to redefine its "exceptional" status to include a territorial conquest of a magnitude previously unknown.

The Senate vote of February 1899 to ratify the Treaty of Paris, which would go down as one of the most significant decisions in the history of US foreign policy, was passed by a majority of only one. What is more, the "Bacon Amendment", which would have defined as transient rather than permanent the American presence in the Philippines, was only defeated by the Vice-President's deciding vote (Abueva 1976: 118).[10]

The public campaign against Philippine annexation was led by anti-imperialist societies. In November 1898, on the eve of war, they organized themselves into the Anti-Imperialist League, with chapters in Boston, Washington, Chicago, and many smaller towns and cities (Kramer 2006: 182). Not all of those involved in the League, and against the Philippine annexation, espoused what would be judged today as admirable motives. The loose coalition drawn together by the movement included white supremacist Democrats and an older generation of liberal Republicans. For many of the latter, the argument against taking the Philippines was based on the danger of "empire" to the US "republican virtue"; for the former, the arguments were explicitly racial – "annexation of the Philippines would lead to the 'corruption' of the US body politic itself through Filipino citizenship and the 'degrading' of US labor by additional waves of 'Asiatic' immigrants" (Kramer 2006: 183). The implication was that the Philippine people's lack of capacity for political rationality would threaten the political institutions of the United States.

For other anti-imperialists, however, the argument against annexation hinged on "the recognition of the Philippine Republic in national terms (as a state)", as Kramer explains "[and of] Filipinos in racial terms (as civilized)" (2006: 183). Once the war began, many stressed the point that the war of liberation had in fact become a war of conquest. They made it known that they did not buy into the rhetorical strategies of McKinley and others, designed to obfuscate realities unfolding on the ground. Additionally, by denying the Philippines independence and freedom, the United States was not only betraying its pre-war promises, but was also stepping into the shoes of Spain (Hilfrich 2012: 20).

Political battles over the United States' status as an imperial power continued to be fought in the lead-up to the presidential election of November 1900. The election became one of the most critical contests over foreign policy in American political history. McKinley ran his Republican campaign for re-election on a pro-expansionist, imperialist policy, backed by some of the wealthiest and most powerful men in the country; meanwhile, the Democratic Party opposition campaign, led by William Jennings Bryan, was built primarily on a policy of giving the Philippines independence. Bryan was a supporter of McKinley's entry into the Spanish–American War, and even supported the ratification of the Treaty of Paris.[11] But it was when the Bacon Amendment failed to pass, and with it an assurance that Filipinos would be allowed to develop a "stable and independent government", that Bryan began speaking out.

Running as an anti-imperialist in 1900, Bryan found his platform supported by the Anti-Imperialist League's most prominent member, the acclaimed author and humourist Mark Twain. Twain wrote letters, essays and pamphlets questioning the Philippine–American War. Like Bryan, Twain had initially supported America's involvement in the Philippines, believing the US to be fighting solely to free the Islands, along with Cuba, from Spanish oppression. It wasn't until he read the Treaty of Paris document, which stated that the United States had paid Spain twenty million dollars for the Philippines, that his private opposition began. This turned public in 1900, at which point his fame drew national attention to his views. He returned from Europe to the US in October, one month before the hotly contested election. As reporters surrounded him in New York upon disembarking from the ship, Twain announced to the crowd:

> I left these shores, at Vancouver, a red-hot imperialist. I wanted the American eagle to go screaming into the Pacific. It seemed tiresome and tame for it to content itself with the Rockies. Why not spread its wings over the Philippines, I asked myself? And I thought it would be a real good thing to do.
>
> I said to myself, here are a people who have suffered for three centuries. We can make them as free as ourselves, give them a government and country of their own, put a miniature of the American constitution afloat in the Pacific, start a brand new republic to take its place among the free nations of the world. It seemed to me a great task to which we had addressed ourselves.
>
> But I have thought some more, since then, and I have read carefully the Treaty of Paris, and I have seen that we do not intend to free, but to subjugate the people of the Philippines. We have gone there to conquer, not to redeem . . .
>
> It should, it seems to me, be our pleasure and duty to make those people free, and let them deal with their own domestic questions in their own way. And so I am an anti-imperialist. I am opposed to having the eagle put its talons on any other land. (Twain and Zwick 1992: 5)

Although it would be McKinley and the imperialists who would ultimately win the 1900 presidential poll, the anti-imperialist campaign had succeeded in putting Washington on notice that its public rhetoric on the annexation of the Philippines needed to align with America's democratic values. They had pushed McKinley's administration to promise that the Philippines would eventually be granted independence (Hilfrich 2012).

Twain's writings in particular had put him at the centre of political debates. Given his popularity, the imperialist press found his views difficult to dismiss (Twain and Zwick 1992: xxxiv). In the months and years that immediately followed, Twain would condemn the racism of US soldiers toward Filipinos and the assertion that Filipinos were not capable of self-government. Ability to govern, he argued, came from strength of character and unfaltering patriotism, not race (Twain and Zwick 1992: xxxii). As Zwick recounts, Twain "thought the many atrocities the United States performed during the war demonstrated that the Filipinos were more civilised than those who sought to rule them", and he based his arguments on logic and circumstances. "Corruption and lynchings were commonplace in the United States", he contended, "but no one argued that self-government should be abandoned, thus why should imperfect conditions in the Philippines preclude self-government there?" (1992: xxxii). The war, for Twain, was loaded with contradictions that he detested, not least the idea of patriotism. After all, the Filipinos were patriots, fighting for the independence of their country; whereas it was a blind patriotism, Twain argued, that was represented by the majority of US citizens supporting the war.

A Cacophony of Alibis

> Did we need their consent to perform a great act for humanity? We had it in every aspiration of their minds, in every hope of their hearts. Was it necessary to ask their consent to capture Manila, the capital of their islands? [Laughter.] Did we ask their consent to liberate them from Spanish sovereignty, or to enter Manila Bay and destroy the Spanish sea-power there? We did not ask these things; we were obeying a higher moral obligation which rested on us and which did not require anybody's consent. [Great applause and cheering] (McKinley 1900a: 187–93)

President McKinley made these remarks to a clearly delighted Boston audience in February 1899. America's unique democratic history had endowed it with an unmatched liberal character so that only the United States "would be able to construct a 'wise and beneficent governmental authority over a rude people' and offer its imperial subjects an 'impulse and guidance toward the attainment of a higher form of life and larger liberty'" (Go 2007: 78).

The United States was not the first empire to believe itself exceptional; indeed, the history of empires suggests this to be a common trait. Yet in reflecting on the distinctiveness of the US empire, it is striking how this sense of superiority and of imperial destiny fed upon a strange brew of religious idealism, racial essentialism, and hard mercantilism. Although incoherent to the outsider, the multitude of alibis used to legitimize conquest of the Philippines from 1899 was bound up in an American sense of itself as the ultimate democracy, and a force for good in the world.

A Divine Mandate

In deliberations over what to do with the Philippines, both sides of the annexation debate invoked the United States' divine mandate to shape the rest of the world in its own image. After all, one of the hallmarks of late nineteenth-century American political culture was the conflation of the twin agenda of religious enlightenment and political emancipation.

For annexationists, the Philippines represented the chance to manifest the mandate from God, "not simply to set an example of progress to other nations but to actively replicate itself around the globe" (Harris 2011: 25). Opponents of annexation also called on America's Christian mission to defend the opposite view. But as occupation and war ensued, religious idealism became central to the enactment of American policy in the Philippines. The possibility of introducing "moral and social progress" and the "effecting [of] change in the individual consciousness" would become a key motivating force amongst Protestant missionaries who went to the Islands (Maggay 2011a: 6–7). In the conquest of the Islands, missionaries proved to be a most effective force. As one high-ranking officer told the visiting Chairman of the Standing Committee on Foreign Missions, Reverend George F. Pentecost, "the presence of a Protestant missionary in any part of the islands was worth more than a battalion of soldiers for all purposes of pacification" (Maggay 2011a: 15). Completely disregarding the Christianity of the Spanish period, not to mention the published theological and intellectual writings of Filipinos themselves, United Brethren missionary Ernest J. Pace wrote to his Board secretary:

> . . . the rising generation of Filipinos represent to us as radiant an opportunity as one could hope for. Unfettered and unwarped as their

fathers were, knowing nothing of the intellectual serfdom of Spanish days, they are being trained under the modern system of education that is creating a new brand of Filipino. He is learning to weigh things with an unbiased mind, to view events in history in their proper perspective. He learns the reasons why nations like America, England and Germany are great, namely, that underneath all is reverence for God. (Maggay 2011a: 13)

Such "benevolent paternalism" was rooted in the conviction held by missionaries at the time that ultimately democracy requires "a political culture whose inward character [is] shaped and transformed by Christ" (Maggay 2011a: 11). Only through their brand of Christian civilization, they assumed, could a country develop the kind of institutions and mindsets that would guarantee democracy. This supported the official government policy that independence for the Philippines could be considered only when Filipinos had demonstrated such behavioural prerequisites as honesty, self-control, and orderliness (Harris 2011).

Whether or not all users of this rhetoric intended it to deceive, the effect was the construction of violence as love – the "peacemaking guns of Admiral Dewey", said Chairman of the Presbyterian Committee on Foreign Mission, "have opened the gates which henceforth make accessible not less than 8,000,000 people" (Maggay 2011a: 5). Or, as Senator Edward W. Carmack from Tennessee passionately argued in the Senate in 1902, "We are killing these people over there for the salvation of their souls. We are extending our Christian civilization in the Philippines over the dead bodies of the Filipinos. We are building up the Church of God out of human bones, cemented together with human blood" (in Harris 2011: 60). What is more, this evangelical mandate was not inconsistent with America's commercial objectives. "The United States could no longer ignore the responsibilities of the 'white man's burden' to civilize and to Christianize less fortunate peoples . . . if, in the course of doing all this, some Americans made an honest profit in the new business fields, so much the better" (Clyde and Beers 1991: 218).

Fighting Savages, for Democracy's Sake

Under pressure from the anti-imperialists over American intentions in the Philippines and reports of US atrocities in the Pacific, President McKinley appointed what would be the first of two "Philippine Commissions." As it arrived in Manila in early 1899, one of the Commission's primary goals was to produce "knowledge" about the Filipino population in order to rationalize the war, its ends and means, for an American public (Kramer 2006: 185). Despite the fact that for at least two decades prior to 1898 Filipinos had been contesting the racial precepts of the Spanish, and the racism which underpinned Spanish colonialism, the Philippine Commission set out to present "facts" that would effectively "tribalize" the Filipino population in scientific terms (Kramer 2006). The construction of a "self" and an "other" that would follow was a case of Edward Said's orientalism par excellence.

The trope of savagery was not unique to American war rhetoric, dating back as far as 1812 when colonial rule was overthrown with a call to arms against British diabolism and the tyrannical and murderous English. The war declared against Mexico in 1846 was similarly portrayed "as a reluctant act of national defence in response to an irrational and evil Mexican aggressor, a belligerent foe that was easily inflamed and as unstable as a violent storm" (Ivie 2005: 56). When the two-year war ended with the annexation of half of Mexico's territory, the Boston publisher and bookseller Nahum Capen (1804–1886) had declared it a victory for "democracy" on the same scale as the battle of the Athenians against the Persians: "The cause of democracy is a universal cause of equal rights and freedom [...] and it is placed with us, more than with any other people, to be protected, preserved, and advanced' (in Keane 2009: 370–1). This kind of hubris paved the way for the quiet occupation of territories in the name of democracy, with the threat or actual use of force.[12]

Five decades later, as the United States was about to enter the twentieth century, President McKinley declared the "savages" of the Philippines would be the beneficiaries of America's "noble generosity" and "Christian sympathy and charity." Descriptions of "natives" were "driven by a logic of difference that established the identities and relative positions of the United States and its other(s) as fixed and natural" (Doty 1996: 36). After being classified in a racial hierarchy (from Negritos at the bottom to the Indonesians of Mindanao at the top), the Islands' population (excepting a small oppressive elite) were described as good but primitive and "densely, inconceivably ignorant" masses, whose ignorance prevented them from even understanding what freedom was (Doty 1996: 37). Filipinos were represented as innately endowed with characteristics that ranged from the more benign, childlike "lacking the rationality generally attributed to adults" and as being "impulsive, unreflective, imitative, and unaware of consequences", to resembling animals more than humans, likened to a "faithful dog", more likely to "feed" than to "dine" (Doty 1996: 39).

These "facts" would become the basis of defence for the Philippine Commission's central ethnological and political conclusion: "The Filipinos are not a nation, but a variegated assemblage of different tribes and peoples, and their loyalty is still of the tribal type" (in Kramer 2006: 187). Written by zoologist Dean C. Worcester, the Report made the argument that "tribal" fragmentation was evidence of backwardness in social evolutionary theory which held that societies evolved from "savagery" to "civilization." Representing the Filipinos as without reasoning processes and intellectual capacity also rendered them incapable of self-government, "in need of guidance, tutoring, and uplifting", and ultimately, "incapable of exercising agency" (Doty 1996: 39–43). As such, it ruled out any possibility of recognizing the Philippines as a nation, or the Philippine Republic as a legitimate state (Kramer 2006). "These Americans told themselves", Harris writes, that "they were doing the Filipinos a great favor, because a US administration in the archipelago would protect the Filipinos from the consequences of their hereditary incapacity for self-governance" (2011: 61).

Filipino racial inferiority was also used to justify the use of force by American troops, in what effectively became a race war (Kramer 2006). US journalists on the ground were struck by the changing language used by American soldiers to talk about the Filipinos. Not only did the term "nigger" come into heavy circulation, the enemy was increasingly defined as the entire Filipino population, and such ethnological homogeneity as a "savage" race made "exterminist warfare" viable (Kramer 2006: 201). Incidents of violence against both Filipino prisoners and civilians, including the use of water cure as torture, became increasingly recorded. Perhaps most striking was the increasing use of the metaphor of hunting animals. Only two months after the fighting began in 1899, Lieutenant Telfer wrote that it was "great fun for the men to go on 'nigger hunts'", a relief from the boredom of guarding the railway at Marilao (Kramer 2006: 204). When the Filipino fighters, out of necessity, turned to guerilla tactics, such methods of combat were seen as further evidence of the savagery of the whole population. Those not fighting a "civilized" war were deemed not worthy of being treated in a civilized manner.

There is no doubt that violence was at the heart of America's early engagement in the Islands. Yet even this became viewed as a case of American goodness. "The warfare that has extended the boundaries of civilization at the expense of barbarism and savagery has been for centuries one of the most potent factors in the progress of humanity", President Theodore Roosevelt told a large crowd gathered at the opening of Arlington Cemetery on 4 May 1902. The cemetery was inaugurated as a symbol of national sacrifice and honour, memorializing "the triumph of civilization over forces which stand for the black chaos of savagery and barbarism." Yes, there had been US abuses and brutalities by American troops in the Philippines, but the noble, universal ends justified the unsavoury means. Keep in mind, Roosevelt reminded the crowd, that for every American abuse, "a hundred acts of far greater atrocity" had been committed by "a very cruel and very treacherous enemy" (in Kramer 2006: 169).

Similar defences could be found in congressional debates of the time. Faced with evidence of American soldiers using the water cure in interrogation to force Filipino prisoners to confess to their part in the nationalist resistance, a Senator from Wisconsin, John C. Spooner, rationalized the events with a line-by-line exegesis of the US Declaration of Independence: when the document refers to "people", Spooner insisted, this related to Americans of English descent, "because only they manifested the homogeneity necessary for self-government"; "Scattered tribes [a designation he gave the Filipinos] do not constitute a people", he insisted, so the Declaration did not apply to them (Harris 2011: 71).

For all the belief in behaviour as demonstration of civic virtue, white America at the start of the twentieth century still doubted that non-whites would ever be capable of ruling themselves. "You may change the leopard's spots", argued Virginia Senator John W. Daniels before the President, "but you will never change the different qualities of the races which God has created in order that they may fulfil separate and distinct missions in the cultivation and civilization of the world" (Harris 2011: 75–6).

Liberty Denied is Freedom Gained

The proponents of annexation manipulated the language of "democracy" to rationalize the objectives of US foreign policy. In particular, the theme of liberation and "liberty" was central. By exploiting ambiguities in the concept of freedom, they were able to justify American sovereignty over the Philippines, while insisting they were guaranteeing Filipino liberty.

First, this was achieved by conceptualizing liberty negatively. Freedom for the Philippines was defined as liberation from the tyranny of the Spanish oppressors. This, according to expansionists, implied a "positive responsibility" on the United States to intervene, and the "impossibility" of their doing otherwise (Hilfrich 2012: 17). The notion of American responsibility, or "duty", became a consistent theme in the rhetoric of President McKinley. In October 1898, for example, even before the official signing of the Paris Treaty, he made a proclamation in Chicago:

> The war has put upon the nation grave responsibilities. Their extent was not anticipated, and could not have been well foreseen. We cannot escape the obligations of victory . . . Accepting war for humanity's sake, we must accept all obligations which the war in duty and honor imposed on us. (McKinley in Hilfrich 2012: 18)

Following the Treaty's ratification by Congress, and the outbreak of open conflict in and around Manila Bay, this liberation argument became the basis for fighting the Filipino forces, and for deeming those resistant to American controls as "ungrateful rebels." If liberty for the Filipinos was the outcome of peace and justice, it was the rebels who were prolonging the resistance and disorder in the Islands' administration, who were to blame for delaying it. It would be against both logic and history, argued McKinley, to contend that the United States had any other agenda:

> We never dreamed that this little body of insurgents whom we had just emancipated from oppression . . . would turn upon the flag that has sheltered them against Spain . . . This nation for nearly a century has not compromised liberty . . . and Abraham Lincoln spoke in 1863 the proclamation of liberty to all men beneath the flag . . . Our flag stands for liberty wherever it floats; and we propose to put sixty-five thousand men behind that flag in Luzon, to maintain the authority of the United States and uphold the sovereignty of the republic in the interest of civilization and humanity. (McKinley 1900b: 280–2)

Once the Filipino forces formally ceded to the United States in 1901, Filipino liberty became consistent with American sovereignty through making the former contingent and conditional upon learning "good government." The violence and subjugation that continued to underwrite the policy of benevolent assimilation was deemed legitimate by virtue of its consistency with the tutelary aim of American colonization. Only by being deprived of their right to positive liberty could the Filipinos' negative liberty be safeguarded. "We do not deny them liberty", claimed Senator Beveridge, "we instruct them in liberty":

> Liberty manifests in just institutions. Equal laws are liberty, we have given them to the Filipinos. Impartial courts are liberty; we have given

them to the Filipinos. Free education is liberty; we are giving it to the Filipinos. (in Hilfrich 2012: 22)

In addition to blurring the lines between positive and negative liberty, the imperialists made their democratic case by linking the idea of liberty to modernization, and to social and economic progress. Promises of economic development – and of a higher standard of living than had been provided by the Spanish – were designed to justify a sustained denial of positive liberty (Hilfrich 2012: 34). It was not only through the instruction for self-government, as McKinley declared in December 1899, it was in the US government's development objectives for the Philippines:

[…] to open the schools and the churches, to set the courts in operation, to foster industry and trade and agriculture, and in every way in our power to make these people whom Providence has brought within our jurisdiction feel that it is their liberty and not our power, their welfare and not our gain, we are seeking to enhance. (in Hilfrich 2012: 34)

The Need for Censorship

For these alibis to be effective domestically at the time, censorship was also required – especially as members of the Anti-Imperialist League were doing their best to distribute information about the harmful effects of the war.

One of the most significant compilations of source material, in the form of personal letters, official reports and media statements, was that collated by Henry Hooker Van Meter. Though some might say it was badly organized, Van Meter's 400-plus-page *The Truth About the Philippines from Official Records and Official Sources* (Van Meter 1900) drew on primary evidence to refute as falsehood McKinley's rhetoric on the Philippines encounter.

One prominent theme in the collection was the censoring of news about the Philippine–American conflict. Military authorities in Manila were under strict instruction to monitor closely news from the Islands travelling back to the American public. This was especially the case during the first year of occupation, and in the lead-up to the hotly contested 1900 election. A one-line letter addressed to Van Meter from the Associated Press in Chicago, dated 27 April 1899, captured the reality from the earliest days of the colony: "Dear Sir. There is a very strict censorship at Manila. Sincerely yours, Melville E Stone, General Manager" (Van Meter 1900: 76). Stone himself knew this, since he was regularly receiving reports from correspondents on the ground. One such reporter sent a note back to Chicago on 30 July 1899, telling the editor:

> The censorship enforced during the war and before the beginning of it was, according to the newspaper men who had worked in Japan, Turkey, Greece, Egypt and Russia in war time, and in Cuba under the Weyler regime, and during our war, so much more stringent than any hitherto attempted that we were astonished that the American authorities should countenance it, and were confident that public opinion would be overwhelmingly against it if its methods and purposes became known. (Van Meter 1900: 76)

General Otis had made the frank admission to them, the same reporter declared, that "my instructions are to let nothing go that can hurt the administration." Any story that could justify support for McKinley's opponent, the anti-imperialist Bryan, was denied.

It was not only a question of winning the crucial 1900 election. For McKinley's administration, it was necessary to maintain unchallenged the claim that the Filipino population was not fit for self-government. First-hand accounts, such as that of the first commander of American troops in the Philippines, General T. M. Anderson, posed a serious threat. Seeking to address the erroneous stories he found being circulated in America upon his return from the Islands, General Anderson wrote:

> I was in the Philippines until the latter part of March, having been sent there in June, 1898, in command of the first military expedition, and during that time I had some chance for studying the Filipino character and mind. I regard the Filipinos, such as have been carrying on operations against our forces in the island of Luzon, as being not far below the Japanese in intelligence and capability of culture. Nearly all can read and write; they have many schools, and there are a number of newspapers. Their cities are populous and well laid out and kept. There are many engineers and artists among the Filipinos. (in Van Meter 1900: 60–1)

Similarly, when Brig Gen Charles King returned to America from service in the Philippines, his frustration with the accounts he found being circulated about Filipino capability was concealed with difficulty in his interview for the Catholic Citizen of Milwaukee. "The Americans here do not realize the truth", he said, "that nine-tenths of the people read and write [but] men have told me again and again that they cannot credit it [...]" (in Van Meter 1900: 62). Letters sent home from volunteer officers in the army documented frustration and despair with the war, and in many cases, were being printed in local and state newspapers. First South Dakota branch volunteer, Sergeant Hugh D. McCosham, sent this letter home:

> Major-General Otis has telegraphed that the volunteers are anxious to remain here, when I know and every officer on the island knows that 95 per cent of the enlisted men in the eight army corps are praying to God to get home at once.
>
> You Americans shudder at the tyranny of Spain and the cruelty visited upon the natives of Luzon and Cuba, but I want to tell you that bright, brave, young Americans who volunteered to defend their country in the hour of peril, are giving up their lives by service in sacrifice to the vanity of star bespangled generals and a fog-headed dollar-hearted bureau of officials at home.
>
> ... You may publish this letter and my name shall be signed. I would face a court-martial willingly and prove more than I write, for I know that it is only by arousing the sense of the States that we can be relieved – and to stay much longer will be death to most of us. (in Van Meter 1900, 167–8)

At the end of the collection, Van Meter bemoaned that "Mr McKinley's promises and American performances are about as opposite as it is possible for professions and practices to be" (1900: 426). He was hopeful of the impact of the material he had collected, being optimistic that "[w]hen the American people know the truth, as they soon will, we will firmly believe the American conscience will right the wrong." For, as he continued, of the infamy of the occupation "enough has been published now to open the eyes of all honest Americans to ascertain the truth of the situation there" (1900: 431). Though Van Meter's efforts did persuade many of his fellow citizens that applying a policy of double standards in the Philippines was wrong, he underestimated the capacity and determination of the American government and public as a whole to hide the looking glass.

The Colonial School of Democracy

The cacophony of alibis offered by the United States about the conquest of the Philippines made the US colonial project self-contradictory to the core: while the divine mandate to "civilize" the Philippines claimed Filipinos could be changed "into proto-type Americans through a benevolent and responsible administration"

(Harris 2011: 67), at the same time, the imperial gaze of the colonizers depicted Filipinos as essentially inferior to (white) Americans. In other words, Filipinos had "not yet reached the pinnacle [of self-government]", but were "constitutionally incapable of doing so" (Harris 2011: 77). Rather than being resolved, these founding contradictions were simply carried forward in the colonial regime's pursuit of its own legitimacy.

From the middle of 1901, as regions were successfully "pacified" by the American military, sustaining the legitimacy of the fundamental contradictions at the heart of US rule was only possible by the deployment of deliberate strategies. The first was the writing of a fabricated story about the Philippines' past. Not only did colonial "knowledge" construe the Philippine population as downtrodden savages, the notion of the Philippines at the turn of the century as an independent nation, with modern governmental institutions such as elections, a Constitution and a Congress, needed to be delegitimized to make way for American benevolence. The second was a program of "benevolent assimilation", through which the native populations were to be domesticated and "reconstruct[ed] into recognizably modern political subjects" (Rafael 2000: 54). Whereas the continental empire was a punitive force, the imperial frontier of the American empire was the site of the bestowal of a precious gift, a "special relationship" with more likeness to "the bond between a parent and child rather than master and slave" (Rafael 2000: 55). In other words, as Rafael surmises, "the culmination of colonial rule, self-government, can be achieved only when the subject has learned to colonize itself" (2000: 22).

The "Nation-Building" Enterprise

There should be no doubt that in the Philippine–American encounter, history-writing was made a central instrument of power (Ileto 2001a). In fact, the effects of US hegemony in the Philippines are perhaps nowhere more discernible than in the construction of a Philippines national narrative. In 1941, American official Joseph Ralston Hayden would boast that "only within the last generation have [Filipinos] become generally conscious of a national history, national heroes, and common aspirations for a national destiny." Hayden was not entirely inaccurate. The American colonial project did create a Philippine national story – one that was revised to the point of "fiction" (McCoy, Scarano, and Johnson 2009: 21), but was "perfectly congruent with the dominant politics of 'constructive partnership' with America" (Mojares 2006: 495).

From the moment American authorities stepped ashore in Manila Bay, they felt the strong need to legitimate their own arrival by reframing the Philippines past. In a 55-volume "reconstruction" of the past titled *The Philippine Islands* (1903–1909), historians Emma Blair and James Robertson ignored three-and-a-half centuries of Spanish colonization by documenting the incompetence and degradation of Philippine society. In so doing, the compendium of US colonial knowledge made way for American imperial rule. It showed, as James Robertson would later write, that the Americans needed to "protect Filipinos from their historic inclination toward 'ineffectiveness and indirection of government' and a proclivity to engage in 'feud and warfare'" (McCoy, Scarano, and Johnson 2009: 21).

In particular, it became strategically important for early American officials and "scholars" of the Islands to reframe the Philippines' revolutionary struggle for national independence, and the nature of the society and the political ideas that had inspired it. Dean C. Worcester, professor of zoology at the University of Michigan and member of the Philippine Commission, had arrived in Manila a year earlier, in March 1899, and witnessed the fighting between the United States and the Filipino forces led by Aguinaldo. For Worcester, the Filipino leaders of the revolution were illegitimate representatives of the Filipino people. After all, according to Worcester and others, there was no such thing as a Filipino nation, only "a heterogeneous collection of imperfectly civilized tribes" (Rafael 2000: 20). Colonial warfare on the part of American forces was not an attempt to conquer the native population but "a kind of police action that would quell the disorder on the islands caused by the stirrings of deluded peasants and workers led by a gang of ambitious, mixed-blood Filipinos" (Rafael 2000: 20)

In the first colonial textbook, written in 1903 by American educator David Barrows, the war between the United States and the Philippines Army was coined "a great misunderstanding." To further make the violent conflict into a non-event, Barrows recorded that "many of the Filipino leaders were necessarily not well instructed in those rules for the conduct of warfare which civilized people have agreed upon as being humane and honorable", while the textbook remained silent on American atrocities. This served to explain why the American intervention was a liberating event for the Philippines. The revolution was a beginning, certainly, but "ultimately a failure." What is more, it had only served to demonstrate why the Philippines could not yet be entrusted with independence. In the end, Barrows wrote, the war between American and Filipino forces was a real "blessing", for "without it the Filipinos would never have recognized their own weaknesses" and the Americans, as entrusted guardians of the

Filipinos, "would never have done our work thoroughly" (in Rafael 2000: 21).

At the same time, Taft, Roosevelt and others were highly cognisant of the need to reshape Philippine nationalism. Aware that the forceful suppression of nationalist sentiments would prove counter-productive in the longer term, their guided nationalism became a key strategy. As early as 1901, Governor William Taft proposed to the Philippine Commission that the Filipinos be given a national hero. "Taft quickly decided", explained former ambassador to the Philippines Charles Bohlen, "that it would be extremely useful for the Filipinos to have a national hero of their revolution against Spain in order to channel their feelings and focus their resentment backward on Spain." But, Taft had added, it needed to be someone "who really wasn't so much of a revolutionary that, if his life were examined too closely or his works read too carefully, this could cause us any trouble" (Constantino 1977: 29).

It was no accident that the US chose José Rizal as the man whose legacy could be posthumously fashioned into a legitimating symbol of their own imperial project. Rizal, himself a medical doctor and skilled writer, was the leader of the Propaganda Movement, a group of European-educated, suit-wearing *ilustrado* elites who, at the time of their emergence in the 1880s, sought assimilation with rather than separation from Spain. In the days leading up to his execution by a firing squad of Filipino infantry, Rizal wrote one final letter, intended as a public denial of the crime of which he stood accused. It would be these last words that would be crudely read in order to shape Rizal the martyr into an effective American sponsor. "My countrymen", he wrote:

> I have given proofs that I am one most anxious for liberties for our country, and I am still desirous of them. But I place as a prior condition the education of the people, that by means of instruction and industry our country may have an individuality of its own and make itself worthy of these liberties. I have recommended in my writings the study of civic virtues, without which there is no redemption. (in Majul 1957: 28)

The US regime appropriated Rizal's espousal of civic virtues and education before independence to discredit the Katipunan Revolution and its more radical leaders, and as a validation of their authority over the islands (Ileto 1998: 70). Rizal did not live to see the American arrival in 1898 and the replacement of Spanish colonial authority with another exercise of colonial subjugation, so his silence on these events could easily be fashioned into consent. To make it clear who was the

Philippine national hero, the US authorities built a towering monument to Rizal in Manila's centre.

The motif of Rizal as a symbol of grateful submission was also used in other ways. In the Civic Education program adopted as part of the colonial public education system, it was made clear that Rizal was the hero that Filipino schoolchildren should emulate. The book *Philippine Civics* (Malcolm 1925) was first published in 1919. By its 1925 third edition, written by George A. Malcolm, Justice of the Supreme Court of The Philippine Islands and former Dean of the College of Law, University of the Philippines, it carried a full-page portrait of Rizal, from the painting by notable Filipino artist Juan Luna, with a quote by Rizal's close friend Ferdinand Biumentritt that he was "the greatest man the Malayan race has produced." The entire book was "reverently dedicated" "To the Memory of Dr José Rizal, Filipino author, patriot, and martyr." Near the end of the volume of more than 260 pages, under the heading "Political Independence", there is a description of the "noble ideal" cherished by the Filipino people – the one for which the Filipinos fought Spanish forces from 1896–1898 followed by the "Filipino-American war." After peace was restored, the text goes on to say, "the people did not forget their ideal of independence." In fact, the author writes, "that beautiful sentiment has found an echo in every Filipino heart." They communicated it to the American people "by means of speeches, articles in magazines, and books", and when the "American people became convinced of the justice of the request of the Filipinos", they made a promise of future independence. After this, the American author makes one last admonition:

> The Filipinos must show the world that they can establish a good and stable government [...] In order that the Filipino people may take their place among the free nations of the world, you must do your part. (Malcolm 1925: 257)

But the final words were left to Rizal himself:

> Our liberty must be secured by making ourselves worthy of it, by exalting the intelligence and the dignity of the individual, and by loving justice, right, and greatness, even to the extent of dying for them. (Malcolm 1925: 258)

There are many ironies in the co-opting of Rizal's legacy as an endorsement for the American colonial regime, one being that Rizal was already a national hero before American sponsorship (Delmendo 2004: 26). But perhaps the greatest relates to language. In his writings intended to subvert colonial power, Rizal had co-opted the term *Indio*, which at the time was a derogatory label used by the Spanish to refer to their native subjects, and turned it into a tag of ethnic pride – what had been a colonial term denoting racial inferiority became not only an assertion of anticolonial nationalism and a symbol of Philippine national dignity (Delmendo 2004: 28), but also a signifier of a common national identity. The ethno-political concept of the *Filipino indio* formed the basis for the imagination of the Philippine nation as a collective identity. A few short years later, American officials would be canonizing Rizal, while using the term *indio* as the basis for the argument of tribal fragmentation and "savagery" on the Philippine Islands, and the absence of a Filipino nationality.

A Manner of Tutelage

As power was handed from the US Army to civilian administrators, so too was a racial essentialism transferred as the basic organizing principle underpinning US colonialism. Though terms like "tutelage" and "uplift" seemed a departure from the mindset of racial exterminism during the war, this was never far beneath the surface. After all, as Kramer pointed out, "'benevolent' assimilation could always, implicitly, be withdrawn for the other kind" (2006: 209).

It was William Taft who was appointed by President McKinley as civilian governor of the Islands. Taft and the Philippine Commission set to work establishing a "tutelary" government whereby under America's "strong and guiding hand", the newly re-colonized Philippine population would receive an "education" in American political ideas, institutions and values (Go 2007: 79). After all, according to colonial experts, the Filipinos might have been incapable of original thought, but were naturally endowed with the skill of mimicry. If only they were associated with enough honourable and upright Americans, they would have a strong tendency to copy (Rafael 2000: 34).

Taft, who would be elected to the US Presidency in 1908, was an imperialist and believed in the permanent retention of the Philippines within the American empire (Mahajani 1971: 233). Yet he was also a skilled diplomat. He set about curing the Filipinos of their demands for independence through a strategy of inducement, indeterminacy and gaslighting.

Inducement. "Schools for kids are the most important action for gaining long-term support: candy for kids is perhaps next best" (US Army Lieutenant-Colonel Charles T. R. Bohannan 1964). Alongside its task of producing "knowledge" about the Philippines and Filipinos for the purposes of establishing legitimacy for its rule, the Philippine Commission that arrived in the Islands during the first months of 1899 was also mandated to support the War Department's "policy of attraction" (Kramer 2006: 183). Officials in Washington had initially believed the Filipino "insurgents" would be easily subdued, but when the violent confrontation did not subside, American leaders concluded that the most effective way to end the insurrection was to devolve power to a civilian government of wealthy landowners who "stood to gain from cooperation with the Americans" (Cotterell 2010: 151).

Making its base the former home of the Spanish Supreme Court, the Philippine Commission held daily sessions which "became the central ritual of urban, wartime collaboration", Kramer explains, "where informants exchanged testimony favourable to US sovereignty for political patronage" (2006: 183). Almost immediately, the Commission's efforts to lure *ilustrado* and *principale* elites away from the Philippine Republic showed promising results. As early as 1901, collaborators who had formerly represented Philippine independence in the Malolos Congress began to produce rhetoric endorsing the opposite. Rather than an enemy, America was "magically transformed" into a liberator, the saviour who would lead the Philippines "along the path to Kalayaan" (Ileto 1979: 179).

One can only imagine, says Ileto, "the surprise and disbelief of the revolutionaries at such co-optation of their language by collaborators in the towns." Macario Sakay was one such revolutionary who made his displeasure known. An original member of the Katipunan society that had led the open resistance to American rule following leader Aguinaldo's capture, Sakay was infuriated by the "alienation of words from their true meanings", not least the abuse of the term *kalayaan* (freedom) (Ileto 1979: 178–9). In the documents and letters of the Sakay-led resistance movement, the word *tunay* (genuine) began to appear, as ideas of "genuine" revolutionaries fighting a "genuine" revolution were cultivated. Any capitulation to the Americans, such as that occurring under the elite-led collaborative government, was a deviation from the path to "true" freedom (Ileto 1979: 176). But Macario Sakay and his followers, and others like them who continued to openly resist American rule, were quickly labelled "bandits", "dissidents", and a "problem" for Philippine hopes of self-governance. Sakay himself was eventually hanged by the American authorities in 1907.

As a domestic political system developed in the early colonial days, it was American officials who defined its shape and the legislation governing it. This included restricted suffrage, with only three per cent of the population entitled to vote. Political participation was made an exclusive domain, with competition for political posts confined to the elite. Even then, the status of elected officials was compromised by American reluctance to concede authority in key arenas of administration.[13]

The administrative arrangements put in place in the first decade of colonial rule, including the setting-up of the Philippine Assembly in 1907, were less a concession to Philippine aspirations of autonomy, and more a means by which Filipinos would become obligated to the United States.[14] During a meeting of the American Political Science Association in 1908, James Le Roy admitted that the inauguration of the Philippine Assembly one year earlier had been an important measure, "even if it proved only a sort of safety-valve for the discharge of Filipino opinion" (Le Roy 1908: 215). What became clear, if it was not already, was that while colonial authorities may have acknowledged local discourses that sought independence and recognition as equals, they did not respect them. "While they deal in high-sounding phrases concerning liberty and free government", Taft said in 1900, "they have no conception of what it means" (Go 2007: 101).

Indeterminacy. Governor Taft firmly rejected the idea of making definitive announcements about the path to independence on the grounds it would cause unrest, and would "change [the Filipinos'] attitude from that of desiring to secure peaceful self-government under our laws into one of agitation for immediate independence" (Mahajani 1971: 241). In 1902, he told the Senate Committee that "the United States should declare its intention to hold the islands indefinitely, until the people showed themselves fit for self-government under an increasingly popular government" (Mahajani 1971: 241). This was a sentiment with which President Theodore Roosevelt agreed. On his return to Manila in 1907 for the inauguration of the Philippine Assembly, despite requests from the newly elected assemblymen, Taft refused to speak of independence, and declared he could not answer the question of how long the process of preparation for self-government might take. He admitted that in his own opinion, he believed the time would be "considerably longer than a generation" (Mahajani 1971: 243).

As the years and decades went on, the focus turned to American intentions and ideal outcomes, with independence becoming something that could be indefinitely deferred. During this time, Roosevelt and others cultivated an association between self-government and the "sober performance of duty" (Mahajani 1971: 245). Compliance with existing structures of power, however subjugating and violent they were, became equated with the behaviour most required of the good student of democracy; to demonstrate a readiness for self-government was to accept discipline and subjugation. Daring to question the situation, or advocating independence, subjected Filipinos to accusations of being anything from mischievous, obnoxious, and ungrateful, to bandits, rebels, and conspirators. It was, in Hau's words, "the vision of a people schooled in political quiescence" (Hau 2000: 39).

There came a temporary reprieve from this staunch position of indeterminacy in 1913, when Woodrow Wilson was elected President. Serving until 1921, Wilson would be the only Democratic President to hold office during the Philippine occupation, until the Commonwealth period of 1935. While in office, Wilson sought to use the Democratic-controlled Congress in Washington to fulfil his party's long-standing campaign promise to prepare the Philippines for ultimate independence. In 1916, the Organic Act (also known as the Jones Law) passed through Congress. If the Senate had had its way, the Act would have gone as far as to fix a date for the granting of independence, but this intention was thwarted by the House. Instead, the law provided for the abolition of the US-controlled Philippine Commission, and its replacement with a 24-member Philippine Senate. The electorate was also extended to include all literate men. Perhaps most controversially, however, the preamble to the Act contained the promise that the intention of the United States was to see the Philippines "fully assume the responsibilities and enjoy all the privileges of complete independence."

Despite remaining vague on the timing, the Jones Law preamble confirmed that independence would come to the Philippines, unleashing fresh hope and increased determination amongst Philippine politicians. Just two years later, in 1918, members of the newly convened Philippine Independence Commission were sent on behalf of the Philippine Assembly to the United States, to make the case in person that they had met the necessary requirements that should trigger the "promise" of the Jones Law.

Meanwhile, Republicans and commercial interests in the Islands were angered by President Wilson's affront to the Republican policy of indefinite retention. According to the influential American Chamber of Commerce in the Philippines, the new legislation represented a "disastrous bit of muddling" (Gardner 1927: 8). Once Wilson was replaced by a Republican President in 1921, restlessness and aggravation over concessions to the Filipinos became much more open. In fact, the Filipino desire to be no longer subject to foreign rule became known in the United States as "the Philippine problem." Promises of independence "so thoughtlessly and heedlessly made", it was argued, had left the US with a mischievous and ignorant ward who would not accept American discipline (Lyons 1924: 34).

Gaslighting. There had long been an argument that the Filipinos' demands for independence were themselves proof of their incapacity for it. "It is the inability of the common people to understand what is in their own interest", Taft said, "that justifies our remaining there" (Mahajani 1971: 257).

In the final year of his presidency in 1913, Taft would write that the continued restlessness in the Philippines over independence was a result of the people being "so densely ignorant" that "it is very difficult to get into their heads" that what America was trying to do was to teach them their rights (Salamanca 1984: 64).

A professor of political science, sent by Taft on a special investigative mission to the Philippines, would similarly lament: "[I]t is a deplorable fact that the people of the Philippines seem unappreciative of our efforts and resentful of our domination" (in Salamanca 1984: 145).

As the years of colonial subjugation turned into decades, the gaslighting by colonial officials relentlessly continued. General Leonard Wood, former Governor of Mindanao, and William Cameron Forbes, former Governor-General of the Philippines, both staunch retentionists, had been sent on a mission by new Republican President Warren Harding (1921–1923) to investigate whether claims for independence were warranted. Though the two men were met with almost universal demands for "liberty" and "independence" during their tour of the Islands, Wood's subsequent report construed this as the "unthinking passion of an ignorant people for some prize whose value or meaning they did not understand" (Mahajani 1971: 261). Despite some praise for Filipino qualities such as self-respect, dignity, and active minds, the report concluded that in giving Filipinos the most advanced form of representative government, the United States had "over-taxed the ability of the people to absorb, object and make efficient practical use of what it has taken other nations generations to absorb and apply" (Mahajani 1971: 261). Freedom in this present backward condition, advised Wood, would be bad for the Philippines. Out of love of liberty, the United States should retain the Philippines and train the Filipinos for another 50 to 100 years.

Undeterred, in 1923 the Philippine Commission of Independence convened by the Assembly sent a declaration to Harding's successor, President Calvin Coolidge (1923–1929), charging the new Governor General of the Islands, Leonard Wood, with "illegal, arbitrary and undemocratic politics." They declared it necessary to make use of "all lawful means within [their] power to obtain the complete vindications of the liberties of the country now violated and invaded", claiming that this "once more demonstrates that the immediate and absolute independence of the Philippines, which the whole country demands is the only complete and satisfactory settlement of the Philippine problem" (in Lyons 1924: 101). In reply, President Coolidge saw fit to remind the Philippine political officials of the correct understanding of history:

> The present relationship between the American nation and the Filipino people arose out of a strange, and almost unparalleled turn of international affairs. A great responsibility came unsought to the American people. It was not imposed upon them because they had yielded to any designs of imperialism or of colonial expansion. The fortunes of war brought American power to your islands, playing the part of an expected and a welcome deliverer. You may be very sure that the American people have never entertained purpose of exploiting the Filipino people or their country.

Coolidge continued:

> In accepting the obligations which came to them with the sovereignty of the Philippine Islands the American people had only to wish to serve, advance and improve the condition of the Filipino people. That thought has been uppermost in every American determination concerning the islands ... In any survey of the history of the islands in the last quarter century I think the conclusion inescapable that the Filipino people, not the people of the United States, have been the gainers.

It was left only to the President to remind the Philippine politicians that, in fact, it was the United States which carried the burden of the engagement, and not the other way around:

> I should be less than candid with you however if I did not say that in my judgement the strongest argument that has been used in the United States in support of immediate independence for the Philippines is not the argument that it would benefit the Filipinos but that it would advantage the United States. Feeling as I do and as I am convinced the great majority of Americans do regarding our obligations to the Filipino people I have to say that I regard such arguments as unworthy. The American people will not evade or repudiate the responsibility they have assumed in this matter.
> The American government is convinced that it has the overwhelming support of the American nation in its conviction that

present independence would be a misfortune and might easily become a disaster to the Filipino people. (in Lyons 1924: 101–5)

There were, of course, American voices of disagreement, exemplified in a journalist's essay in 1923 entitled "Filipinos Understand Democracy":

In America most folks believe that democracy has yet to be taught to these poor, unenlightened creatures as you teach tricks to a dog – take them in hand, show them one thing at a time and lead them by slow degree up to that high level of political sagacity whereon we now sun ourselves. This is a notion that might as well go to roost in the belfry with our other dear old delusion about the headhunters and cannibals. (Russell 1923: 9)

Such counter-narratives remained marginalized for the most part, however, and ineffective in terms of changing policy.

Summary

Director of American Studies at Stanford University, Shelly Fisher Fishkin, recently asked of Mark Twain's anti-imperialist writing: "Why was it not featured more prominently in American literary history – and American social and political history? And why was the Philippine–American War itself so off the radar screen not only when it came to criticism by America's most famous author, but in American history textbooks as well?" (Fishkin 2010: 23). In answer, Reynaldo Ileto would reply that the myths of "benevolent pacification", "benevolent assimilation", and "a splendid little war" persist because they help to conceal the profound contradiction that was perceived, even by American officials at the time of invasion, that the gap was all too clear "between the official discourse of a civilising mission, and the actual behavior of [the] army" (2001b: 107). Or, as Van Meter wrote at the time, "A false policy has compelled its promoters to defend it by a campaign of falsehood from first to last" (1900: 431).

For more than four decades, American authorities in the Philippines dictated the boundaries of correct "democratic" political attitudes and behaviour, while defining this not as domination, but as a benevolent path to freedom. What was labelled "democratic tutelage" and "benevolent imperialism" involved the equating of democracy with the acceptance of the need for discipline, the development of self-restraint, and with a dutiful quiescence to imperial power.

For a nation on the brink of self-determination and self-definition, the phenomenology of subjugation and humiliation in the name of democracy would have a lasting impact – on the languages through which people lived democratically, on the presumptions associated with notions of freedom, democracy and independence, and on the construction of the subjectivity that was deemed entitled to these promises. It was an experience that laid the foundations for a middle-class ambivalence around democracy: a schism, between a revolutionary impulse determined to chase the democratic dream on the one hand, and an acquiescence to imperial authority on the other.

Democracy & Duress

Duress ... is neither a thing nor an organizing principle so much as a relation to a condition, a pressure exerted, a troubled condition borne in the body, a force exercised on muscles and mind [...]

Duress rarely calls out its name. Often it is a mute condition of constraint . . . . But it is productive, too, of a diminished, burned-out will not to succumb, when one is stripped of the wherewithal to have acted differently or better.

(Ann Laura Stoler 2016: 7)

CHAPTER 2

The Colonizer Outside
Living Democratically in a Paradox

In 1901, the first Prime Minister of the revolutionary Philippine government, Apolinario Mabini, known for his intransigent views on independence, was faced with a conundrum. After almost three years of coordinated resistance to America's imposed sovereignty, he was forced to concede that a majority of people had come to prefer acceptance of American rule rather than prolonging the struggle. Writing after the concession, and once American sovereignty was firmly established in the Islands, Mabini reflected on the decision in this way:

> We fought under the conditions that our duty and dignity demanded of us, the sacrifice of defending while we could, our liberties . . . War became, then, unjustified from the moment when the majority of the people preferred to submit to the conqueror and many of the revolutionists themselves passed to his ranks, because, not being able to enjoy their natural liberties while the American forces prevented it, and not having the resources for removing this obstacle, they deemed it prudent to yield and have hope in the promises of the people of the United States. (in Majul 1957: 82)

Having realized the armed struggle against American forces was over, various Philippine groups formed in Manila to continue to fight for independence using legal means. And yet, as soon as the colonial administration was established in 1901, the United States government passed the Sedition Law, declaring unlawful "any attempt on the part of any person or group to advocate independence for the Philippines or separation from the United States, even by peaceful means, as long as the war or 'insurrection' against the United States was not proclaimed officially at an end" (Majul 1957: 87). Thousands of Filipinos considered to be anti-American were prosecuted under this and the Libel Law. Even once the Sedition Law was formally set aside upon official termination of hostilities in July 1902, authorities continued with covert operations, including surveillance and infiltration, to demoralize and destroy any groups or organizations promoting nationalist sentiment (Terami-Wada 2014: 210).

Almost all accounts of this period of American rule suggest that within a few years of the administrative takeover, elite and middle-class Filipinos were successfully integrated into the new colonial program. Historian Michael Cullinane, for example, argues that by 1910, "although dissent continued among many working-class sectors in the urban areas, especially through labor unions and working-class organizations", among both the wealthy classes and the middle sectors, anti-American sentiment had dissipated. He attributes this to two early American policies. First, Governor Taft's "policy of attraction", which inducted the *ilustrado* class into national and local politics. Even before the establishment of the Philippine Assembly in 1907, municipal elections were held as a reward for towns conceding to American authority. The interests of national and municipal elites, Cullinane and others argue, turned to political struggles against one another: "The political enemy quickly became other Filipinos and the illusive colonial masters were transformed into distant arbiters of policy and appeal" (Cullinane 2014: 95). Alongside this was the American policy of expanding and "indigenizing" the colonial bureaucracy. Resistance was evident at the start of American intervention amongst a middle sector that was behind the dissemination of nationalist and anti-collaborationist discourse through newspapers, organizations and other endeavours, but after 10 years of American rule, the initial instigators of the anti-colonial revolution had "ceased to be a threat to the American colonial administration" (2014: 93–4).

There is no doubt that Taft's two-pronged "policy of attraction" proved successful, not only in attracting the *ilustrado* class into a tamed national politics, but also in bringing an end to open rebellion by those in the middle. Yet a straightforward narrative of elite collaboration with American imperialists and the integration of a self-interested middle element overlooks the evidence of alternative dispositions and moods incited by the US colonial program at the time. While the political elite would become masters at manipulating the constricted domain allowed them by the new colonizers, this followed a period of vocal resistance during which the defamation of personhood implicit in colonial discourses and practices were thoroughly and sagaciously rejected.

In this chapter I navigate the languages, incidents and failed attempts by the middle class to negotiate the terms of democratic life during the period of formal colonial rule – dynamics that have too often been subsumed within a narrative of middle-class cooperation with the colonial project.

One of the complexities of the American colonial period was the way in which the middle classes, reared as they were under an intensive process of Americanization, began to imbibe the colonists' democratic discourse while never fully capitulating to the colonial program's underlying tenets. Bringing this "messier" history to the fore not only demonstrates the deep indignation persisting long after the formal acceptance of American sovereignty, and the canniness sometimes employed in trying to hold the colonizer to account – it also reveals the complicated way in which Filipinos practised living democratically within the colonial democracy paradox. This was less a simple case of inculcation of colonial rhetoric, and more a story of recursion, capturing the way the middle class began to inhabit the colonial condition in an effort to eradicate it, laying the groundwork for the democratic ambivalence that would subsequently materialize.

Indignities and Indignation

The first national political party organized under American rule was the Partido Federalista (Federal Party), established on 23 December 1900, under the leadership of T. H. Pardo de Tavera and with the blessings of Governor William Taft. Pardo de Tavera was the original "Americanista", a term used to describe Filipinos who supported American policy in the Islands, and his Partido Federalista advocated a form of Philippine statehood within the United States.[1] Going further than advocating an end to conflict, acceptance of American sovereignty, and the admission of the Philippines as one of America's states, three of the most prominent members expressed their aspirations in these terms:

> Peace being secured, all the efforts of the party will be directed toward the Americanisation of the Filipinos and the spread of the English language so that by this medium the American spirit may be infused, its principles, political usages, and grand civilization adopted, and the redemption of the Filipino people be radical and complete. (in Salamanca 1984: 138)

With the protections and favours extended by the American colonial government, the Partido Federalista thoroughly dominated

Philippine elections until 1907 – helped by the fact that its opponents, those who advocated independence, were obstructed from organizing themselves into parties. Governor Taft ruled that groups advocating independence were too radical for politics.

The early party platform of the Partido Federalista proved unsustainable, however. As early as 1904, Pardo de Tavera explained to his old friend Governor Taft that advocating a form of Philippine statehood within the United States was dead. Shifting positions, he informed Taft that "should I, at this time, try to resurrect [the old party platform], I could not gather around me more than a few adherents." By 1907, the party had changed its name from Partido Federalista (Federal Party) to Partido Nacional Progresista (National Progressive Party), the change explained by a high-profile member Benito Legardo in the following terms:

> It must be kept in mind . . . that if this government is to proceed within the bounds of reason, there is not at present any person of any class whatsoever, no matter how popular or great he may be, who can prevent public sentiment from favouring Philippine independence . . . (in Salamanca 1984: 139)

Whatever the precise motivation of Pardo de Tavera and his fellow party leaders, they were correctly reading the public mood. The program of independence had enormous appeal in the electorate.

While Pardo de Tavera's Partido Nacional Progresista conceded that, in "due time, the government of the Philippines may be an independent republican government, maintaining, if necessary, such political relations to the government of the United States as both countries may adopt by mutual agreement", they campaigned against "immediate" independence. In contrast, the opposing Partido Nacionalista, a coalition of parties excluded by Taft until 1906, declared its aim as "the immediate independence of the Philippine Islands . . . under a democratic government", asserting that this was not only the natural right of Filipinos, but also something they "desire and are ready to receive at any moment." One position proved the clear winner. In the National Assembly elections of July 1907, the newly formed Partido Nacionalista secured 65 per cent of votes, and won 59 of the total 80 seats available (Salamanca 1984: 141).

The United States, for its part, regarded the results of the first Assembly elections, and the majority win by the Nacionalistas, as "an inconclusive index of the relative strengths of the political parties" (Salamanca 1984: 141). Despite the fact that both major political parties, even the one-time pro-Americanistas, were openly advocating independence, and regardless of the shift in leadership to the more "radical" Partido Nacionalista, the United States held strongly to its original policy of indefinite deferral. In the context of American domestic politics, the strategy was unsurprising. Governor William Taft was being groomed by President Roosevelt as his successor, and as one of the chief architects of the United States' Philippine policy, it was in Taft's interests to play down the idea of independence as a popularized issue in the Philippines, and to assure the President all was well.

If antagonism between Americans and Filipinos already existed, these events only exacerbated the tension. Even the prominent collaborator T. H. Pardo de Tavera believed the mistrust and disillusion was not due, as American officials claimed, to "bad government" by Filipinos. Rather, he explained:

> It is simply this persistence in not saying in a clear and frank manner that some day independence will be given. Naturally, upon seeing that there is a desire to elude making [a] declaration, it is understood that they do not wish to promise that which they do not wish to concede. This is the source of the mistrust . . . (in Salamanca 1984: 145)

One decade after US arrival, rather than dissipating, indignation within the Philippines had in fact reached a peak, inflamed by the American government's relentless double talk and obfuscation on the issue of independence. It was at this moment of heightened enmity between the Philippine Assembly and the colonial administration that the United States Secretary of War, Jacob M. Dickinson, visited the Islands. The most distinguished American official to have made the journey from San Francisco to Manila Bay, the Secretary spent 40 days in the new colony – 13 of those in Manila, while he used the rest of his stay to visit the capital's surrounds and other islands, travelling as far south as the volcanic islands of Jolo in the Sulu Archipelago. Reporting directly to the US President, who by this time was the former Philippine Governor William Taft, Secretary Dickinson's assessment of America's new possession would be compiled into an official 16-page report (Dickinson 1910). In the report's appendix two documents can be found that provide an insight into the mood within the Philippines at the time. One was a letter from the Nacionalista Party addressed to the US Congress, and the other, a full transcript of a public hearing held on the eve of the Secretary's departure, in which members of the middle class take the opportunity to voice their views and concerns.

In Defence of the Filipino Character

By the time of the US Secretary of War's visit to the Islands in 1910, the Partido Nacionalista boasted a party committee in almost all towns throughout the archipelago, having dominated seats in the Philippine Assembly since its establishment three years earlier. The platform of the party since its inception was a demand for immediate independence. The Nacionalista party's executive used the occasion of Dickinson's visit to submit a 22-page letter, signed by its President, Sergio Osmeña, and translated from Spanish into English, intended for the audience of not only the Secretary of War, but for the American President and Congress in Washington (Dickinson 1910: Appendix C).

Upon the Secretary's arrival in Manila, American Governor of the Philippines William Cameron Forbes, who held this position from 1909 to 1913, warned him that the Philippine Assembly was "getting a little out of hand" with "a number of turbulent spirits." Not least of these was President of the Assembly, Sergio Osmeña, whom Forbes described as "clever enough to put himself in the forefront of the popular movement in order to hold his power" (Salamanca 1984: 143).

Osmeña and his fellow leader of the successful Partido Nacionalista, Manuel Quezon, would go on to become two of the most significant Philippine politicians of the American period. Both were provincial politicians: Osmeña was from Cebu in the Visayas, while Quezon came from the small village of Tayabas, in the north-east corner of Luzon. Quezon's parents were Spanish Mestizo, while the Osmeña clan were a prominent Chinese Filipino family. Both belonged to the highest stratum of Philippine society, having met while studying at college in Manila in the 1890s. Both were part of the independence movement alongside Emilio Aguinaldo. A few years later, they set up the Partido Nacionalista to compete for power with the Manila-based politicians of the Partido Federalista. In the 1907 Philippine Assembly election, both won seats under the Partido Nacionalista banner, with Osmeña elected as the Assembly's first Speaker, and Quezon sent to the US House of Representatives as one of two resident Filipino Commissioners between 1909 and 1916.

Both Osmeña and Quezon have become implicated in the prevailing, uncomplicated narrative of the Philippines' early political class. The narrative asserts that their early public declarations of the need for Philippine independence were self-serving, designed only to win domestic support for themselves. Governor Forbes claimed at the time:

The most prominent leaders [Nacionalistas] . . . are some of them, very particular friends of mine, and I have asked them what their idea is in case they win – whether they are going to make any move to get independence – and they practically admitted to me that it was really a catch way of getting votes; that what they wanted was office, not independence. (in Salamanca 1984: 147)

During their long political careers, these two leaders would indeed learn to cannily play to American and Filipino audiences. But their attitudes to colonial relations, particularly in the first decade and a half, were more complex than assumed in the collaboration narrative. Certainly, there is reason to question Forbes's claim. First, such early stories of Nacionalista party political leaders are based on American accounts. Early colonial officials such as Taft, Forbes and others, had good reason to play down any notion of resistance, or to portray it as isolated instances of radical uprisings by undisciplined and dangerous bandits. Second, the stories are complicated by the fact that at least until the First World War, the party leaders spoke assertively and provocatively about Philippine independence to American audiences, including in the United States. If the motives of the leaders were as simplistic as Forbes suggested, their oratorical performances and written statements to non-Filipino listeners would make little sense.

The letter sent back to Washington in 1910 with the visiting Secretary of War provides a defensive argument, in nature and scope, that seems to clash with the assumption that the party leaders, in their calls for independence, were simply playing political games.

From the outset, the premise of the letter was clear: on behalf of the leading political party in the country, the authors set out to defend the "character of the Filipino people." The reasons that had been given for the existing colonial policy of denial of Philippine independence, the letter argued, included claims about "the lack of preparation of the Filipinos for the exercise of the responsibilities and powers inherent in such governments on account of defective conditions." Such derogatory accounts by American observers, the authors stated, which implied an inherent "lack" in "the nature of the Filipinos", were not statements of fact but themselves evinced vested interests in not conceding independence to the Philippines. What is more, it was not to American kindness or benevolence that the party appealed to claim independence for the Philippines; it was to the fact the Filipinos were "endowed with those conditions necessary to establish and maintain a stable government of law and order", a fact that had "been proven by the existence of what was the government of the Filipino republic in the years 1898 and 1899." Revisiting the crucial events of the final years of the nineteenth century, culminating in the overturning of Spanish authority and the establishment of the Philippines' own government, the letter stated:

> The fact that the Filipinos had refused to re-establish old institutions, and that they have created others – new ones – made it clear that the Filipinos not only had their own political ideas, but likewise that their ideas are the most advanced that the progress of time has shown. (Dickinson 1910: Appendix C 62)

The letter demonstrated that the party executive understood all too well the contradiction at the heart of America's colonial policy – between behaviourist arguments about nurturing change, and essentialist arguments of racial deficiency. They embarked on a criticism of the ambiguity of American alibis, and against the US drive for homogeneity in its own image. Nor did they shy away from holding up a looking-glass to the United States. To the accusation of the Philippines' incapacity for self-government, based on the claim of too little political experience, they replied that the United States itself was evidence that such an argument had little force. Before the British colony declared itself independent, it had no such experience. Furthermore, the political experience of American statesmen to date has been only in domestic affairs. And yet, since the war with Spain, they had declared themselves capable of a colonial administration of new people.

To the accusation of "caciquism", and the claim that democratic institutions and principles will not withstand the practice of oppression and crime by local caciques, they responded that the instinct of profiteering at the expense of another, or of taking advantage of others, is hardly a quality peculiar to Filipinos. It is a universal human sentiment, and one that "in one form or another [...] exists among all people, whether they are civilized or not." What is more, the instances of cacique abuse in the Philippines are "assuredly less scandalous than those which are told of officials of independent countries who enter into illicit combinations to permit gambling houses or houses of prostitution, in the profits of which they participate" (Dickinson 1910: Appendix C 74).

The letter concluded with a detailed outline of at least three ways in which the United States' denial of Philippine Independence, and its policy of "indefinite retention", was not only hypocritical, but in fact causing the Philippines harm. First and foremost, the United States had removed the dignity of the Filipinos, and in so doing had undermined their stated objectives of progress and wellbeing. The letter attempted to convey to its American audience what it was like to endure ongoing subjugation. Consider, the authors wrote, the way the Filipino is treated by American residents of the islands. In their attitudes, ideas and actions, they convey a message that the Filipinos "are not to be, nor will ever be independent; that the American flag will never be lowered there, where it has once waved." Few care to hear the demands of the Filipinos for their independence. Quite the contrary, "many of them laugh jokingly at it as at a thing impossible." Notwithstanding the statements of US authorities that the established government is for the "interest and benefit of the Filipinos", few Americans living in the islands try "to intimately know the Filipinos or to gain the friendship of the latter"; rather, "many of them have displayed egotistic and personal motives [...] sometimes publicly indicating that the Americans have come to the islands to better their purses and interests, and at other times depreciating the association of the Filipinos, or in a thousand ways treating them depreciatingly" (Dickinson 1910: Appendix C 77).

No doubt the text was referring to recent events, including the enactment of a law (Act no. 1696) in August 1907, in response to petitions by American residents of the Islands, that made use of the Filipino flag an illegal act, penalized by fine and imprisonment. Governor-General Cameron Forbes had also specifically ordered that when municipal authorities held ceremonies to receive him, the American march must always precede the Filipino. Such symbolic indignities lay on top of instituted differentiation, such as the difference in civil service salaries paid to American and Filipino employees. Together, they served to humiliate and denigrate the status and intelligence of all Filipinos.

Second, the authors wrote, the cost of America's denial of Philippine sovereignty was not only the indignity of the experience. It was the inflamed antagonism and mistrust between the Philippine government and the public. The constant criticism by American authorities of Filipino politicians as "propagators of evil doctrines", as "obstacles to the execution of the plans of the government", and as "the most dangerous enemies of its own people", legitimized the view that the proposals or complaints of the Filipino leaders, as representatives of the Filipino people, should not be taken seriously. Furthermore, this constant criticism was undermining the close union between the Filipino government and the people, and breeding suspicion and mistrust. The division between Christian and non-Christian Filipinos was also being exacerbated, since the jurisdiction of the Philippine Assembly did not extend to the Moro Province of the

South, damaging the Philippine sense of being one nation, and one community of citizens, despite the geographical and religious differences (Dickinson 1910: Appendix C 80). American control was in fact distorting the very idea of democratic representation. The majority of government was American, and they acted according to the interests of the American community, but the public "form among themselves the opinion that the government does not listen to the voice of the Filipinos" and "gives no attention to the development of the Filipinos' own economic interests" (Dickinson 1910: Appendix C 77).

Worst of all, the letter concluded, was that all of these forms and processes by which the Filipino people were made "forcibly subject to an exclusively American type" were conveying a "lack of confidence in the capacity of the natives" and preventing Filipinos from indigenizing democracy themselves. "Little effort has been placed", the authors argued, "that the Filipinos themselves might form the legislation with reference to the conditions and customs of the people. The legislation now in force has been constructed on purely American lines without exact knowledge of the character and peculiarities of the inhabitants of the country. Such legislation", they continued, "is not the work and product of circumstances and convenience of this people, but a copy and imitation of laws taken from a people with different characteristics and a distinct type of civilization" (Dickinson 1910: Appendix C 79–80). This process itself undermined the stated intentions of the US to prepare the Filipinos to exercise self-government. To the contrary, the existing US policy in the Philippines was paralysing the country's democratic development. "For all these reasons Mr Secretary", Sergio Osmeña signed, on behalf of the Filipino people, "we respectfully charge you to be the interpreter of the feelings of the Filipinos to President Taft, to whom we desire to transmit a copy of this document, and to the American Congress, to each one of whose members we likewise desire to transmit copies of the same" (Dickinson 1910: Appendix C 81).

"Excuse Me Sir, We're not Stupid": Public Representations to the US Secretary of War

Just two days before his scheduled departure for San Francisco, the Secretary of War held a free public hearing in Manila. It was a Thursday morning, inside the grand Marble Hall of the Ayuntamiento building, with lavish European furniture and wood-panelled rooms which had, a decade earlier, been the site of the official signing of change of colonial power from the Spanish Governor General to American General Wesley Merrit.

Beginning at 10 o'clock, Secretary Dickinson's brief opening address to the men gathered in the hall was translated into Spanish by Mr Rupert D. Fergusson, chief of the translating division of the executive bureau. He began with a clarification. "It has been erroneously stated", the Secretary announced,

> [...] that during my stay in this country I would at all times be surrounded by public officials and by Americans who would not allow me to hear the voice of the people. That is not true [...] I have at all times endeavoured to come in contact with the people without any official intermediary . . . I have always believed in a full and free discussion of public matters.

He then offered an open invitation to hear from the public in attendance about matters affecting their interests, and with an assurance that he had come to the meeting "for the purpose of listening to any representations which any of you gentlemen may desire to make" (Dickinson 1910: Appendix B 41).

The success, or lack thereof, of the morning's interventions in modifying colonial policies and practices is not the reason for its significance. Rather, this lies in what it reveals about the contested logics at play. Employing the democratic aspirations that had inspired the Philippine Revolution prior to America's arrival, and the promises embedded within American democratic discourse itself, these actors challenged the contradictions and anomalies they saw around them, and were unwilling to concede to the defamation of Filipino subjectivity implicit in America's colonial project.

First to speak was Mr Leocadio Joaquin, who also began with a clarification: could representations be heard, he asked, only by "those persons who are able to show that they represent some element in the community, or some party or some interest?" He promptly received the assurance, after translation, that the Secretary intended to treat everybody in the hall on the "same footing", and accord "equal rights to all."

Mr Joaquin went on to present his concerns regarding agriculture, and in particular the onerous requirements under the recently enacted land registration system. Most lands, he explained, have titles derived under the Spanish government. The process for obtaining the new Torrens title now required was a restrictive one that was not only paralysing agricultural work but was also excluding many who could not get the necessary paperwork completed. What is more, Mr Joaquin informed the Secretary, more than a thousand surveyors duly qualified by accredited colleges had, in the two years since the new law was enacted, been disqualified, leaving but a hundred surveyors certified by the new government in the whole Islands. On top of this were the restrictions on capital available to small landowners. "It is for this reason that scarcely one-tenth of the arable lands of the Philippines are under cultivation [....] I have been over many of the provinces and I have found that there are very many families who are able to eat only one meal a day because they have not got money or food to eat oftener", Mr Joaquin reported. A remedy, he implored to the Secretary Dickinson, "is as urgent for the agriculture of the country as a cure would be for a man who is about to die for want of medicine" (Dickinson 1910: Appendix B 42).

Mr Joaquin had another issue to raise before the Secretary, again questioning the imposition of American systems on what were already established institutions in the Philippines. This time it regarded equality before the law for Filipino citizens. "During the Spanish Government", he explained, "there was a certain number of attorneys who were paid by the Government to devote their services free to poor clients." Tell him, Secretary Dickinson instructed the translator, that the practice everywhere in America is that the courts assign lawyers if a man is not able to employ counsel. "The lawyer is a sworn officer of the court and he is bound to defend without charge any person not able to defend himself", pronounced the Secretary, no doubt pleased by his own response.

"That is the practice", Mr Joaquin responded, "and it is a bad practice to be sure." It had been introduced in the Philippines following the establishment of the American government, but as he explained in full frankness to the distinguished guest, "the results [were] deficient in practice." He went on to outline the inequity of a prosecuting attorney, on the one hand, who has probably spent a month preparing the case, versus a lawyer for the defendant who has just been brought into the case at that very moment. When the Secretary asked Mr Joaquin what he considered the remedy for this, the latter replied, "I would recommend that the old Spanish practice be adhered to." He went on to explain that under the former system, a lawyer was appointed by the government to defend all poor defendants in criminal cases. He was paid a salary that was comparable to that of the salary for the prosecuting attorney. How is it fair, he propositioned, that the government "maintain an office for the prosecution of crime and at the same time maintain no establishment in defence of poor defendants" (Dickinson 1910: Appendix B 44–5).

Next to rise and speak before the Secretary was a journalist from the *La Vanguardia* newspaper, a Spanish language daily that had begun printing in February the same year. Mr Gonzalez Liquete addressed the guest: "I simply came here to get the news of this transcendental event, but as I have seen that none of the persons who devote themselves to politics has come forward today to give expression to his opinions, I should like to fill this vacuum by making a few remarks." Mr Liquete brought to the attention of the Secretary the discrepancy between the "principles and promises" so often repeated by the American administrators about encouraging the "Filipinisation" of the civil service, and the reality of seeing Americans supplant Filipinos in public organizations.

Following Mr Liquete came Mr Lorenzo Tatlong Neri, from Santa Rosa in La Laguna, who explained to the Secretary how 200,000 hectares of land in his town had been monopolized by the Philippines Sugar Estates Development Company. The company had purchased the land from the old friar estates. The American administration had mandated that these friar lands be sold to the government. However, the Philippine Sugar Estate Development Company had been excluded from selling, and about a month ago the company had written to all tenants currently occupying the lands saying that they were being dispossessed, since the company intended to start cultivating the land for its own benefit. Mr Neri explained that he hoped the Secretary would use his influence in favour of these people, to persuade the government to purchase the land, rather than exclude it for sale, in order to sell it back to the tenants. Secretary Dickinson responded that he couldn't help, and that the matter should be taken up with the Governor-General (Dickinson 1910: Appendix B 47–8).

Next was Mr Montenegro Reyes, a soldier, who was humbled by the opportunity to speak face to face "with the highest representative of the Sovereign Government", but who declared without hesitation: "The nobility of the soldier, such as I am, demands that I should talk with clearness and frankness, and to say that my people want immediately independence." At this, the audience in the hall launched into a spontaneous applause that required no translation for the Secretary. Soon to be shut down, however, by the velocity of Mr Dickinson's reply: "Tell him there is no probability of that either today or in the immediate future. Tell him he has spoken frankly and I would not be just with him if I did not also speak frankly to him." After a brief exchange about the *bandolerismo* act, which still prosecuted farmers for feeding alleged "bandits" even though the Islands were now supposedly "at peace", Mr Reyes returned to the issue at heart: "I thoroughly understand", he said, "that you can not settle this question of independence; that you have not the legal power to do so, but we wish you to be the voice of the people." "Tell him they have representatives in Congress for that very purpose", was the Secretary's final response (Dickinson 1910: Appendix B 48–50).

After a brief break during which written messages were handed to the Secretary, the next to rise was physician Mr Marcelo Eloriago. The doctor's message about independence was cannily parcelled in an exaggerated reverence that managed to subvert the balance of power, even if just for that moment, and to lay bare the ridiculousness of the circumstances at hand:

> It is not my purpose to speak to you of the independence of the Philippines, for although I, like all Filipinos, am possessed by the desire for a government of our own, because we contend that the Filipinos are prepared – not only prepared now, but have for a long time past been prepared and competent – to rule ourselves, but I have not come here to ask you for this independence, nor to speak about it, because it does not live in your hands to grant it to us; nor shall I speak of this independence, though it is a very beautiful thing to those here present and to all Filipinos in general. Not only do we deserve it very much, as your honor must have heard in your trip through the provinces of this Archipelago, where you have seen reflected this desire in the faces of all Filipinos, but you have heard it from the lips of all who have expressed themselves with sincerity. Nor do I come here to lay any complaint before you, though I, like the majority of Filipinos, would complain of the administration, not on account of the goodness or the badness with which it is carried on in the hands of the present public functionaries, but because in our judgement, a radical change is necessary; that is to say, we want self-government. This you will call a political question, and as regards political matters, I repeat honourable sir, I have not come to take up your time. (Dickinson 1910: Appendix B 50–1)

The incisiveness of Mr Eloriago's remarks continued. He explained that what he had come for, in fact, was to speak on behalf of those who, though committing no crime, languish in jails under the charge of sedition, rebellion, conspiracy, and *"bandolerismo"*. Though illegal, he explains, the acts committed by these people were impelled "by an idea for the welfare of their country." Now that peace is a reality in the country, the imprisonment of these people is without reason, he argued, and cannot be justified (Dickinson 1910: Appendix B 50–1).

Finally, the most extraordinary exchange of the morning occurred between labour organizer Mr Jose Turin Santiago and the Secretary of War. Having first politely requested that the Secretary relate back to the American Congress the deep desire in the Philippines for autonomy, Mr Santiago said: "There are laws that exist in the Philippines, that are not only not agreeable to the Filipino people, but will be the cause of general future discontent." When asked what laws he referred to, Mr Santiago explained that in the constitutional bill of the Philippines, it was prescribed by American Congress "that here in the Philippines no law shall be enacted which shall restrict the liberty of speech or the press"; and yet, a libel law and a sedition law were enacted as constitutional measures. "I wish to say", pronounced Mr Santiago, "that they are contrary to the purposes of the act of Congress of July 1, 1902."

In response, the US Secretary instructed Mr Santiago that if he believed the laws mentioned to be unconstitutional, then he had a plain remedy available to him – to "get the thing settled if you think your rights are infringed under those laws" – which was to take the case to the Supreme Court of the United States and "have it decided." But it was not the improbability of access for a man such as himself to the highest court in the United States to which Mr Santiago responded, but to a point of democratic principle and dignity:

> In my private opinion, it should be taken before the Philippine Assembly [...] I am thoroughly convinced, as are also my associates, that the remedy lies in our hands, and for this reason our desire is that our popular chamber be converted into a genuine representative of the Filipino people, a genuine parliament. (Dickinson 1910: Appendix B 51–2)

The Secretary seemed confused and asked for clarification of what Mr Santiago meant when he said that the remedy lay in "our" hands. As the exchange continued, and then neared a close, things reached a more remarkable point. "Finally", Mr Santiago said:

> [...] it is the general conviction of all Filipinos and of all men who love freedom and who believe that they were born free and should live free, that they shall never be happy, and that the benefits of liberty will never be theirs so long as they are considered as colonists of another government – as men inferior to others. We reject with all the strength of our souls every assumption and every intent on the part of any sovereignty on earth who should come here to implant, as sovereign in these islands, a colonial government, because we Filipinos are not agreeable to colonial government and we do not wish it.

The Secretary curtly accused Mr Santiago of making "an unfounded and reckless statement": "Have you ever seen anything coming authoritatively from Congress or the President indicating that they are going to implant a colonial government here?" Without hesitation, Mr Santiago replied:

> Two thousand six hundred and twenty-seven American employees receive P7,000,000 and 4075 Filipinos receive P3,000,000. These data, taken in conjunction with the libel and sedition acts and other acts that in future we can foresee, and considering the position occupied by the Philippine Assembly – its lack of prestige – we believe, we fear, that the noble words of the unfortunate President McKinley, like the sacred and historic words of Philip II, will not be complied with in the Philippine Islands.

The Secretary was aghast: "You reject the sincerity of statements on the part of the President of the United States, who really is the one who has been the principal exponent of those expressions?" "I base my fears", said Santiago, "on the fact the Filipinos do not need to be prepared for self-government; that they have already proved by the past that they are fit for self-government." What followed, as the Secretary's final statement to Mr Santiago, seems best described as an object lesson in gaslighting:

> Then, because President Taft has announced the policy of preparing the Filipinos for self-government and you think that you are now prepared for self-government, you think that the continuation of that policy on the part of President Taft indicates a purpose to colonise the Philippines? [...] I think you had better wait until the American people do something to indicate that they have the intention of colonising the Philippines. I do not think it does any good, when declaration has been made by Presidents McKinley, Roosevelt, and Taft, and have been apparently sanctioned by Congress, indicating a purpose to bring these people up to a standard of government whereby there will be devolved upon them the responsibilities of their own government, to sow the seeds of distrust in the American people and to impugn their good faith. (Dickinson 1910: Appendix B 54–5)

In all, the session lasted almost three-and-a-half hours. A stenographer diligently recorded the transcript of the hearing, which was included in the appendix of Secretary Dickinson's official report to US President Taft.

Realising the Limits of Democratic Agency

By the 1920s, when for most the memory of the Philippine–American War had significantly faded, the relationship of the Philippine middle class to its colonizer took on a new shape. The growing middle class, many of whom were employed in various facets of the colonial bureaucracy, became the primary beneficiaries of an English-language colonial education system, one goal of which was the intensive Americanization of its Filipino students.

As the corruption and chicanery of the Philippine political elite increased (as they manipulated the constraints of participation in the colonial system to their own advantage) the culprit became more difficult to identify. Was the United States to blame for the Philippines' lack of independence, or was it the immorality of the political class? Through an imported American framework, it was the latter that appeared the chief concern, given the central message that democratic freedoms were conditional upon the performance of dutiful citizenship and moral probity. Under the surface, however, there still ran an undercurrent of resentment to American sovereignty, which from time to time erupted in indignation, movements of nationalistic spirit, and in "bold acts of refusing to abide" (Stoler 2016: 4) with colonial subjugation.

National Humiliation Day

Three decades into the new century, and the US public had officially cooled on the question of keeping the Philippine Islands. The Wall Street crash of 1929 had extended into American agriculture, and there was a diffuse sense that the overseas commitment in the Philippines was making the Depression worse. Lobbyists "stepped up their demands on Congress to block Philippine imports", while the American Federation of Labor and other "self-styled patriotic movements" rallied against the flow of "cheap farm and domestic workers" who, they argued, in the midst of escalating domestic unemployment, had "become pariahs" (Karnow 1989: 252).

On the other side of the Pacific, the Philippines' most senior political figure, Manuel Quezon, with National Party colleagues Sergio Osmeña and Manuel Roxas, were increasingly concerned about being cut off from the US market. However genuinely Quezon and his colleagues desired it, the idea of Philippine independence from the United States had become an increasingly precarious prospect. As far back as 1909, the National Assembly had protested against the free-trade program imposed on the Philippines under US colonial policy on the grounds that "in the long run [it] would be highly prejudicial to the economic interests of the Philippine people and would create a situation which might delay the obtaining of [...] independence" (Jenkins 1954: 33). Two decades later, these early fears had proved well founded. The free-trade program had resulted in a Philippine economy that was almost entirely dependent on the American market, both in export and import terms. It was a radical shift from the Spanish regime, where Philippine commerce was divided amongst a number of different countries, including Spain, China, the US, the United Kingdom, and India (Jenkins 1954: 38). What was more, the economy was concentrated on a few specialized export crops such as sugar, copra and hemp, requiring large numbers of unskilled labourers earning low wages.

In Watsonville, California, in early January 1930, amidst the growing desperation of the Great Depression, racist sentiments against Asian immigrant workers had reached boiling point. Five nights of bloody riots resulted, in which a mob of 500–700 Caucasian men went on a rampage, targeting the homes of Filipino residents, and beating some of them along the way. In the midst of the violence, one Filipino resident of Watsonville, Mr. Fermin Tobera, a 22-year-old lettuce picker who had come to the United States two years earlier, was shot dead. Though several arrests were made, Tobera's murderer was never charged. This was unsurprising, as the trial judge, who was also head of the Chamber of Commerce, had only a few weeks earlier "passed public resolutions . . . filled with racist anti-Filipino comments" (Terami-Wada 2014: 11–12).

When news of the killing reached the Philippines, the incident was almost universally condemned – by the Philippine government, leading business people, students, and ordinary Filipinos. Thousands of students and faculty members of the University of the Philippines gathered for a rally demanding "the immediate emancipation of the Philippine Islands", while members of the municipal board in Manila planned a memorial service, and even drafted a manifesto urging all Filipinos to peacefully protest against this act of racial degradation by observing 2 February 1930 as "National Humiliation Day" (Terami-Wada 2014: 12).

On the nominated day, around 15,000 people gathered at the Rizal Monument in Luneta Park. People also simultaneously gathered in the town plazas of other Luzon provinces, and even in California where 1,000 people marched (Terami-Wada 2014: 12–13). Like Rizal just over three decades earlier, young Fermin Tobera became the embodiment of the heroic sacrifice of Filipinos for the cause of liberty. Speakers, including well-known poet José Corazon de Jesus, made impassioned calls for immediate independence from the United States. When Tobera's body was finally repatriated, a procession of thousands of mourners lined the street to see the remains and pay their respects. In the speeches of politicians and labour leaders that marked the occasion, Tobera was declared a national hero.

American authorities watching the public unrest dismissed the events as a continuing "silly" agitation for independence, and did not bother to cable reports of the happenings to Washington (Terami-Wada 2014: 15). But the incident in Watsonville had lifted anti-American sentiments to a new level. It had emboldened Filipinos to speak out against ongoing racial prejudice in the archipelago.

Students at Manila North High School, for example, staged a walkout, organized protest rallies and circulated a petition calling for the dismissal of an American teacher, Mabel Brummit, whom the students accused of consistently directing at them a barrage of derogatory remarks, saying for example that "Filipinos were unfit to be *coheres* (drivers of horse-drawn vehicles); it would be better if the Filipino students went and ate *camotes* (sweet potatoes); and [that] it was a mistake for the US government to spend so much money trying to educate Filipinos for they would never learn English" (in Terami-Wada 2014: 13). The students were determined to see their case through and refused to return to class until the matter was resolved. By the time Ms. Brummit was finally dismissed by the department, as many as 10,000 students and supporters had become involved, although the student leaders who orchestrated the strike action were also expelled by the Bureau of Education (Terami-Wada 2014: 14).

Other incidents, occurring around Manila, including a violent clash between US navy soldiers and Filipino civilians in the port area, attested to a deep frustration that was bubbling to the surface.

The Sakdalistas and Middle-class Led Protest

Benigno Ramos was one young government official who was deeply stirred by the unfolding incidents sparked by Tobera's murder. At the time, Ramos was working as director of the Senate Clipping Division. Though he had associated closely with Senate President Manuel Quezon for almost a decade and a half and had become one of the Nacionalista Party's most valued orators, they clashed over the response to the students' strike, leading them to fall out irretrievably. While Quezon had been pleading with students to keep the issue from flaring up and to return to class, Ramos advised the students not to listen to Quezon. When Ramos refused his mentor Quezon's request to withdraw from these activities, including his advocating of a boycott of foreign-made goods, he was told to resign from his government job.

Ramos, however, was just getting started. In response, he launched his own platform in a weekly newspaper titled *Sakdal* ("to accuse"), in which he began to question the leadership of Quezon and the Nacionalista Party. Mastheads for the new paper carried the slogans "Independent, with No Master but the People", "SAKDAL, the Mouthpiece of the Oppressed Citizen", and "The Newspaper of Truth." Ramos "attributed the sad plight of the poor and the desperate economic condition of the country to foreign domination", and advocated independence as the only solution (Terami-Wada 2014: 148). His own experience gave him a unique advantage: not only did Ramos have access to Quezon and the Nacionalista Party, his middle-class status made him well placed to reach out to educated people, ordinary folk, and even the "spiritually inclined." Ramos knew personally some Filipino communists, he was acquainted with Western radical anarchist ideas, and he even relied on the work of José Rizal at times to make his points (Terami-Wada 2014: 153–4).

Within its first year, *Sakdal* had an average print run of more than 15,000, and a circulation that came close to matching that of the "well-established commercial newspapers with strong financial backing" such as *Taliba* and *The Tribune* (Terami-Wada 2014: 16). So inspired were the readers and subscribers of the newspaper that they transformed themselves into a loosely organized movement – the Sakdalista.

While most studies have described the Sakdalista as a fringe peasant movement similar to subsequent agrarian movements in Central Luzon, this was not the case. Notwithstanding its strong magnetism amongst the poor, the movement was broad-based, with well educated professionals and people of means, including "landlords, town proprietors, lawyers, medical doctors, writers, school teachers, and office workers", on its list of members (Terami-Wada 2014: 6–7). What is more, national and local leadership of the movement was distinctly middle class (Terami-Wada 2014: 138). The Sakdalista was a national protest movement of those outside the elite that would challenge the elite dominance of elected positions. With copies of the group's publications passed around among people and families in the provinces, observers soon noted that this was the first serious attempt to form an alliance between the middle classes and the masses.

The significance of the Sakdalista lay not in its success, as in a short time it would be crushed. Rather, it was the way the movement reflected a process of self-construction, occurring particularly within the middle class – a refusal to tolerate the subjugation and indignity of the colonial condition, yet a form of resistance that began to reflect the embodiment of colonial tutelage. The United States was neither entirely rejected, nor unconditionally embraced. What emerged was a more complex sentiment.

First of all, it was racial dignity, a feeling of self-worth, and the love of freedom that inspired members to join the mass movement. The words "honor and dignity" appear in numerous pages of the party organs, manifestos, and memorials sent to the US officials (Terami-Wada 2014: 163). Eliminating poverty was one way to recover dignity, it was believed. The leaders also focused on restoring the value of the "Filipino culture." One of the things, the leaders argued, "that [led] the upper classes astray, in addition to their love of money and lack of compassion for fellow Filipinos, was their excessive attachment to foreign ways, goods, and markets", most especially American (Terami-Wada 2014: 161). They insisted "that political freedom rested on economic independence, which should be obtained through love, sacrifice, action, and education" and was linked to the promotion of Filipino-made products, which would "revitalise livelihoods and commerce" (Terami-Wada 2014: 22–3).

Alongside the agenda of economic nationalism, the principles of the movement had a distinctly moderate character, reflecting its bourgeois influence. Leaders promoted a frugal lifestyle, and emphasized "morality" and "traditional family values", even issuing moral guidelines for members which highlighted, for instance, that "children were expected to love and respect their parents and to help the aged; men were expected to show respect to women; young girls were expected to be modest; and everyone was expected to keep the traditional Filipino customs" (Terami-Wada 2014: 47). It was this moderate approach, with its emphasis on hierarchy and order, that would cause increasing hostilities with the Communist Party.[2] By 1934 the Communists were accusing the Sakdalistas "of being the puppets of the imperialist and capitalists", "a mouthpiece of the bourgeoisie" and "not truly revolutionary" (Terami-Wada 2014: 94).

Taking on the elite. In the meantime, Speaker of the House Manuel Roxas had returned from Washington, where alongside Senate President Sergio Osmeña and with US Senator Harry B. Hawes, he had agreed to a drafted outline of legislation which provided for the granting of Philippine sovereignty. But not only did the agreement concede a 10-year period of preparation, the proposed legislation came with economic conditions. Free trade was to continue until 1940, although while there were restrictions placed on the quantity of Philippine products entering the US duty free, no such restrictions were applied in the other direction. In return, the

Philippine legislature was authorized to convene a constitutional convention, towards the formation of an interim Commonwealth government. In the 10-year transitional period, American sovereignty was protected by a number of key provisions, including retention of US control over Philippine foreign affairs, equal rights in the Philippines for American citizens, and a provision that the US Supreme Court retained the power to review all decisions by Philippine courts (Jenkins 1954: 36).

The Sakdalistas staunchly opposed the bill, believing that 10 years was too long to wait for independence. After the original bill's passage through US Congress but before successful ratification in the Philippines, Benigno Ramos himself, having raised the necessary funds from the membership, travelled to the United States in March 1933. He declared to the American leaders he met on behalf of the Sakdalistas that this was the "last stand" by Filipinos, "for their God-given right to live free so that they could shape their own destiny" (Terami-Wada 2014: 33).

When he returned from Washington, he and others began the process of transforming the movement into a political party. It seems the advice of the American leaders was for Ramos and his compatriots to challenge the government of the day through electoral means. When the Sakdalista Party announced its platform in late 1933, it declared in its preface: "Our freedom of '96 is here, not through war but through elections" (Terami-Wada 2014: 36). The party declared itself committed to openness and transparency, to spreading its aims "through newspapers, public speeches, and campaigns." Not beholden to any imposed ideology or system, it would seek "to establish a government that would be neither capitalist nor communist but fully and wholly Filipino in its origin and objectives" (Terami-Wada 2014: 38).

Curiously, and again suggesting the influence of Ramos's recent US trip, the party announced in its platform that America was not the enemy. Rather, it said, all Filipinos, rich or poor, literate or illiterate, should unite to "help the great America in fulfilling our independence" (Terami-Wada 2014: 38). The Party's platform included the removal of the offices of resident commissioner and the commercial representative of America in the Philippines, and an investigation into the condition of Filipino workers in the US and Hawaii; other than these, America was not the object of indignation. The enemy, to the extent that there was one in the Sakdalista discourse, was the Philippine government itself – not only over charges of corruption and self-enrichment, but in its willingness to consider a "temporary status of autonomy" in the form of an interim period of Commonwealth government, rather than demanding immediate independence (Terami-Wada 2014: 21–3).

While observers, including journalists, struggled to understand where the Sakdalista representatives fitted in the existing political architecture, they did recognize that their success represented the "little man" refusing to stay forgotten, using the limited ballot that even colonial democracy had provided as a weapon. In the lead-up to the first contest of the 1934 election, the party appealed to its members by emphasizing that "the election was an effective weapon for changing the present situation and achieving independence" (Terami-Wada 2014: 42). It seemed they were not wrong. Despite the ineligibility of many of the Party's supporters to vote due to the literacy qualifications for voter registration, in June 1934 the Sakdalistas managed to send three representatives to the national legislature, along with one elected governor and numerous local-level politicians. The new delegates took to Congress 17 reform bills they planned to present to the legislature, among which was a rejection of the Tydings-McDuffie Act,[3] a bill for immediate independence, promotion of native industries, investigation into ownership of friar lands and so on.

The paradoxical circumstances really surfaced in April 1935, when the Secretary of Agriculture issued a memorandum to the American Governor General expressing his concern about "the intense anti-government propaganda campaign being waged by the Sakdalistas." The Secretary urged that these "irresponsible" orators be arrested, and that "the Department of Labor mobilise its agents to track every movement of the Sakdalistas and other radicals" (Terami-Wada 2014: 61). The call from government for a more oppressive stance was heeded by officials. Speaker Paredes returned from a speaking tour so alarmed by the support he had encountered for the Sakdalista Party that provincial executives were asked to redouble their efforts against "the revolutionary rhetoric being preached by the 'disgruntled groups'" (Terami-Wada 2014: 60). Quezon even mounted a personal attack against his once loyal right-hand man Ramos, trying to smear his reputation.

The attack was not limited to accusations and rhetoric. The Philippine Constabulary was ordered "to closely monitor the Sakdalistas' meetings, speeches, and other functions" (Terami-Wada 2014: 55). Local authorities refused to issue meeting permits, or disrupted meetings so that Sakdalistas had to begin meeting in private homes, and a mailing ban was placed on the *Sakdal* weekly (Terami-Wada 2014: 57).

Harassment also extended to the Assembly itself. Not only were the Sakdalistas' proposals not well received, the Party Platform was ridiculed "as utopian promises of betterment for the poor, thus sowing the seeds of discontent among the poor by means of this unrealistic, utopian vision" (Terami-Wada 2014: 56). The proposal for a salary reduction for lawmakers so offended other legislators that "members of the majority party drew up a petition to oust the Sakdalistas from any committee chairmanships they held" (Terami-Wada 2014: 48). Sure enough, just three months after they had been nominated, the two Sakdalista representatives were removed from their chairmanships.

The American authorities did not need to directly intervene in events to stave off the threat from any of the Sakdalistas' proposed reforms. Though the colonial system had provided the Sakdalistas with the space to contest the hegemony of the existing Philippine elite, they had also ensured that such actors would be forced to endure the repressive misdeeds of the elite rather than turn to protest. Time and again, the message of the colonial administration had been that disturbances and agitation might jeopardize the granting of independence. The Sakdalistas themselves acknowledged the impossible bind in which they found themselves – that continuing their attempts to participate in the political process might in fact harm prospects of the ultimate goal, that is, the granting of independence (Terami-Wada 2014: 213–14).

By late 1934, two factions of the Sakdalistas had emerged in response to the crackdown. One vowed to continue towards independence using existing methods, while the other, which included Ramos (who had done a turnaround from his commitment to change through legal means), vowed to overthrow the government by force. On both sides, criticism of the US again increased. Quezon's government, they claimed, had become simply an instrument of the American colonizers.

Ramos himself took a leading role in preparation for a May 1935 uprising. On the evening of 2 May, as many as 68,000 Sakdalistas gathered at pre-agreed locations ready to charge at municipal offices. But the uprising plan had been leaked to the constabulary intelligence by planted informers. Despite being the largest uprising in three decades, the insurgence was crushed immediately, with around 60 people killed and hundreds injured (Salonga 2001: 9). Ramos and more than 100 other leaders were charged with sedition and tried, while local authorities continued to be vigilant, organizing and arming citizen bands with shotguns for night patrols to intimidate the remaining Sakdalistas (Terami-Wada 2014: 76).

Elite Mastery of Double Talk

Accompanying the emerging inner tension within the middle class between a rejection and acceptance of imperial authority, was a strategic deployment of the contradictions and ambiguities of imperial governance by the political elite. The Sakdalista episode had demonstrated the way in which the rhetoric and practices of the Philippine elite had come to mirror the strategies of colonial governance. Nowhere was this more evident than over the long political career of the Philippines' foremost colonial era politician, Manuel Quezon.

In 1907, despite knowing only Spanish, Quezon asked Sergio Osmeña to send him to the American Congress as Filipino Resident Commissioner, a post he held between 1909 and 1916. Within four years he had learned English, given speeches and actively participated in discussions about the Philippines. This experience would stand him in good stead.

In 1916, the same year that the US Congress enacted the controversial Jones Law, which replaced the unelected Philippine Commission with an elected Senate, Quezon had returned to Manila, where he was elected to the new Philippine Senate, and subsequently elected as Senate President, a position in which he served until his inauguration as the first President of the new Commonwealth Government of the Philippines in 1935.

Reflecting on the political genius of Quezon, Teodoro Agoncillo wrote:

> Quezon's political sagacity and his mastery of the art of intrigue and double talk had their beginnings in the cloak rooms of the American Congress. A keen observer and a born psychologist, Quezon learned the science and art of politics not on the floor of Congress but in the offices of the American congressmen and senators. (Agoncillo 1974b: 8)

Quezon's journey into colonial politics is perhaps best analysed in two phases. During the first, which followed the first decade of colonial administration, the former soldier and guerrilla fighter in Aguinaldo's resistance army began to embrace the ambiguity at the heart of America's colonial policy in the Philippines. He took on board the Janus-face of notions such as conquest for the sake of liberty, "rights" guaranteed but temporarily suspended, partial sovereignty, contingent and deferred promises of independence, even "benevolent assimilation" and "democratic tutelage."

It was no coincidence that this change in Quezon took place at the same time American domestic politics was undergoing a shake-up. A few short years after Secretary of War J. M. Dickinson's 1910 visit to the Philippines, Woodrow Wilson became the first Democratic President of the United States since Grover Cleveland in the mid-1890s. This was greeted with jubilation in the Philippines. The Philippine Assembly "unanimously passed the resolution congratulating Wilson and expressing the wish of its members that his administration would recognise Philippine Independence, in accordance with reiterated petitions of the Philippine Assembly." They were not disappointed. In one of his first speeches, the President-elect declared: "The Philippines are at present our frontier but I hope we presently are to deprive ourselves of that frontier" (Salamanca 1984: 146).

One year before Wilson's successful campaign, and aptly timed to fall on the 4 July Independence Day in 1911, Quezon had addressed a sympathetic crowd in Tammany Hall, New York City. Speaking of the "overwhelming influence" of the American Declaration of Independence, Quezon told the crowd that "even in the Philippines where the people's clamor to be free is so deeply felt because the desire to breath the wholesome air of freedom is innate in the human heart, we argue in the very words of that Immortal Document."

There began to emerge in Quezon's political discourse a level of equivocation that saw him express gratitude for the stated American policy of helping the Philippines, while still insisting it was release from this very same policy that Filipinos most needed and desired. Democracy had become a language by which Quezon could both affirm the intent of American presence in the Philippines, while at the same time reject it. Such malleability even enabled Quezon to go so far as to assert that, despite their contrary identities as colonizer and colonized, it was the love for democracy, freedom and liberty that bonded the two countries (Quezon 1924: 94). He claimed this despite the fact that for one, democracy was the alibi for forced subjugation; while for the other, it was providing the basis for resistance against this very condition of constraint.

By the late 1920s and early 1930s, a second striking characteristic had begun to dominate Quezon's governing logic – the use of the imperial tools of exemption and exception, by which sections of the populations are differentiated from the rest, defined as exempt from democratic principles, making way for the creation of spaces in which exceptional power becomes legitimized.

During the first half of the 1930s, Quezon had successfully eliminated the threat from the popular movement behind the Sakdalistas, but the danger was far from removed. As 1936 drew to a close, an editorial in the *Philippines Free Press* made a significant prognosis. "Unless all signs fail", read the article, "there is going to be something like a revolution soon in the Philippines – a revolution in the sense of a change – and that is on the land" (Editorial 1936: 28).

Although always appalling, conditions for the average farm worker, particularly on the plains of Central Luzon stretching 200 kilometres north of Manila Bay, had worsened still further by the mid-1930s, exacerbated by the global slump in commodity prices. As the strengthening of local elite political power and the onset of the modern market economy disrupted the traditional tenancy system, another phenomenon emerged from these developments – the creation of a peasant "class" whose circumstances and grievances were becoming increasingly uniform. Organizing this agrarian class became much easier (Kerkvliet 2014: 300). The history of agrarian unrest in the modern Philippines dates back to earlier in the twentieth century, when anger at conditions resulted in scattered and relatively small-scale peasant uprisings. But by the mid-1930s, "discontent had grown to rage" which in turn "united a few hundred thousand peasants in the important rice-and sugar-producing plain of Central Luzon" (Kerkvliet 2014: xxiii).

Having virtually eliminated all political opposition parties after the Commonwealth was established, Quezon turned on this growing opposition movement north of Manila, censoring information broadcasts in the guise of a National Information Board, and even using the Assembly to extend the law of sedition. He showed no tolerance for dissent. In his message to the National Assembly, at the opening of the First Session in June 1936, Quezon told his colleagues and a wider Filipino audience:

> Let this new democracy of ours show the world that Democracy can be as efficient as Dictatorship, without trespassing upon individual liberty and the sacred rights of people. (Quezon 1936: 35)

In the same speech, Quezon boasted that the country had never been freer of "armed bands and outlaws" as under his Presidency. Just two hours after being inaugurated, Quezon announced, "I had a conference with the governors of Laguna and Tayabas and the Chief of Constabulary, and I instructed them to spare no effort for the capture and extermination of these outlaws." Proud to announce that all such resisters had been since captured or killed, he went on to say:

> [...] there is still a danger of possible sporadic public disturbances like the uprising of the Sakdalistas which took place a year ago last May. Professional demagogues who make their living by exploiting the good faith of the uninformed or the real or fancied grievances of the discontented, are exciting the masses with incendiary speeches and literature. Communism has also been active during the last few years and while their propaganda has not been particularly effective the forces of law and order have been constantly on guard. (Quezon 1936: 7–8)

As the Sakdalistas had perceived, the awareness of being watched, of needing to practise democracy correctly for a US audience, was used as a threat to quell dissent, and as a legitimating basis for crushing the opposition of such "radical" elements altogether, lest it jeopardize the cause of achieving the ultimate goal of independence.

Such a threat was not new. Even before the official surrender of the Malolos government to American forces at the turn of the century, the provincial governor of Manila, Ambrosio Flores, is recorded as telling employees of foreign-owned companies who were striking over deteriorating labour conditions in the American-occupied city:

> [...] can you not understand . . . that at this time when the future of the country is being decided, when the civilized world has its eyes fixed upon us to see if we possess the requisite ability and culture for self-government and if we sufficiently guarantee order to protect foreign interests in our country; can you not see, I repeat, that at this precise moment the disturbances you cause by these strikes, your reasons not being known to the outside world, may give rise to false impressions concerning the depth of our national character? (in Ileto 1979: 123)

More than three-and-a-half decades later, Quezon explained why it was so crucial for "disturbances of public order" to be eliminated:

> One of the few cases which may give occasion for American intervention is the failure of the Government to preserve order and to protect life, property and individual liberty. The world is watching this experiment in Filipino self-government, and the confidence and respect which in the future the nations may have in the Philippine Republic will depend in large measure upon our ability to maintain peace and order and to extend effective protection to all the residents of the Islands during the transition period. (Quezon 1936: 7–8)

At the same time, Quezon attempted to proactively defuse the increasingly antagonistic relationship between capital and labour. From the first session of the new Assembly, he put the "agrarian problem" front and centre in his political discourse. Soon afterwards, he would formulate his Social Justice program, expressing his ambition that "the Philippines shall become a country where poverty is unknown, where justice is the watchword, and democracy and freedom the motto" (in Lopez 1951: 22). Under the influence of Roosevelt's New Deal, he reached out to organized labour in an unprecedented way, bringing into place new legislation including the Collective Bargaining Law and the Eight-Hour Labor Law. No doubt Quezon and others in government believed such measures would effectively answer the challenges from class restlessness, although this would prove not to be the case.[4]

The main beneficiaries of political and economic progress under American rule, Quezon claimed, had been the rich and the middle class. Sad to tell, he said, "the men and women who till the soil or work in the factories are hardly better off now than they were during the Spanish regime":

> The Filipino worker has heard, if he not able to read, of the equality before the law of the poor and the rich. He has heard of democracy, liberty, and justice [...] And yet, what does he actually see? [...] His hopes have been raised, his vision has been broadened, and his outlook has been painted in bright colours. But thirty five years of American regime has brought him only disappointments and sometimes, despair. (Quezon 1937)

What was his solution? To trust that he was, in fact, the people's true representative, and would deliver the economic and social development that the country so badly needed. While "misguided group[s]" needed to feel the full force of the government, those who were attracted to these groups, particularly peasantry and labouring classes, needed to look no further than Quezon himself, who saw the injustices suffered by farm labourers and tenants, as well as urban industrial workers. In order for his government to succeed in this mandate, Quezon claimed it relied not on brute force, "but on the undivided loyalty of every citizen to the Government – a loyalty founded upon individual consciousness that this Government is his, and that it exists only for his protection, for his liberty, and his happiness" (Quezon 1937).

This authoritarian manoeuvring, positioning submission to authority as the pathway to progress, reached a peak in 1939 and

1940. Addressing audiences at the two Manila universities, Quezon began what would be more than a month of public debate on his theory of "Partyless Democracy." The basis of justification for this proposal was that democracy in the Philippines had been improperly handled, producing inefficient government and inequalities of wealth. In an address entitled "The Essence of Democracy" delivered on 16 July 1940, Quezon expounded his own theory with its call for three "radical revisions" to democracy. First was the need to discard the theory that democracy needs political parties:

> A nation is like a family, multiplied a thousandfold, and just as it is impossible for a family to be happy or to make progress when there is a division among its members, when father and mother and children are at cross-purposes so it is impossible for a nation to grow strong and accomplish great ends if the people are always divided, if they are taught to believe that patriotism means division. (in Pascual 1952: 271)

Political parties, he argued, arose out of "fundamental disagreements on political institutions, or on social and economic philosophies"; and such differences of opinion, he believed, were the enemy of democracy. What was more, under his current government, Quezon asserted, "[i]n as much as there are . . . no essential differences on these matters among our people, there seems to be no reason for the existence of different political parties."

His second point concerned liberty in democracy. "We must revise the view", he said, "that in a democracy liberty must not be restricted." Liberty in a democracy, he argued, needs restraint. Liberty was threatened by the abuse of liberty, and "organized society is predicated on the willingness of men to limit their freedom of action in the interest of the well-being of the entire community in which they live" (in Pascual 1952: 273). Third, in regard to private property and the contest between capital and labour, it was the government's role to intervene so as to avoid concentration of wealth in the hands of a few. The government, Quezon argued, was to be trusted as the protector of social justice, which was consistent with his dismissal of the class-based peasant and labour movements.

In reality, all three "revisions" were already being implemented by the President. The advocating of the "theory" simply brought the actions of his government firmly within a democratic discourse. And although most of what Quezon proposed was challenged by the students, professors and journalists in the audience, he remained undeterred, stressing that his main aim in proposing this exceptional form of governance was social justice – the need to overcome the self-indulgence and social hierarchism that was destroying the Philippines (Friend 1988: 174).

Against the backdrop of the Second World War, and on the eve of the United States' (and subsequently, the Philippines') involvement in the conflict, Quezon was forced to concede that it would be rash to proceed at that point with the experiment of partyless democracy. Nevertheless, the episode exemplified eloquently that within four decades, the Philippine political elite had learned to manipulate, even to mirror, the contradictions of "colonial democracy." Quezon demonstrated the capacity to control and ultimately confine democracy by rationalizing anti-democratic politics as a pathway to democratic evolution. Like the colonizers themselves, Quezon and other elite used the language of democracy to lend legitimacy to practices of exclusion and the exercise of exceptional powers. All the while, the promises and aspirations of the American democratic discourse had not materialized. But as later chapters in the book go on to show, it was a strategy that would prove effective, at certain key moments, in mobilizing middle-class democratic ambivalence in order to consolidate power.

Summary

The experience of subjugation and humiliation inherent in the colonial condition nurtured a deep-seated indignation within the Philippines. Despite their relative success at integrating themselves into the colonial apparatus through public education and employment, a growing middle class made attempts to defend the character of the Filipino against pronouncements of naiveté and childishness, and to assert not only their desire for independence and autonomy, but the terms by which such autonomy should be organized. As the decades passed, however, the underlying sentiment of indignation became entangled in a process of recursion, in which middle-class actors attempted to work within the constraints of the colonial order in order to overcome it. The response to the abuses of power by local political elites revealed the complex position in which middle-class citizens found themselves – constrained by the very colonial order that nourished their democratic aspirations; and caught between the desire to pursue these aspirations and the fear of sabotaging the chance to be truly free. Living democratically within the colonial democracy paradox began to take on an ambivalent quality – of working with and against the existing structures of power – that would manifest even more clearly in the immediate post-war period.

CHAPTER
3

The Colonizer Within
Imperial Recursions in Imaginings of Democracy

On a rainy 4 July morning in 1946, thousands of jubilant Filipinos packed Luneta in Manila to witness the transfer of sovereignty from the United States to the Philippines. General Douglas MacArthur had flown from Tokyo to be in attendance with new Philippine President Manuel Roxas and former US High Commissioner Paul McNutt. It was MacArthur's address that most captivated the crowd. The son of General Arthur MacArthur – who had led American soldiers into the islands almost half a century earlier – declared that the moment signalled "the end of mastery over peoples by force alone – the end of empire as the political chain that binds the unwilling weak to the unyielding strong" (in Karnow 1989: 324).

Just months before the Japanese occupied the Philippines in December 1941, MacArthur had been recalled from retirement and stations in the Philippines as commander of the USAFFE (United States Army Forces in the Far East) command, which incorporated the Philippine Army. One day after Japanese forces attacked the US fleet at Pearl Habour, Clark Air Field, north of Manila, was attacked, along with three other US military installations in the Philippines. General MacArthur lost control of the air space, and Japanese forces began to make landings in Luzon. Within weeks, both American and Filipino troops had retreated from Manila to Bataan and Corregidor.

As the Japanese took control of media and public utilities, the commander of the invading troops, General Masaharu Homma, proclaimed that Japanese imperial forces were in the Philippines "to emancipate the Filipinos from the oppressive domination of the USA" and help them to establish a "Philippines for the Filipinos, develop their own culture, and attain prosperity through their membership in the 'Greater East Asia Co-prosperity Sphere'" (Salonga 2001: 12). For most Filipinos, however, the abuses and atrocities, along with the arbitrary commandeering of private homes and buildings for "military needs" meant permanent allegiance to Japan was unthinkable. At the same time, they found themselves demoralized by the fact that the Americans, whom they had believed unbeatable, had indeed been driven out.

It would not be until 21 September 1944 when American planes would again be seen flying above Manila, bombing Japanese military sites. But even then, the Japanese command in the Islands did not retreat. When American GIs made it to Manila early February 1945, guided by Hukbalahap guerillas, they released thousands of Americans and other foreigners who had been interned, and took possession of the presidential palace. But the Japanese admiral in charge defied superior orders and decided to fight on. Numbering 20,000, Japanese naval forces blew up bridges as they retreated across the Pasig River. "The ghastly, horrendous battle for Manila south of the Pasig River began", writes Jovito Salonga in his memoir about the time (2001: 37). Civilians killed in the battle for Manila numbered 100,000, and reports of rape were rampant. Over the period of a month, whole districts of the city were turned to rubble of concrete and steel. Except for Warsaw, no other city was razed to the ground as devastatingly as Manila (Salonga 2001). When General MacArthur walked ashore at Leyte in October 1944 and uttered the famous words, "People of the Philippines: I have returned", it was an exhilarating national experience. The years of Japanese occupation, for most Filipinos, were brutal and full of suffering. In contrast, the "liberation era", as it became known, was an extraordinary period of what historian E. P. Patanne called "stateside guzzling", when the ingesting of American-labelled commodities was "a form of ritual" designed to reassure the Filipinos about the "good old days" (Patanne 1960: 111). And with the imperial US voluntarily relinquishing the Philippines and peacefully transferring sovereignty to an independent government, the Philippines once again appeared to be cruel colonialism's benevolent exception.

The period around and immediately following the Philippines' second independence, between the end of Japanese occupation and the arrival of Cold War politics in the mid-1950s, was a critical juncture in the nation's history. The long-awaited status of an independent self-governing nation was finally achieved amidst recovery from the devastation of the war, and post-independence relations between the US and the Philippines were being negotiated, especially in relation to America's trade and military access to the newly sovereign islands. This period would also be the one that demonstrated most viscerally the protracted nature of American rule.

Even before the United States' entry into the Second World War, the Philippine political class's reverence of all things American had reached lofty heights. "The very air that is breathed there", declared Laguna's Congressional representative Dominador M. Tan to the National Assembly in early 1941, "gives abundant proof of the innate goodness of democracy" (Tan 1941: 59). But nothing would demonstrate the complex and entangling American love affair more eloquently than the speech by the first President of the new Philippine Republic on the occasion of the 4 July 1946 granting of independence.[1] Not only was the day a celebration of the noble ideal of democracy, well-travelled from ancient Greece, via Europe, then the United States, to reach even the shores of the Philippines; according to the new President, the day of independence was also a day of vindication – not of Filipino people, and their resilience in the face of colonialism, quite the contrary, it was vindication of the United States' assessment of the incapacity of the Philippines to reach the point of freedom by itself. Roxas elaborates: "As the spokesman for America predicated half a century ago, the Filipino people now look back with gratitude to the day when God gave victory to American arms at Manila Bay and placed this land under the sovereignty and protection of the United States" (Roxas 1946: 11–12).

According to Roxas, the Philippines history of colonial relations with the United States did not simply stay in the past. It left indelible marks on the newly independent state. First, "the greatest ornament of our independence", Roxas told the crowd, lay outside the Philippines itself. It was nothing intrinsic to the Philippines of which the people could be proud. Rather, it was its special "friendship" with America which raised the country "far above the level of our intrinsic power and prestige." It was the American Declaration of Independence and the American Constitution, furthermore, that the new President declared the source of his government's authority, not the will and consent of the Filipino people themselves.

It was not only amongst members of the Philippine elite that the imperial framework had developed roots. In the early 1950s, Professor Emeritus of History Claude Albert Buss,[2] from Stanford University, summarized thus the success of America's oversight of the islands:

> In the short span of a half-century Americans brought better health, wider education, and a common English language. They not only gave a superficial physical stamp of Americanism to city and country but also invigorated a whole people with a yearning for and devotion to 'the American way of life.' No amount of economic maladjustment

or social inequity could erase the fundamental spiritual tie of the Philippines to the United States [...] (Buss 1954: 3)

While the account of Professor Buss describes the "spiritual tie" between the United States and the Philippines as an invigorating "uplift", Elenita Mendoza Strobel's description of the lived experience captures something entirely different. Elenita grew up in a newly independent Philippine society. She lived with her Catholic mother and Methodist father in the town of San Fernando, Pampanga, only 16 km to the south of the largest US military base in Asia, Clark Air Base. Reflecting on childhood memories, Elenita remembers vividly the way her early life was filled with symbols of white middle-class Protestantism. Friday evenings were family concerts featuring Bach and Mozart, singing harmonies to Cole Porter and Irving Berlin. The household radio played Frank Sinatra and Nat King Cole. Bedtime stories were Hans Christian Andersen fairy tales. Even as a child, Elenita recognized the dissonance of living this lifestyle "in the midst of a neighbourhood where the women sat on their front steps picking each other's lice while they talked about the latest *tsismis* [gossip], where the men squatted on the sidewalk stroking and cuddling their fighting cocks, drinking beer, smoking cigarettes."

Elenita's sister was employed at the Clark Air base school as a teacher of "Filipino culture", where she met a "Yankee" from Maine. Elenita recalled graphically the time her father invited her sister's American friend to visit the family home:

> I was assigned to make sure the house was clean, especially the toilet and the toilet bowl. When no amount of muriatic acid would erase the yellow stained bowl, my sister handed me a copper penny. Here, she said, use this to scrape the stains. I sweated for hours on my knees scraping the yellow. Yellow isn't good enough. Only white will do. (Strobel 1993: 9)

Reflecting four decades later, Elenita acknowledged the indelible mark these childhood experiences had left on her soul. "I made sure that I was liked by all the white missionaries and Peace Corps volunteers who came to visit us", she recalled. "Reaching out to white folks, hoping for whiteness to rub off and to test one's self and measure it by how well you could maintain their friendship and interest while waiting to hear some affirmation of your friendliness and the infamous 'Filipino hospitality', became a full-time preoccupation." "I wanted to belong", said Elenita, "and I thought the only way to belong was to be like someone else." Many years later, Elenita would liken the experience to a process of "becoming a split subject" (Strobel 1993: 11). Her story resonates with Caroline Hau's characterization of the postcolonial Filipino as a "doubled subject" – one which is, on the one hand, "free in its capacity to strive for perfection and respond to its existing conditions", and yet at the same time "irreducibly constrained by these determinants and her history" (Hau 2000: 27).

Though material constraints of colonial rule had been removed, within the space of "everyday discourses and practices", in the categorizations and logics people used in everyday life (Stobbe 2005: 107), the colonizer remained. The "differential knowledge" (Said 2003) that had rationalized the colonial system still permeated the post-independence public sphere. Through a process of internalization, the complex of images upon which imperial power was based were reproduced and reinforced. It was as if the source of imperial duress was no longer external (Stoler 2016), but imposed through a process of self-scrutiny and self-judgement. Amongst the middle-class public in particular, anxiety remained over the Filipino subjects' capacity for transformative thought and action, which in turn continued to nourish the indignity of the colonial condition, and to fuel the democratic aspirations for genuine freedom and independence. It is in these simultaneous deferential and defiant impulses that the foundations of an ambivalence that had taken root in the middle class's imaginary of democracy can be located.

Emotional Economies of the Post-War Public Sphere

By the time of the country's second independence, although government, both in the capital of Manila and in the provinces, remained exclusively in the hands of Filipino landowners and businessmen, the middle class had grown considerably in size since the turn of the century. An expanded American education system as well as development of occupations "in the state bureaucracy, the professions, and private corporate development" (Pinches 1996: 109) was largely the cause. While the assumption predominant in Philippine studies is that this middle class remained immersed in clientelistic networks until the 1970s (Kimura 2003), in fact the post-war middle class was already socially, economically, and culturally independent from the landed oligarchy and political elite. At the same time, they represented the most Americanized generation in Philippine history (Satoshi 2004).

One of the clearest indicators of an independent and politically engaged middle class was the existence of a vibrant civic sphere, consisting of a mix of media and forums discussing, in English, the state of politics and social issues in the newly independent country. As far as newspapers at the time were concerned, the *Philippines Free Press*, or *Free Press* as it is commonly known, was considered then, and for decades following, to be the leading national weekly.[3] With its broad circulation, it was perhaps the most important public space for the discussion of national politics, and debates about the nation's entrée into democracy, and it was widely considered the best guide to understanding the country's political and social issues.[4]

Readers of the *Free Press* valued the publication for its "impartial and fearless" reporting (David 1948: 54), and its daring exposés of scandals and rackets by government officials. Over its history, the publication had many libel cases brought against its editors. Both editor and manager had been imprisoned during the Japanese occupation. During the early years of Ferdinand Marcos's presidency, the paper became known for its fierce and unrelenting criticism of the administration. No sooner was martial law declared on 21 September 1972, the *Free Press* (with other outlets) was closed down, and its editor and leading writers arrested and imprisoned without charge.

The paper's subscription-based model, which required readers to pay six or 12 months in advance for their weekly copy, meant that the readership was predominantly middle-class, although stories were told of the paper being routinely circulated and shared among households in the *barrios*. Containing regular editorials, cartoons, and feature articles by its staff writers, the most prominent of whom was Teodoro Locsin, the paper was also dedicated to publishing reader contributions in the form of letters, essays, poems, and even satirical pieces. Approximately one quarter of its content was contributions from its loyal readership.

The findings in this chapter are based on analysis of the discussions in the *Philippines Free Press*. As mentioned in the introductory chapter, a discursive practices approach was employed to analyse the discourse in the newsmagazine over a five year period, from 3 January 1946 to 30 December 1950. The focus of this method, borrowed from the work of Roxanne Lynn Doty (1993) is on the linguistic construction of reality, and production of meaning. Its usefulness for the current study is its emphasis, not on the motivation or intention of writers of the text, but on what work discursive practices in the text do, and how they make certain relationships or practices possible, while precluding others. Rather than presupposing as unproblematic particular subjectivities, backgrounds, or meanings, these are denaturalised. Attention is paid to the way discursive practices – in particular predication, presupposition and subject-positioning – are used in the texts, and applied to specific historical, political and social contexts.

110 | *Democracy & Duress*

For it is through such textual mechanisms that meanings and subjectivities are created, and subjects are positioned vis-à-vis one another.

A sequence of steps was taken in applying this method to the *Philippines Free Press*. First, the corpus of data for analysis was selected. This included both staff-authored pieces and the many letters, poems, essays, and notes sent in and republished on behalf of readers (see Table 3.1).

Table 3.1 *Philippines Free Press* 1946–1950, Inventory of texts analysed.

Category	Description	Number
COVERS	Short front cover editorial, including the accompanying weekly cartoon illustration (staff-authored only).	226
POLITICS	Reportage, opinion, letters, poems discussing democracy, elections, government, nationhood (staff and public-authored).	195
HUKS	Reportage, opinion, letters discussing the Luzon peasant movement (staff and public-authored).	213
	Total	634

Next, the selected texts were manually coded. This involved a process of extracting the textual mechanisms applied to each of the five subject identities chosen for analysis: (1) the United States, American; (2) the Philippines, Filipino; (3) Citizen, public; (4) Politician, elected official; and (5) Huk, Central Luzon peasant. Three categories of textual mechanism were identified: (1) Predicates, which include labels, qualities, or attributes attached to the subjects with the use of adverbs or adjectives; (2) Presuppositions, which refer to the background knowledge that is assumed or implied by the text; and (3) Subject-positioning, which refers to the way the relationships between subjects or subjects and objects are represented, such as oppositional, similar, or complimentary.

Finally, the coded extracts were analysed for coherence and recurring meanings, identities and positioning, in order to examine whether there existed in the text a coherent "logic" suggestive of a dominant discourse.

America, Light of Liberty, and Our Corruptible Selves

What is revealed through analysis of the *Philippines Free Press* discourse is the way the voices continued to construct the subjects of the United States and the Philippines in a way that reflected the same differential identities and racialized distinctions that appeared within the American account. The United States was represented as "benevolent", "patient", "divine." In its relationship to the Philippines the US was depicted with attributes such as trustworthiness, fairness, generosity, and eagerness to help. "Mother America" and her "good intentions" were "to be treasured." Conversely, the Philippines was continually described in negative terms, as "sick", "infected", "diseased", and with compromised agency, represented as childlike, with infantile capacities and attributions such as "easily wooed", "immature", and even "foolish-fond." A simple count reveals that two thirds of all descriptors or predicates relating to the local subject were derogatory. Of the one third that were positive, all but a handful are drawn from the Philippines' special relationship with the United States, with the local subject's own value being derived from favour shown by its former colonizer: that the Philippines "owes thanks", for example, for being "illuminated" and "made free" by the former guardian.

Tables 3.2 and 3.3 show the descriptive characteristics attributed to the United States/American and Philippines/Filipino subjects over the first five years of independence. The predicates hang together in a clear way, suggesting a coherence and shared logic that formed the dominant public discourse at the time. What is more, this coherence extends across both the staff-authored cover stories and those from the public readership.

The reproduction of binary oppositions in the *Free Press* discourse further suggests that middle-class Filipinos had come to absorb a view of the Filipino subject as the colonial "other." These binary oppositions not only positioned the subjects vis-à-vis one another in a hierarchical arrangement, the subject positioning implied two distinct temperaments or dispositions, suggesting as "natural" the type and degree of agency that could be assumed by both. The United States was bestowed with an unbounded amount of agency. Its subjectivity was constructed in such a way that its exercise of authority over the Philippines was principled, legitimate, and warranted. Juxtaposed was the positioning of the Philippines as inferior to the United States, with little to no agency. What was more, the construal of the Philippines/Filipino subjectivity as corrupt and inept meant that the level of agency accorded to it was deemed reasonable in light of its premised capacity

The United States / The American	The Philippines / The Filipino
• Deserving of Philippine gratitude; • Has lofty and noble ideals; • Is enlightening the world, illuminating dark places, bringing light and hope and inspiration to the downtrodden and oppressed; • Is a benign power; • Has exchanged imperialism for a new gospel of political liberty; • Its actions are ordained by destiny; • Is benevolent; • Uncle Sam; • Is becoming weary, impatient with helping the Philippines; • Proud of the Philippines progress; • Parent-like; • Capable of determining the destiny of Philippine presidents; • Is trustworthy; • Has a record of dealing generously and justly with the Filipino people; • Is hearing about lawlessness in the Philippines; • Its army is a source of irritation and resentment in the Philippines; • Judge;	• Infested; • On a political merry-go-round; • Of doubtful capacity for self-government; • Reeking of scandal; • Rotten; • Where lawlessness reigns; • Defenceless against graft & corruption; • Antithesis of America; • Seen as exemplar, bulwark of democracy in the Far East; • Its democracy is being raped by those chosen to defend and uphold it; • A bastion against communism; • Has become an international cynosure; • Owes thanks to the United States; • Illuminated by the United States; • Light of Asia, helping United States bring light and liberty to oppressed people around the world; • Has become unvirtuous; • Immature, infantile in capacity for self-government; • A disappointment to the United States, needing to impress;

Table 3.2 *Philippines Free Press*, Predicates from staff-authored cover stories, 1946–1950.

- Good; - Plays the role of Santa for the Philippines; - Feels friendship, sympathy for the Philippines; - Is eager to help the Philippines; - It stumbled upon the Philippine Islands; - Has left a positive legacy in the Philippines; - Is cherished by Filipinos; - Is a champion of the cause of all people who would live in justice, decency and liberty; - Pro-Filipino; - Is hoping to save the Philippines from chaos and ruin; - Good, ever accommodating; - Has demonstrated genuine altruistic spirit; - Has shared its lifeblood with the Philippines; - Has earned the right to supervise and monitor in the Philippines; - Coldly critical, sophisticated.	- Infested with a special breed of rats; - Notorious for corrupt politics; - Mocking the hope, breaking the heart of past hero Rizal; - Full of evils; - Has as its greatest intangible asset, American interest and goodwill; - America's Pearl of the Orient; - America's noble experiment of democracy in the East; - Characterized by corruption, looting and nepotism; - Plagued by thousand and one ills; - Free, but shaky, overwhelmed by new status; - Progressed under American rule; - Pro-American; - Taken America's cause as its own; - Was made free; - A sick man – anaemic, emaciated and enfeebled – in urgent need of help; - Ravaged, demoralized; - In need of saving from chaos and ruin; - In a tragic position; - Normally peace-loving nature beginning to be corrupted; - Passionate;

The United States / The American	The Philippines / The Filipino
	• Simple;
	• Have a gloomy future
	• Hoping the world is impressed by its progress as new Republic;
	• Shamed by improprieties of government;
	• Idolize and cherish the word "independence";
	• Greatest day was day United States granted them independence;
	• Overcome by frenzied pursuit of wealth;
	• Afflicted with the psychology of greed;
	• Childish, easily entertained;
	• Takes things personally;
	• Held by superstition;
	• Easily wooed;
	• Cherishes the American way of life and have made American ideals their own;
	• Prostrate;
	• Foolish-fond.

to exercise it correctly. The "ends justify the means" argument became endorsed and reified in the discourse, the American project considered legitimized by its divine and moral objective.

The binary between the US and the Philippines was reinforced through the repetition of metaphors which represented the nature of the relationship. The parent/child binary appeared repeatedly within the text – the Philippines was constructed as having the capacity and agency of an infant or child, immature and dependent while in contrast, the United States was represented as the parent, or overseer, a patient guide and teacher, nurturing yet also disciplining the

The United States / The American	The Philippines / The Filipino
• The preferred source of capital for the Philippines, America has a splendid record in the Philippines; • Benevolent and altruistic; • Under American rule the Philippines made progress; • Benefactor, liberator; • Owed the Philippines undying gratitude for benevolent tutelage, honoured the Philippines dream of independence; • With good sense and good judgement; • Not to be treated by Philippines as an entirely foreign country; • American spirit; • Foreigners; • Its greatness lies in the people and the way they think; • Benevolent, supervisor, Mother, all-knowing, ready and able to help.	• Handle politics disastrously, regard politics as profitable industry, every nook and corner of country invaded by politics, forgetting politics original import, its slow progress can be attributed to politics, diseased, cannot distinguish right from wrong because diseased by money-making politicians; • A country in danger, its only salvation is the sure and swift action of the President, in deep affliction; • Need the right man to break the chains off dear Filipinas; • A prostrate country; • Cannot progress without outside capital; • Its democracy modelled on American ideals and principles, but now ruled by manipulative politicians; • Filipinos often whimsical and vacillating, gullible during elections, have the government they deserve; • Like a child lost in some unexplored jungle of Borneo; • Suffering the sins of corrupt officials; Being watched by Americans – their conduct, manners and faults are being observed; • Found fine and acceptable the American way of life and the ideals professed by America;

Table 3.3 *Philippines Free Press*, Predicates from public-authored texts, 1946–1950.

The United States / The American	The Philippines / The Filipino
	• A country in danger;
	• A Christian democracy, the only one in the Orient;
	• America's fiesta-loving ward, drifting towards Red disaster;
	• Of questionable fitness to live in a democracy;
	• Easily persuaded.

Philippines with its childlike characteristics, until it could take responsibility for itself, and understand the consequences of its actions; a proud father, who "remembers with pride" the "steady progress of its former ward toward independence and freedom" (Editorial 1949d: 1). Also found were core oppositions of good/evil, male/female, light/dark, judge/parolee. Such binaries became the basis on which meanings and identities were built, so that the asymmetrical relationship between the two subjectivities – the American and the Filipino – became reified and naturalized as if representing the innate and essential quality of each. If the United States was a steady hand, wise, rational, reasoned, and fixed, in direct contrast, the Filipino sense of "self" was unanchored – fickle and impulsive, undisciplined and prone to chaos. As the superiority of Uncle Sam was rendered permanent in the discourse, the inferior character of the Filipino subject became a permanent flaw.

What is more, the distinction drawn was not only between the two subjects of the American and the Filipino, but also between two different types of nation-states. While one signified democracy, the "good guy", the world's guide and protector, the other was deficient in comparison, floating around the fixed signifier but not yet grounded. It is possible to imagine, given such logic, how the American colonial period could be celebrated as a kind of "rite of passage" for the Philippine nation in its desire to reach the goal of freedom. Circularly, however, to memorialize history in this way was to legitimize and perpetuate a narrative in which the Filipino subject was constructed as being of dubious suitability for self-government, prone to misbehaviour and vice.

Independence as a gift. The representational practices identified in the text are exemplified by discussions around the Philippines'

Independence Day, which by no coincidence was celebrated on 4 July. On the cover of the first post-war issue of the *Free Press*, published on 23 February 1946 – the first edition since confirmation that the United States would finally grant Philippine independence on 4 July that year – the editorial read:

> In years gone by, in the press and on the platform, we were frequently and flatteringly warned that 'the eyes of the world were upon us', that the whole world was looking our way. Not always justified then, the phrase may, with much better grace, be used now.
>
> For that, let us thank the United States – the United States and its lofty and noble ideals as embodied in the Statue of Liberty – the Goddess of Liberty – Liberty enlightening the world.
>
> [...] And today, divine transition, the benign rays from that symbol are flooding the Far East, illuminating the dark places, bringing light and hope and inspiration to the downtrodden and oppressed [...] But for the Philippines and the advent of America in the Far East, the peoples that now hail the dawning would still be fettered by the past, dreaming, hoping, aspiring, striving. (Editorial 1946c)

Figure 3.1 Izon, Esmeraldo. "The One Year Old." Cartoon. *Philippines Free Press*, 28 June 1947.

Or consider the edition marking the first anniversary of Philippine independence, published on 28 June 1947. The cover featured a cartoon entitled "The One Year Old" (Figure 3.1), along with an accompanying text that read:

> And what now, little man? Going it alone, legs a bit shaky and steps a bit uncertain, but getting along, head in the right direction and hand tightly gripping the flag [...] (Editorial 1947e)

Philippine Independence Day was, for many Filipinos, all about America. Whether looking backwards or looking forward, the country's independence was defined by its relationship to America. In an "Open Letter to Uncle Sam" published on 1 July 1950, Mr Leopoldo Sanchez from the National Orthopaedic Hospital said that on this fourth anniversary of Philippine independence, it was of "the great American nation" and "the Stars and Stripes waving in Freedom's air" that he was thinking. After all, not just once, at the turn of the century, but again against the Japanese in the recent war, the Philippines was indebted to American sacrifice. Great was America, he said, "not only in armed might but in the things which make for greatness – democracy, fairness, goodness, and love." He finished the letter with a humble offer of "lasting gratitude" to Uncle Sam, before signing off, "Sincerely, A Filipino" (Sanchez 1950).

The protracted asymmetry between the United States and the Philippines post-independence was not only legitimate, according to this discourse; there was a permanence implied about the way the Filipino looked upwards towards his or her American benefactor. As part of commemorations to mark Independence Day in 1948, the editor dedicated a full page to the reprinting of a poem sent in by reader Mr Treyes of Bacolod City. Entitled "We Will Not Forget" (Treyes 1948), the poem declaimed:

> Now, when we look upon our flag as it waves
> Proud, free, resplendent in the boundless blue,
> We still see the banner that once flew by its side.
> We still see the blaze of color that it made
> In the sky with its red, white, and blue.
>
> We will not forget, America!
> Think not that we may forget; no, even if we tried.
> Your flesh has been grafted into ours; and there,
> It has taken root, and grown, and flourished.
> We know you, America!

You may not know our Lapu-Lapu, our Rizal;
But we know your Lincoln, your Washington.
The Longfellow that you know, we also know –
We love them as you love them.

You may not know our history, our traditions;
But we know your history, your traditions;
And they form a part of what we love, what we treasured!
And, better still, the ideals that you cherish, the hopes,
The dreams that you have dreamed through the years,
We have made ours.

On the day your flag was lowered,
It was not 'mid-the roar and din of revolution,
As it often is, at the birth of a new nation;
And as it slowly descended, the eyes of a grateful people
Followed it and tears flowed freely . . .

Think you, then, that we will forget?
No, America, we cannot, not ever forget!
You gave us freedom. You gave up power;
But you hold within your hands something mightier –
A people's heart, a nation's trust!

According to the author, as a branch owes its entire existence and being to its trunk, so the Philippines has been born out of America. This sapling relationship means not only will the branch always be a branch, rather than seeing itself as directly planted in the ground, but there is also a definite direction in the relationship that is implied. While the trunk does not need the branch to survive, the reverse is not true.

The enemy within. A tone of self-flagellation also appeared in these early post-independence discussions. Rather than scrutiny being placed upon the former colonizer, the United States, for the disruption of the Philippines' democratic aspirations, the negative appraisal was almost always reserved for the Filipino subject itself. Striking about this judgment, which at times reached the point of self-loathing, is the way it exhibited a distinct middle-class character. While flaws in the Filipino subject were associated with those above as well as those below, the voice in the text – sometimes referred to as "the public" and at other times, the "honest" or "right-thinking" citizen – is of one who is "caught in the crossfire" (Editorial 1947d), rendered powerless and impotent by the political machinery of the elite above, and the "foolishness" of the masses below who perpetuate the elite's power.

Figure 3.2 Izon, Esmeraldo. "New Gulliver." Cartoon. *Philippines Free Press*, 7 August 1948.

There is little doubt that it was for the political elite that this public discourse reserved its most disparaging anger and blame. The promises of political contenders were like "iridescent soap-bubbles blown with such ease to delight and deceive the foolish-fond electorate" (Editorial 1947c). Elections were described as a time when "a glorious and usually unfounded conviction fills the mediocre and inept that he can lead the country out of difficult straits"; the "venal and corrupt" candidates were likened to "the vulture [that] circles with unerring instinct over the prostrate form of a dying man" (Editorial 1949c); and their rivalries compared to a town-fiesta game when "gentlemen" run madly around the plaza in an attempt to be the first to catch the greased pig (Editorial 1946b).

It wasn't only those above who bore the force of judgement in the texts. Juan de la Cruz, the fictional name given for the common *tao*, the person on the street, also contributed to the construction of a flawed Filipino subjectivity. Though described in pitiful terms – the "forgotten man", the "little man" who tills the land, works hard, only to be submerged by the corrupt landed political class – the common *tao* is also gullible, simple, too forgiving, and easily led astray. This Filipino subject failed to meet the standards of citizenship required by democracy – "high intelligence, public spirit, and civic virtue." Instead, out of indolence, they "neglect[ed] to inform themselves of public issues" (Chavarria 1949).

It was not simply passivity that was blameworthy, according to the readers. It was the naiveté of Filipinos, of "the fair Filipina", "often whimsical and vacillating", and "easily wooed." The Filipino "people" were "quick to resent, but especially quick to forgive and forget" and could be easily won over "by gentle persuasion and love and they will give you the very shirt off their backs" (Anonymous 1949). They "readily swallow[ed] [the] glittering promises" of unprincipled politicians during elections, one writes: "Thus the saying", the reader concludes, "that we have the government we deserve" (Nuera 1946).

It was this constructed Filipino subject, one which excludes the middle-class "citizen", that became the chief object of blame. There was no doubt whatsoever that the government was indefensibly corruptible. But such corruptibility reflected the state of the people. "Who is to blame", asked one reader in 1948, for the failings and anomalies of the Philippine government, but "the people" who even upon realizing their mistake in electing crony officials, "just watch and wait" (Borromeo 1949). It reflected, according to another, a "morass of moral bankruptcy" in the Philippines' "national soul" – a "tragedy" of "our people's own doing" (Aquino 1947).

Indignity Compounded, Anxiety Inflamed

The narrative of failure and blameworthiness not only conjured feelings of shame, it aroused reminders of the indignity that was a present companion in the colonial condition. While the United States had proved itself the benevolent tutor with altruistic motives in helping the Philippines achieve freedom and progress, the "Filipino" subject, it increasingly seemed, had failed to prove itself worthy of such a privilege. The whole colonial project had been based on a rationale of preparing the Philippines for self-government. Freedom was conditional upon the Filipinos "learning" how to manage the responsibility of being free. Half a century later, so embarrassing was the state of the newly independent Philippines, a front-page editorial wrote, that it mocked the life of that cherished national hero and martyr José Rizal. "If he were alive", and "if he could see the evils under the

Philippines sun", his "heart would break" at the sight of corruption, superstition, and violence (Editorial 1949a).

As conditions in the new Republic became increasingly degraded, with electoral violence and rampant government corruption, the feelings of shame and humiliation were augmented by an innate, visceral sense of being watched. Even Filipino citizens in the United States were "being watched by Americans", according to one such Filipino studying in New York during 1947. The Filipinos' "conduct, their manner, and their faults are being observed. We, the Filipinos in America, are the ambassadors of goodwill of our people" (Velarde Jr 1947). "Let us not give Mother America and the world the painful and shameful impression that we are corrupt, degenerate people", Florentino Pamor urged his fellow citizens the same year (Pamor 1947). From the Filipino Club in New York, Julio Villa Jr wrote a letter to the *Free Press* editor, published on 22 July 1950, in which he warned his fellow countrymen:

> Knowledge of the corruption in the Philippine Government today is beginning to spread to America. The June *Reader's Digest Time Magazine* of June 3, the World Telegram and Sun of May 26, not to mention the dispatches to the New York Herald Tribune and Washington DC papers, have presented the hard-hitting facts to the American people . . . (Villa Jr 1950)

The deeper the political crisis that emerged in the country during these early years of post-independence, the more it seemed to reflect not only on the innately corrupt character of Philippine politicians, but on the foolishness of Filipino voters, a narrative that continued to reinforce the colonial construction of the "inferior" Filipino subject incapable of self-government. Every report of government wrongdoing was experienced as a defamation of the Filipino people, and a loss of esteem not only in the eyes of Americans but the whole world. "Our national soul", wrote journalist Melchor Aquino, "can only be as good as that of our citizenry, in the same way that our government can only be as good as the people make it. Bitter as the truth may be, our national soul and our government are floundering in the morass of moral bankruptcy. This tragedy is our people's own doing" (Aquino 1947). Living up to the standards and expectations of the former teacher and benefactor proved a seemingly impossible task.

Was the granting of independence premature? This was the question being discussed four years into America's Filipino "experiment." Mid-1949, Mr Williams, from Negros Occidental, wrote a letter to the *Free Press* in which he compared "those days when an American governor was in Malacañan", a time when the country "was enjoying peace and prosperity through American benevolence and supervision", to the days of post-independence status, with a government "run like hell." He said it was fortunate for his country, that "Mother America" ignored the earlier "pestering" of the Philippine politicians for independence: "The USA knew well what would happen to her fiesta-loving ward once beyond her control. Hence the transition period. No wiser move could have been made" (Williams 1949). If McKinley had not annexed the Philippines, the islands would have fallen into anarchy and misrule. Yet even after half a century of American tutelage, as Locsin put it, the events following independence appeared to confirm that the Filipinos remained "untrained in self-government" (Locsin 1950b). "We need and want democracy: but are we ready for it?" was the question being posed.

Figure 3.3 Izon, Esmeraldo. "Democracy Gone Mad." Cartoon. *Philippines Free Press*, 14 November 1953.

In just five years, pride had turned to desperation. The 1949 election had been the dirtiest and most violent yet, and the sentiment circulating was that democracy in the Philippines had been "murdered." Democratic politics in the hands of Filipinos, it seemed, had become dangerous. Democracy may even have been causing more harm than good. If it were "productive of good, of some tangible benefit for the people", one writer reflected, "then the merry-go-round on which Philippine leaders are riding with such carefree abandon would be justified." But it is not serving the public good, he scorned, only an exchange of rank between men of power (Dian 1949). "Democracy in the Philippines", wrote Damasco Suyko of Bantayan in 1949, "has assumed a new concept. It embraces non-compliance with the will of majority, disrespect for the rights of the minority, and reliance on force to influence public opinion" (Suyko 1949). "Is this democracy in action", asked staff writer Teodoro Locsin, "or merely bedlam?" (Locsin 1949).

Figure 3.4 Izon, Esmeraldo. "Execution." Cartoon. *Philippines Free Press*, 15 October 1949.

The Material Costs of Indebtedness: The Parity Provision

It was an undeniable reality – the continuation into the independence era of the United States' influence over Philippine domestic politics. At its most basic, the lesson in practical politics was outlined in a *Free Press* editorial of 1949: "All a Philippine President needs to be assured of re-election is somehow to get an invitation to Washington shortly before Election Day. He whom America favours, or merely seems to favour, will win" (Editorial 1949b). Yet the effects of colonial entanglements during this period were more complex, and insidious, than even this scenario suggests. The naturalizing of the asymmetrical relationship between the United States and the Philippines continued to constrain Filipino imaginings of their own democratic agency, while at the same time enabling the United States to exercise a level of sovereignty over the Islands without needing to claim the status of sovereign power. How? The language of gratitude and indebtedness made certain policies and practices in the independence era possible, even imperative, while it precluded others. Post-war negotiations between the US and the Philippines over the terms of the latter's independence would demonstrate this clearly, and none more so than the controversial parity provision.

Philippine independence was subject to two conditions. The first was the continued presence of US military bases throughout the archipelago. Second was a package of economic concessions favouring the US. The Military Bases Agreement was signed and ratified by the new Philippine Senate on 26 March 1947, granting to the US 99-year leases along with full jurisdiction over American and Filipino personnel on a total of 22 military sites (Salonga 2001: 43). Though a Philippine panel set up to negotiate the military bases had attempted to restrict extraterritorial jurisdiction over the sites, US Ambassador Paul V. McNutt threatened to withdraw all US forces if the newly independent Philippine Congress would not concede to American demands. Capitulation followed, although the issue would again be revisited by the Philippine Congress in 1991, after the EDSA "revolution", with a different outcome.

More controversial at the time were the economic concessions demanded by the US. On 30 April 1946, two months before Philippine independence, the US Congress passed the Bell Trade Act. The legislation outlined the terms on which trade between the two countries would be governed following America's relinquishment of sovereignty, and it outlined the provisions that would be contained within the executive agreement on independence, to be signed on 4 July. Along with provisions guaranteeing favourable trade conditions for the US, such as tariff reductions, the most controversial part of the Act was the grant of rights to US citizens and corporations to the archipelago's natural resources in parity with the rights of Philippine citizens.

When passed by US Congress, the parity provision contravened the 1935 Philippine Constitution. At the time of drafting, the constitutional convention in the Philippines had agreed on inclusion of the following clause in an effort to safeguard the country's resources from future foreign control:

> All agricultural, timber, and mineral lands of the public domain, waters, minerals, coal, petroleum and other mineral oils, all forces of potential energy, and other natural resources of the Philippines belong to the state, and their disposition, exploitation, development, or utilisation shall be limited to citizens of the Philippines, or to corporations or associations at least 60 per centum of the capital of which is owned by such citizens, subject to any existing right, grant, lease, or concession at the time of the inauguration of the Government established under this Constitution . . . . (in Jenkins 1954: 67)

While this must have been deemed by Washington as satisfactory protection of US interests in the Islands at the time, in 1946 the drafters of the Bell Bill believed the future of existing American business required more protection. Thus, section 341 of the new Bill stated:

> The disposition, exploitation, development, and utilisation of all agricultural, timber, and mineral lands of the public domain, waters, minerals, coal, petroleum, and other mineral oils, all forces and sources of potential energy, and other natural resources of the Philippines, and the operation of public utilities, shall, if open to any person, be open to citizens of the United States and to all forms of business enterprise owned or controlled, directly or indirectly, by United States citizens. (in Jenkins 1954: 67)

Not only would the new Republic be obliged to revise its Constitution to accommodate the parity provision, but also no reciprocal rights were offered to Filipinos in the United States. In fact, the Bill contained other provisions that made the notion of "parity" quite absurd, not least the open discretion granted to the United States President to impose additional trade restrictions where deemed necessary to protect American interests against Philippine manufacturers.[5] The policy was aimed at encouraging the continuation of extractive industries, such as mining, instead of manufacturing goods for the domestic market. In effect, it also "encouraged monopolistic control by giving the few pre-war firms practically exclusive rights to export of major commodities" (Jenkins 1954: 67). Moreover, the Philippine peso was irrevocably tied to the dollar, so that the new Republic "was not free to manage its own currency as changing conditions and national needs might dictate", nor could exchange controls be imposed to regulate the flow of capital (Jenkins 1954: 68). Thus, the

Philippines would remain dependent on American investment, while investors themselves could withdraw funds at any time. In short, as Jenkins explained, these arrangements "encouraged the continuation of the pre-war situation in which the Philippine economy had suffered from overspecialisation and from too great reliance on the American market – conditions not compatible with economic independence' (1954: 66).

The Bell Trade Act required ratification by the Philippine Congress, along with a successful nation-wide referendum to approve the constitutional amendment. Yet this element of Philippine agency in the decision was seriously compromised by the fact that US funds, pledged under the Philippine Rehabilitation Act to help with post-war recovery, including rebuilding the devastated Manila, were made conditional upon acceptance of the Act. "No parity, no money", as President Roxas put it at the time (Salonga 2001: 45).

Leading up to the congressional vote and the National Referendum, public discussion of the issue was widespread. The *Philippines Free Press* newspaper covered the debate closely. The editorial position was quite clear. The worries of some, that the Bell Act resembled a "Trojan horse", were misplaced. Against the warning to "beware . . . the Greeks bearing gifts", an editorial of 15 January 1947 read:

> [...] it is pointed out that for some 40 years now America has been 'bearing gifts' to the Philippines and that the Philippines has immensely benefited thereby [...] The plea of those sponsoring the Bell Act is that it will make for 'economic security.' To those who question that, the answer may be summed up in the well-known words: 'Oh, ye of little faith!' (Editorial 1947f)

A few months later, as discussion continued, another front-page editorial weighed in on the debate between American High Commissioner Paul McNutt, who was defending the deal by saying "there is no intention to compromise future sovereignty", and Filipino nationalists, who "fore[saw] American businessmen, armed with tremendous capital, taking over the mines, land and other natural resources, and the Filipino, with little capital, helpless to check the complete economic domination of their country by another." The question put to the Filipinos, the editorial continued, was "will it end well?" Or were Filipinos "mortgag[ing] their future, beyond redemption?" (Editorial 1946d).

Following the ratification by the Philippine House and Senate later that year, the paper reported that "the die [had been] cast [...] Whether the future will justify such phrases as 'selling one's birthright for a mess of pottage' or 'bartering away one's patrimony' only the future can tell." But, it added, "judging by the past, there is no reason for excessive pessimism" for "the record of the American congress, and behind it the American people, is one of dealing justly and even generously with the Filipino people" (Editorial 1946a).

But the parity provision still required the public's approval of the constitutional amendment. As the 11 March 1947 plebiscite approached, the *Free Press* had been reporting readers' opinions on the issue. In an initial report on 11 January, the paper had tallied opinions in the total of 88 letters received: 16 were undecided, 47 in favour, and 25 against (Editorial 1947b). But since that time, the editor noted, the paper's mailbag "continued to bulge with unsolicited letters, articles, poems on the much-debated question." Of the 74 new letters received from readers across 25 different provinces nationwide, 35 expressed views in favour, 31 declared the intention to vote "no", while 8 remained unsure (Editorial 1947a).

The paper could only republish a sample, but the extracts of readers' letters illuminate the rationale behind citizens' positions on the issue. Of those who were for the change to the Constitution in favour of US citizens' parity rights, one explained that his "yes" vote was for the sake of their children, who by the time they "come of age, milk and honey will be flowing in our country" (Editorial 1947a). For most others, the vote in favour was not so much about the economic concessions themselves, as it was an exercise in loyalty. "To reject parity to our benefactor and liberator (America)", wrote one, "would be tantamount to violating the essence and principles of character training" (Editorial 1947a). Another explained being glad for the chance to show to America his "undying gratitude for 42 years of benevolent tutelage, for the redemption of the promise of liberation after three and a half dark years of Japanese oppression, and for their honoring [the Filipinos'] long-cherished dream of independence" (Editorial 1947a). Mr Gonzales of Bohol had a message for his fellow citizens who feared America's intentions:

> Read the history of Filipino-American relations since the inception of the American regime to know the real intentions of the American people. You will learn some concrete facts about the benevolence and altruism of the American people. (Editorial 1947a)

Amongst those in favour, it was possible to detect the way concepts central to democracy, such as sovereignty and freedom, were being negotiated and where necessary, recalibrated, in order to accommodate the circumstances. Freedom, that inalienable right that should be defended at any cost, "cannot be preserved by simple wishful thinking", wrote Juan Hilario, former columnist for the *Manila Daily Bulletin*, to the *Free Press* editor. Freedom demanded from "each and every Filipino", he continued, "civic courage coupled with hard work." What is more, Mr Hilario wrote, "For a prostrate country like ours, it would be dangerous to seek mere survival and security only [...] progress and opportunity can be had only with the indispensable aid of outside capital and know how. To me American capital and know-how should be preferred because of the splendid American record in our country." To the critics of the Philippine Trade Act with the United States, Mr Hilario had the message that such "pessimism and defeatism" as to expect the worst at this critical moment in the country's history would be disastrous (Hilario 1947).

Those against, on the other hand, expressed determinedly that the vote symbolized the Philippines' continued dependence on foreigners, which offended the "dignity, honor, welfare and interests of the Filipino people." Mr Restituto A. Buenconsejo from Cebu City said he could "hear millions of unborn cursing the present generation for its injustice to them if it approves parity" (in Hilario 1947). The agreement "contradicts the principles of democracy", wrote Miss Josefina Cube y Aguas from Manila, and she felt sure that, for this reason, "the American people would never approve such a proposition for their own country" (in Hilario 1947). What is more, regarding the assumption that the deal was already done, since the Philippine government in ratifying the parity agreement in Congress had already committed the country to its approval, an anonymous reader from Malabon in Rizal wrote that it was the job of the Philippine government to "represent the desires of the people. At least that is what my textbook says. That, too, is what the Constitution means when it refers to sovereignty of the people" (in Hilario 1947).

The March national plebiscite to approve amendment of the Philippine Constitution would record a clear result – 79 per cent voting "yes", and only 21 per cent "no." The days and weeks that followed, however, featured stories of irregularities, intimidation and fraud. A teacher from Bohol told of the Senate President and Secretary for Agriculture's visit to the island. The Mayor of one town had used the occasion to declare that "he would not permit discussion of the parity question because he was the only person in town who understood it." He was followed by the Governor, who "denounced vigorously some teachers who had been reported to him to be against parity", claiming that those teachers "had no right to remain in their positions" (Anonymous 1947).

130 | *Democracy & Duress*

Figure 3.5 Izon, Esmeraldo. "Hocus Pokus!" Cartoon. *Philippines Free Press*, 5 April 1947, p. 17.

Discussion of the parity issue in the *Free Press* had provided a glimpse, not simply as to why the plebiscite ultimately gained a majority amongst the voting population (not discounting the role of electoral fraud), but also as to how such an inherently unbalanced policy was deemed reasonable and legitimate by a large proportion of the population. At the same time, the experience had given further cause for cynicism about democracy in the Philippines. This sentiment is captured in a letter by Samuel R. Capistrano of the Central Philippine College in Iloilo on the day following the plebiscite, published in the *Free Press* on 5 April. Titled "To an American Friend", the open letter read:

> The plebiscite is over. For the next 28 years you will have equal rights with us in the development of our country.[6] As the saying is, 'The people have spoken.' In this case, however, it seems to me that this means, 'The people who compose the Board of Election Inspectors have spoken for the people who did not vote.' [. . .] At college this morning, three friends of mine said that they had voted 'No.' But the board of elections reported no 'No' votes were registered . . .
>
> Dear American friend, I have written you this because you might find your way to our shores during the next 28 years – to help develop our country, to help build a better Philippines. Should you sense a

feeling of resentment on the part of some Filipinos over your presence, do not take it for ingratitude. Try to understand with characteristic American broadmindedness. Remember the story I have told you in this letter.

And if within your lifetime it again becomes necessary to defend democracy with blood and powder, remember how democratic processes are being 'reprocessed' after this latest war and cease to wonder why democracy has to be defended on the average of once every 25 years. Our next defense may not be against a foreign power! (Capistrano 1947)

The Ambivalence Effect: Securing Democracy by Constraining Bandits

Despite the prevalence of a conservative and counter-revolutionary discourse in the post-independence civic sphere, it would be a mistake to characterize this period of politics as one of acquiescence. Quite the contrary, while American colonial rulers and Filipino national leaders were absorbed in negotiations about the terms of independence and the future relationship between the new Republic and its former warden, domestic political issues were reaching a peak. Not only in Mindanao, with the Muslim resistance to Christian Filipino nationalism, but closer to the national capital, Central Luzon had become the site of intensified agrarian unrest. In fact, the Republic entered its new life marred by internal conflicts: how to deal with the issue of Japanese collaborators amongst the political elite; and what to do about the wartime guerilla fighters with links to the Communist Party who were successfully mobilizing the biggest peasant unrest in history. The Japanese occupation of the Second World War had given rise to an oppositional movement that would present the greatest threat to the stability of the existing system of government in half a century. To further complicate matters, these internal difficulties were being played out in the context of early geopolitics of the Cold War.

Reflecting on this period, it was not the success of a popular grassroots political movement that would stand out as significant. Ultimately, they would suffer the same fate as agitators before them. But the period would bring to light two dynamics in particular that characterized the political environment of the time. First, the elite engaged in manipulation of democracy to legitimize their anti-democratic politics, while democracy was also the language within which the opposition were fighting for recognition and change. The outcome of the struggle would determine how "legitimate" democratic politics was framed.

Second, by tracing public discourse at the time in the *Free Press*, it is possible to see how a middle-class public, despite (or perhaps because of) its democratic aspirations, was willing to accept an anti-democratic politics that was based on the same imperial governing logic of the colonial era – namely, the differentiation of certain groups to rationalize their exclusion from democratic rights, and the subsequent acquiescence to the exercise of exceptional forms of state power. It was the ambivalent character of a simultaneous praise for democratic principles and consent to authoritarian over-reach that helps to explain the middle class's support for the government's program to eradicate oppositional politics. Ultimately, the events and the mood of the period would pave the way for American troops to re-enter the Islands in a counter-insurgency mission to quell the peasant rebellion in the Central Luzon region.

The Hukbalahap and the Democratic Alliance

During the war, and especially as the conflict was drawing to an end, both American and Filipino elites feared the potential political strength of a popular nationalist movement, especially given its organized base among the masses, its determined and politically savvy middle-class leadership, and its association with communism. The Philippines' political system had never tolerated more than the most moderate and controlled forms of non-elite participation.

The base of the resistance movement was located in the villages of Central Luzon, where during Japanese occupation, the existing peasant networks were transformed into the "Hukbalahap" (Huks), an abbreviation for Hukbong Bayan Laban sa mga Hapon (People's Army Against the Japanese). For peasants of the Central Luzon region themselves, as well as providing local policing in the absence of either Filipino or Japanese authorities, the Hukbalahap "was a network through which people tried to undercut the Japanese and to govern themselves" (Kerkvliet 2014: 82).[7]

Even during the occupation and resistance, leaders of the Hukbalahap were discussing how to influence the Philippine government upon its return, and how to push for a more progressive agenda on the social, political and economic issues confronting the nation. "We figured", said leader Peregrino Taruc, "that because of the Hukbalahap's achievements and its political strength at least in Central Luzon, the Osmeña government would have to take us into account" (Kerkvliet 2014: 123). In reality, however, the occupation period drove a deeper wedge between the peasant movement and local elites. Whereas most villagers had no choice but to remain on the land during the war despite Japanese oppression, and to defend themselves by forming local Hukbalahap squadrons, most landlords had abandoned their tenants, fleeing to the cities where, in many cases, they collaborated with the Japanese regime (Kerkvliet 2014: 108). What is more, American troops on the ground had, as David Bernstein put it, "no patience with social-minded guerrillas" (in Lopez 1951: 35). The Huks were too political, too radical to be trusted. Even during the War, USAFFE guerillas were sending messages back to the US Pacific Command that the Hukbalahap was "Anti-Democratic", that it was "modeled after the communistic organizations of China", and that it was "motivated by purely personal and political objectives" (Kerkvliet 2014: 131). One leader of the Central Luzon USAFFE unit even wrote to the US in January 1945 that the Hukbalahap was "subversive . . . a radical organization", whose "major operations and activities of carnage, revenge, banditry and high-jacking" have never been seen in the history of the Philippines (Kerkvliet 2014: 131).

When the United States Army returned to Luzon at the end of the war, USAFFE officers were put in charge of disarming the Huks. This saw US Armed Forces return to what they had been doing half a century earlier – going hunting for Huks and killing them like animals.[8] Having returned to their land, local landlords, backed by American troops and Philippine constabulary, also victimized Hukbalahap participants, along with any villagers who supported them. The local elites blamed all crime in the region, including murders and robberies, on the Hukbalahap veterans (Kerkvliet 2014: 165). As Kerkvliet writes of American and Filipino elites: "Perhaps they simply feared the Hukbalahap movement's potential political strength in the post war years [...] [T]he villages in the Hukbalahap had guns, and they had learned guerrilla warfare. . . . They imagined that the worst would happen unless they took direct action against the Hukbalahap. So much the better if they could also argue that this was a communist movement. . . . (Kerkvliet 2014: 133–4).

One of the most significant developments of the occupation period was the convergence of the Hukbalahap peasant movement of Central Luzon, and a more urban-based group of progressives, concentrated in Manila, consisting of groups and individuals, including civil libertarians, nationalists, trade unionists, socialists, and communists, who were, as Kerkvliet describes, "discontented with the regime, disgusted with the major political factions in the country, and in favour of making the government more representative of Philippine society"

(2014: 111). The two movements were concerned with both the vast social and economic challenges facing the country, and with the question of independence. In early 1942 they had joined forces to become the United Front.[9]

Despite the growing repression in the countryside, members of the United Front formally organized as the Democratic Alliance (DA) in April 1945, with the purpose of running their own candidates for political office. The alliance consisted of the "Free Philippines", comprising some very high-profile "Civil Liberties" advocates, the Hukbalahap, and a number of other small resistance groups "of conservative as well as leftist leanings that chose opposition to the Nacionalista Party rather than submission to its monolithic rule" (Locsin 1946a). As Locsin reported at the time, "despite its rather radical cast, DA succeeded in attracting to its fold some businessmen and middle-class professionals." One year after its formation, it had established regional chapters in Luzon and the Visayas and had become the strongest minority party in the country. The new party had big aspirations, expecting it would in due course become the dominant political party in the Philippines (Locsin 1946a).

Despite intimidation, threats and actual violence, the April 1946 election was a decisive victory for DA candidates for congressional representatives in Central Luzon (Kerkvliet 2014: 144). Though the DA-endorsed candidate for President, Sergio Osmeña, had lost the national race, six DA candidates won seats in the House of Representatives, including leader Luis Taruc, who without delivering a single speech beat his rival by 29,000 votes (Karnow 1989: 340). Yet in a repeat of the Sakdalista era just over a decade earlier, state-led repression continued to escalate. The DA headquarters was destroyed by Military Police, with several officers arrested and killed. No amount of placating, even Luis Taruc's appeal to the likes of the Manila Rotary Club, would challenge the claims of government officials that their actions were justified as a defence "against communism and terrorism" (Kerkvliet 2014: 167), in the name of protecting democracy.

The ultimate blow came in late May. President Roxas had been sworn into office, and the country was only five weeks away from the declaration of independence by the United States. In the first session of the new Congress, the six DA congressmen-elect from Central Luzon, including Huk leader Luis Taruc and one other known to be sympathetic to the peasant movement, were refused their seats without so much as a resolution being passed. It was alleged, by President Roxas and other members of the House of Representatives, that "these congressmen had used terror and other illegal means to win"

(Kerkvliet 2014: 171). The move not only solved the problem that President Roxas had not achieved a two-thirds majority in the lower house; more importantly, it eliminated from the chamber members who would have opposed the ratification of the Philippine Trade Act (Bell Act) that gave favourable conditions to American manufacturers and investors in the post-independent Philippine economy, not least the controversial "parity" clause. Roxas and his allies were right to believe that, if the DA congressmen had remained in their elected seats, the Act would have failed to achieve the necessary votes. As it was, even without the seven congressmen and another three senators being unseated, the vote passed by a majority of only one.

Meanwhile, in the countryside of Central Luzon, the moderate demands of the Huk movement were becoming increasingly radical. It was, as Kerkvliet describes it, a vicious cycle: "Violence had pushed the peasants to rebel. More violence compelled them to continue the rebellion and in turn become more violent themselves" (Kerkvliet 2014: 216). When the decapitated body of the peasant movement's leader, Juan Feleo, was found floating down the Pampanga river, a murder that was suspected to have been ordered from the very top of government, the trigger for full-scale rebellion had been pulled. According to the Roxas administration and the local and provincial elites, the only way to deal with the revolt was to crush it.

In the name of democracy. Immediately following Feleo's kidnapping, Taruc wrote a letter to the President in which he said, "[…] under the guise of crushing lawlessness, the MPs, civilian guards, and some of your provincial and municipal officials have trampled in the dust our Constitution and suppressed every democratic right of the peasants." After informing the President he would cease direct negotiations and instead go back into hiding in the mountains of Central Luzon, Taruc presented the President with an ultimatum:

> You have your choice, Mr. President – to be a real liberal and a true leader of Filipinos and rest assured of our cooperation. But be an imperialist fascist agent and you will find that there are enough Filipinos who have learned a lot in the last war and who will not give up in peace social gains acquired during that war […] extremists may want you to order the bombing and cannonading of the poor – to kill them by the thousands . . . But they should know that they can never bomb out the people's new-found hopes and convictions – that democracy, freedom and a lasting peace are for all, including the commoner who feed the nation when it is starving and fight for it when it is in danger. (Kerkvliet 2014: 177)

Simultaneously, the government argued that it was they who were waging the fight to defend democracy from its enemies. Arrests, executions, burning of houses, and intimidation continued. The administration justified the violence and force by labelling the armed peasants as "dissidents" and "terrorists" who were holding the new nation hostage with their banditry and murderous behaviour. What is more, it was alleged these bandits were "communists" who had in mind the destruction of democracy in the Philippines, and who sought "to establish their own government with the help of force and fear" (Kerkvliet 2014: 219). By March 1948, President Roxas had declared the Hukbalahap and the National Peasants Union "illegal associations" in a move deemed necessary to defend the Philippine Republic from the threat of being overthrown by this unlawful, subversive and destructive movement (Editorial 1948).

Though predominantly fighting for reform rather than revolution, the Huk peasants became implicated in the emerging Cold War narrative. In March 1947, President Truman announced to the world that America would support "free peoples who are resisting attempted subjugation by armed minorities or by outside pressures" (Karnow 1989: 336). "It soon became axiomatic in Washington" explains Karnow, "that the Russians managed Communists everywhere, and that America's duty was to stop them" (1989: 336). It was no surprise then, that the Philippine government's accusations and actions against the Huks were fully supported by American officials. As one peasant reflected years later, "Nobody would give us our rights or hear our demands. They said we were communists. I didn't even know what Communism was, and I still don't. But they called you a Communist, and that was that. It made no sense to deny it, because they wouldn't believe you" (Karnow 1989: 342). By the end of 1947, though the Huk rebellion in Central Luzon continued, the Democratic Alliance had all but collapsed, largely as a result of ongoing repression, and the splintering of the alliance on the question of how to confront the unrelenting state force.

"They must live within the folds of the law or be hunted down like dogs." In his exclusive interview with the *Free Press* during 1946, Taruc laid out his belief that the peasants were being "forced to the wall" by landlords' violence, the intention being "to compel them to retaliate in self-defense and thus provide an excuse for declaring the whole peasant movement outlaw" (Editorial 1946e). Taruc's forecast would turn out to be an accurate one. Acts of state violence that had been perceived in the first days and months, at least to a portion of the public, as an unreasonable use of force against poor peasants who were protesting their destitute conditions, would become legitimate within the middle-class civic sphere. Returning to a close reading of the *Philippines Free Press*, over the five years from 1946 to 1950, there certainly were voices sympathetic to the Huks' cause.[10] Yet these voices were greatly outnumbered. A simple count of articles or letters on the situation over the five years reveals a bias towards negative, unsympathetic representations of the Huks; this negative bias was moderated in 1948, the year President Roxas was attempting amnesty negotiations with Taruc and the Huk leaders, but worsened in the years after.

Table 3.4 Analysis of *Philippine Free Press* entries relating to the Hukbalahap, the National Peasants Union or the Democratic Alliance.

Year	Positive / Sympathetic	Negative / Unsympathetic
1946	8	22
1947	7	17
1948	10	11
1949	2	6
1950	2	6

The reason for the decline in articles and letters relating to the Huks in 1949 and 1950 was because the paper had stopped dedicating as much editorial or discussion space to the topic, and instead started a regular column at the back of every single edition entitled "Late Flashes from the Huk Front." This took the form of brief articles that resembled war updates, celebrating successful raids and counts of the numbers killed. The image in Figure 3.6 features (from left to right) the Policeman, Chief, Captain and Lieutenants of the 77th Police Constabulary, standing behind their latest capture. The man squatting in front of them is 32-year-old man Pablo Carlos from Pulongmaba, Porac in Pampanga, who was caught taking food to two other "Huks" who were waiting at his home.

The same labels used by both the Filipino and American elites – of Huks as "terrorists", "bandits", communists – were found in a middle-class discourse used to justify violence and force to exclude and eventually exterminate this perceived enemy of democracy.

The patronizing middle-class voice in the characterization of the country's agrarian problem was also striking. Even within the first year, many readers expressed views that the issue was not an agrarian

Figure 3.6 "Huk Captured." *Philippine Free Press*, 9 July 1949, p. 44.

one, but a case of "professional agitators" and "communist propaganda"; that there was no agrarian issue, as tenants were "enjoying the best of relations with landlords" (Alcid 1946). The Huk followers, furthermore, are "quiet" with "no gripe against anyone." The grievances were wholly contrived (Anonymous 1946). Western Batangas is a "tenant's paradise", wrote one man, with no restriction on the amount of income a peasant could earn with a measure of "industry, thrift and enterprise" (Calabang 1946). "For ages he has been cultivating the little piece of land he inherited from his forefathers", wrote Ramon Silen of Agoo La Union:

> If the produce of the land is not sufficient to make both ends meet he finds a way, an honest way, to make them meet. He does not blame the government for his misfortunes. He does not wait for somebody else or his government to solve his personal problems. He solves them himself. If the reward for his honest efforts is still not sufficient to meet his prime and immediate needs he takes his family with him and goes in search of greener pastures. (Silen 1946)

The striking way Huk subjects were represented was equalled by the extent to which they went unrepresented. Only two articles were published in the first few years mentioning the violence of the military police in the Central Luzon region against alleged Huk guerillas, their supporters and families. When these articles did appear, readers accused *Free Press* journalists of being "left-leaning" and sympathizers with the communist agenda.

The influence of a US disseminated Cold-War rhetoric was unmistakable. Peasant agitation was framed as sitting outside the democratic pale. "Within the framework of democracy", wrote Mr Vilamin, "they can find their progress and happiness" (Vilamin 1948). The idea that the Huks wanted a share in governing power, through the Democratic Alliance, was rejected outright. As Mr Angeles from San Fernando said, it isn't land reform that is wanted, it is "power to establish their economic ideology through the PKM, and power to rule the people Gestapo-like through the Huk army" (Angeles 1947). The fact that communism was the opposite of democracy meant "compromise [was] impossible." The only answer, according to Mr Fernandez of Camiling Rural High School in Tarlac was that "They must live within the folds of the law or be hunted down like dogs [...] Every bullet fired at the Huks brings gain to the people" (Fernandez 1947).

What might a few years earlier have been considered a legitimate questioning of America's continued role in a post-independence Philippines was now considered dangerous, anti-democratic propaganda. Claims against America became claims against democracy, and in favour of the Communism of Russia. "We Filipinos found fine and acceptable the American way of life and the ideals professed by America and went to war side by side with America", wrote Irene Ramos Estabaya of Cebu City to the editor in December 1947, "Today if we feel the same way, it is time – NOW – to douse for all time the fires of Communism in the Philippines" (Estabaya 1947). Then there was the fact that in the eyes of the world, and especially the eyes of America, the Huks were causing "embarrassment" to the Philippines, as America's model of democracy in the Far East (Ty 1947).

There was a minority voice in the *Free Press* during the time, expressing less forceful views. In December 1949, for example, following the most violent election period in living memory, Tomas Matic Jr from Far Eastern University had his letter published in the *Free Press*, "A Citizen Writes to the President": "[I]t would seem, Mr President, that the degree of political persecution and defilement of human freedom exercised by your henchmen is in direct opposition to the loudness of your protestations for peace and democracy." "The man on the street", he continued, "expects consistency between the hand and the mouth." The recent election had "bred a deep undercurrent of discontent", he told the President. "We fought for freedom during 300 years of Spanish oppression. We fought for freedom during four years of Japanese bestiality", he said, with a telling omission of the Philippine–American War. "Must we now fight each other again for that self-same freedom that we have so clearly wrested from foreign hands?" (Matic Jr 1949). But it seemed the answer was already decided. In April the same year, a rogue band of insurgents ambushed a motorcade carrying the widow of former President Manuel Quezon, with her daughter and 10 other passengers. All were shot at close range. Huk leader Taruc "blamed the crime on bandits and decried the government for 'creating national hysteria' by implicating his followers" (Karnow 1989: 344), but it was too late. Public sentiment turned irrevocably against the Huks and in favour of an unmitigated military offensive, for which the US would be welcomed. back

Welcome Back America

As the months went on, the public's growing loss of faith in democracy was only intensified by the unprecedented level of corruption within the Quirino government. Combined with the perceived threat to democracy from the Huk movement, the way was opened for a return to overt US involvement in Philippine politics. "It is true", wrote Far Eastern Affairs veteran Harold Isaacs in June 1950, "that American motives have come to be broadly questioned, that anti-Americanism lives side by side in this country with a surviving sentimentalism about some American ideas and institutions." But affairs in the Philippines were so bad, Isaacs continued, "[a]lmost every Filipino I have talked to has testified to a readiness to respond to a clear and strong lead that would open the way to reform, including one that would come from Washington" (Isaacs 1950).

In early 1950, US President Truman sent an economic mission to the Philippines, under the direction of private banker and former Treasury undersecretary Daniel Bell. In the report that followed, Bell stated that "the profits of businessmen and the incomes of large landowners have risen very considerably", but in contrast, he went on, "the standard of living of most people is lower than before the war." What is more, Bell sent cables to Washington describing Filipino politicians as "self-seeking and unscrupulous men", the most "evil" of whom was the Philippine President Quirino himself (Karnow 1989: 345). Officials in the US were persuaded of the need to deploy clandestine operations to see a change of leadership, lest the success of the American "experiment" with democracy in the Philippines be further called into question. A US military report in the same year had also directed that "the use of U.S. leadership [in the Philippines] should be clothed in every manner possible with the pretense of local action and responsibility" (in Doty 1993: 315). As it turned out, America need not have been so concerned about concealment. The Bell mission had stoked local anxieties about how the Philippines looked to the rest of the world. "What must the members of the mission think", read the front page of the *Free Press* in August 1950, "as they read of the very things that are making the country so fertile a field for communism [...] What are the members of the Bell mission to think about Philippine prospects under the circumstances? Is the Philippines worth saving? They must wonder" (Editorial 1950c). When recommendations of the mission were submitted a few months later, including financial assistance to be delivered on the condition of reforms, and the appointment of US advisors in all key Philippine agencies, including the Central Bank and the Armed Forces managed under US supervision, there was little tolerance in the public sphere for the questioning of US motives. The front page of the paper reflected on the prospect of renewed intervention into Philippine affairs by the US and the complaints from some quarters about the "strings attached":

> The Philippines is a sick man – anemic, emaciated and enfeebled, in urgent need of a blood transfusion. Our good, seemingly ever accommodation Uncle Sam has again demonstrated his genuinely altruistic spirit by sharing what may be called his life's blood to save the prostrate Juan. But Uncle Sam reserves to himself the right to say who shall superintend or perform the transfer operation. (Editorial 1950a)

The pacifying moderation of Ramon Magsaysay. The man that would be chosen as "America's boy" was Ramon Magsaysay. After a chance meeting of Magsaysay with CIA operative Edward Lansdale in Washington, the latter had informed President Quirino that the arrival of US aid was contingent on Magsaysay's appointment as the new Secretary of Defense. After this, things moved swiftly. Magsaysay assured the Philippine Congress that he and his men "would go to any extent to wipe out dissidence, by any means" (Editorial 1950b).

In contrast to other political leaders of the time, however, to the staff and readers of the *Free Press* Magsaysay epitomized the "honest citizen." To his multitude of middle-class admirers, Magsaysay represented a new type of elite politician in place of the "traditional" elite class – one whose upright and decisive leadership could address the socioeconomic and political issues plaguing the newly independent nation, while fending off the revolutionary impulses "from below." Not only did he address the indignity and embarrassment caused by the incompetent and corrupt Quirino government, he spoke as one who understood and identified with the economic and social injustices that had provoked the peasant rebellion. He proposed concrete reforms to address the underlying problems. Never mind that his reform agenda was being funded and backed by the United States.

There was little doubt amongst Filipinos that Magsaysay was "America's proxy", but rather than hide the fact, Magsaysay revelled in it: "What do you know about Filipinos?" he said to US officials, "They like Americans. They like to see me with Americans" (Karnow 1989: 346). Even Magsaysay's opponent in the 1953 race, President Quirino, whose party Magsaysay had abandoned in order to run against him, labelled his competitor an "American puppet." Yet the factor that elsewhere in Asia would have spelled a politician's ruin, Karnow reflects, "to be called 'Amboy' – 'America's boy' – was a halo" (Karnow 1989: 353).

During the 1953 presidential campaign, Lansdale began grooming Magsaysay for the win in an exercise, by his own admission, in "symbol manipulation." Magsaysay was awarded a US Army medal in 1952, named "Eisenhower of the Pacific" by *Time* magazine, and pro-Magsaysay pieces were distributed to local news outlets through the Philippine News Service, also part of the CIA front. On election day, Magsaysay was aboard one of the American warships anchored in Manila Bay to hear the results. He had won nearly 75 per cent of the votes.

Through a combination of the promise of wide-scale agrarian reforms, along with intensified and US-backed military attacks, the Huk rebellion would finally come to an end in 1954. Despite Magsaysay's reforms failing to deliver any substantive change, his leadership, especially his emphasis on "good governance", would be remembered by the middle classes three decades later in the rejection of Ferdinand Marcos and the deifying of Corazon Aquino. For the Americans, the episode had boosted the illusion that insurrection and social unrest could be dealt with by "a reshuffling of the cards" at the top (Karnow 1989: 346). It gave them "erroneous confidence that they could solve social problems elsewhere in the world with the same American way of democracy" (Satoshi 2004: 150). The early 1950s in the Philippines would become known, infamously, as the episode "preceding the gravest failure of America's Cold War" (Satoshi 2004: 150). Edward Lansdale would leave the Philippines in 1953 for Saigon, where he would attempt to duplicate his success by turning the "austere" President Ngo Dinh Diem of South Vietnam into another Magsaysay (Karnow 1989: 354).

Summary

The protracted temporality of the colonial period, and the way the legacies of four decades of American rule took on fluid forms within the Philippine democratic imaginary, is most palpable in the period immediately following independence. Yet as the discourse in the postwar civic sphere demonstrates, the independence era Philippine love affair with America was far from straightforward. It carried within it a complex web of emotions – from pride at being America's star in the East, to the shame of failing to meet the standards of democratic politics, to anxiety and self-doubt over the ability of the Philippines to overcome its own internal flaws in order to make democracy work, all of which perpetuated the indignity of the colonial condition and kept alive the desire to chase "real" freedom.

The memorialization of the American period as the pathway to freedom not only legitimized the ongoing middle-class construction of a Filipino subject of dubious self-governing capacity, it also delegitimized attempts to overcome this – by defining democracy for an "Americanized" middle class, not as a dynamic mediating space for contested thoughts and action, but as the product of the performance of the ideal "moral" citizen. The middle classes, through their democratic discourse, began to apply to those above and below the same type of observation and scrutiny that had been central to America's implicit control of the Philippine subject during the colonial period. All the while, the middle class remained driven by the demands of dignity to realize democratic freedoms and the "paradise" of equality for all in their newly independent country.

The democratic ambivalence that was produced manifested itself in material form by constraining the nature, shape and scope of democratic politics. It wasn't that the desire for genuine sovereignty and independence had diminished: it was that these aspirations remained coupled to a willingness to concede to the imposition of arbitrary authority. In the pursuit of democratic aspirations there was an acquiescing to imperial forms of governance, not only in the acceptance of America's continued restriction of Philippine sovereignty, but in the limiting of the space for participation and dissent. The Filipino oligarchy, propped up by American economic and military power, used this ambivalence to consolidate its own power, and to avoid resolving key issues facing the new Republic.

Democracy & Ambivalence

About democracy, I would have two things to say. The perception that was implanted in me, as I was growing up, was that democracy is the way to have a free life, is a way to enjoy a life that is not controlled or constrained by evil and powerful people. I think the backdrop for that is the Cold War, I mean my teacher in school would always compare the US with communist Russia, and how everything in Russia was controlled, everyone was monitored, and how in the US everything was so loose and free, you could actually set out who you want to be.

The other one, when I started to think about it more closely, is that democracy is really a way to have the people govern themselves . . . At least the people get to choose who is going to run the affairs of the country [...] It's very useful that we have a subject in school called, 'Philippine Constitution and Government', and they made us memorize the preamble to the Constitution, and that Government is 'by the people, for the people, of the people.' That it's actually us who are in charge.

But as I experience it, perhaps there's a third one. It's a different type of democracy. It's a democracy that's only good on paper. But it doesn't really happen in reality. I think for me, democracy is a dream that every Filipino would want, but it is also a nightmare that we wake to every day. We want to dream of that, but we end up having a nightmare, because such a dream is not possible given the kind of set up that we have now.

I think those three strands, or experiences of democracy, have shaped how I think about it.

(Rei Lemuel Crizaldo 2015)[1]

CHAPTER

4

Searching for a Revolutionary Break with the Past

As early as 1950, at a symposium on the future of democracy held at the University of the Philippines and sponsored by the Philippine Civic Organization, Congressman Arsenio Lacson made the following prediction:

> One of these days, the Filipino people will fully realize the depths to which their democratic way of life has sunk. And then procuring new vigor from that realization, drawing strength from their heroic past, they will develop the will to fight and the will to resist, and to prove to all that they are not apostate to the spirit of their race [...] It could be a violent revolution, it could be a peaceful revolution, but it will be a revolution in any case; a revolution directed against the scoundrels who would fatten themselves on the misery of our people. (Locsin 1950a: 2, 63)

Sitting alongside Lacson as one of four invited speakers at the event was Congressman Ferdinand Marcos.

Despite the forecast, in the decade and a half following the mid-century, the Philippines seemed a model of modernization. One of the fastest-growing economies in the region, it comprised "a rising class of manufacturing entrepreneurs, a substantial salaried middle class, a growing working class, a high level of formal education and a political system organised around electoral democracy" (Pinches 1996: 105). Leonides Virata, director of the Chamber of Commerce and a well-known economist, described the emerging "new middle class" as "self-assured, optimistic, exuberant and expansionary." It is a class, he said, "that wants to make a try at those roles and functions which in yesteryears were the exclusive preserve of the wealthy, the socially prominent and the highly educated", determined to "come in to what it thinks its own." "[T]he class that has been hiding for 50 years", he declared, "has at least emerged" (Editorial 1959: 11).

It wasn't only in the national economy that the presence of the middle class was being felt. In small numbers, they began to get involved in local politics, running for such positions as city counsellor. Inspired by the late President Ramon Magsaysay, they became, to quote one journalist at the time, 'enthusiastic fathers of the "good government" movement', with initiatives such as the Quezon City League and the Citizens League in Makati (Editorial 1959: 12).

It was during the same period that the Filipino "search for identity" was emerging as a predominant theme of politics. "The Filipino as Spaniard, the Filipino as American, the Filipino as Japanese", journalist Teodoro Locsin wrote at the time, "when is the Filipino going to be himself? [...] We have become slippery characters, and it can't be helped. The Filipino as eel which eludes the foreigner's grasp – this is a possible portrait of the Filipino as a people" (Locsin 1969: 22). The 1950s saw the strong resurgence of nationalist discourses, from within the state itself and in the political narratives of revolutionary and reform groups working against it (Hogan 2006: 2). The political landscape of the time was marked by interpellations of the Filipino nation" and "people", especially in regard to the Philippines' position and identity vis-à-vis the United States, that provided fertile terrain for populist-nationalist narratives claiming that a reconciled and restored "Filipino people" could be brought about by resolving the ambiguities of the past, offering "a promise of emancipation after a long journey of sacrifice" (Panizza 2005: 23), and imbuing "the people" with the long-held dream of dignity. It was within this context that the project of reconstituting the national identity became conflated with the search for "true" democracy (Curaming and Claudio 2010).

At the same time as the imperative of radical transformation kept alive the task of the "unfinished revolution" and the need to "exorcise the ghost of colonialism" (Hau 2000: 280–1),[2] self-doubt and self-flagellation continued. As Locsin again would reflect, "[t]he 'benign' imperial rule of the United States resulted in what might be described as happy self-depreciation. If Americans could do everything, Filipinos could do nothing. Of course, one must be superior in something – let it then be in vice" (Locsin 1969: 24). The tension that resulted, between the desire for radical transformation and the beating of self, further nurtured, and indeed sustained, the existing feelings of ambivalence towards democracy. As Caroline Hau poignantly put it: "Our dream of nation is from its origin compromised by our colonial and neocolonial history [...] But it is, paradoxically, the compromised nature of our nationalist imagining and practice that keeps the promise of the nation alive and burning" (Hau 2000: 281).

In the meantime, US disillusion with Philippine democracy was deepening. American scholars began expressing criticism of "Filipino" politics. Echoing the discourse of half a century earlier, political scientists began to conclude that the continuing domination of the political arena by a self-interested elite, with the failure to achieve substantial socio-economic reform, represented an innate flaw in Filipino political culture (Satoshi 2004). This criticism reflected the broader academic discussions within political sociology and political science at the time that accompanied the emergence of modernization theory and the "civic culture" argument. The prevailing belief was that "viable political development" was only possible with a "suitable cultural framework" – that is, a political culture that imitated countries of the democratic West (Usul 2011: 1694).

The Nationalist Turn

From the early 1950s, Filipino writers and intellectuals within the burgeoning middle class began to try in earnest to grapple with the "haunting" of the Philippine nation, and "the tendentious issue of how to think about the impact of the 'foreign' on Philippine culture" (Hau 2000: 117). The "nationalist project" that these writers and scholars subsequently undertook sought to interrogate the uncritical narrative of colonialism's legacy on the formation of a Filipino national identity. While not all of this new intellectual stratum embraced Marxist ideas, many did, and in the international context of the Cold War and assertive nationalisms, they were critical of America's ongoing military and economic presence in the Philippines, and of the seeming meaninglessness of the United States 1946 grant of independence (Ileto 1993: 64).

For leading nationalist historians such as Claro Recto and Renato Constantino, the foundation of Filipino nationalism was the rejection of American influence. To be for the Filipino nation was to be anti-American. "We have not yet recovered from the spell of colonialism", said Recto in a 1957 speech (Constantino 1986: 86). "This self-delusion", he asserted at the time, "is one of the greatest stumbling blocks to the full realization of Filipino nationalism and the ultimate attainment of complete and real sovereignty" (Constantino 1969: 292). In 1969, Constantino wrote:

> Twenty-three years after independence, why are we still concerned with national awareness, why are we still unsure of our Filipinism? Why is there still a need for a nationalist movement? The answer lies

in the fate that overtook our anti-colonial struggle [...] American colonization['s] facade of benevolence and altruism and, above all, the systematic miseducation it subjected us to, finally blurred its identity as an enemy [...] Nationalism is above all anti-imperialism [...] [T]he real Filipino [is] the decolonized Filipino. (Constantino 1977: 116)

Within this context, the writing of Philippine history itself became a key area of contestation, as nationalist historians tried to claw back a Filipino dignity and political agency all but lost in colonial accounts, especially in relation to the events of the late nineteenth century and the anti-colonial revolution. The task of reclaiming Filipino agency in the context of US historical narratives became an ideological battle – a crusade of "reeducation" and "new consciousness." Another one of the principal proponents of the project, historian Teodoro Agoncillo, laid out the case in 1960:

[...] there abounds in our midst printed books apparently dealing with our history. Here, as in other fields of endeavour, the tyranny of number is keenly felt and exercises a function that stultifies intelligent thinking. What is meant is that we have mistaken the number of books written on Philippine history for achievement and have lulled ourselves into complacency . . . we find even apparently intelligent and highly educated Filipinos thinking in a vacuum, for their minds have been conditioned by that 'tradition' which recognizes no deviation however slight. (Agoncillo 1960: 116)

Agoncillo and others believed there was a need to "rewrite and reinterpret [the Philippines'] history from the point of view of the Filipino" in order to re-orient the "collective mind" and to "formulate a way of life that is free and basically democratic in spirit and outlook." It would not be easy, Agoncillo conceded, as "there are powerful vested groups interested in maintaining the status quo, that is to say, in making us wallow in the delusion that we are free, independent, democratic, prosperous, and such catchwords as would make us relax in sheepish abandon." But "[t]o free this mind and liberate its energies in a manner conducive to the national welfare is the supreme task of the Filipino historian today" (Agoncillo 1960: 119).

It was not only an anti-Americanism upon which this nationalist history project turned. It also hinged on a class war, as Ileto defines, between "the educated, articulate elite (*ilustrados*) who [had] left behind most of the documents, and the inarticulate 'masses' who fought and died in the various wars" (1998: 1). Nationalist scholars sought to invert the way in which American colonial writers constructed Philippine society at the end of the nineteenth century as a divide between oppressed people and a tyrannical elite, recasting the Filipino "masses" "not as passive followers of 'great men', but as the true subjects of Filipino history, the true agents of social transformation" (Hau 2000: 125). Why did school textbooks mark the significance of the public execution of Rizal, they asked, and not that of Bonifacio, "plebian" leader of the Revolution? Just as the American colonial narrative had insisted on a simplistic reading of Philippines history as a struggle between a small elite and the greater masses, so too these nationalist writings perpetuated this dichotomous interpretation, neglecting the complexities of modern Philippines society, and obscuring in particular the role of a middle element dating back to the membership of the Katipunan. Instead, events at the turn of the twentieth century were framed as centred on an ideological class struggle between the conservative elite reformists and populist revolutionary masses.

As a result, the nationalist project not only became conflated with democracy, where "true" democracy was anti-American; the nationalist movement was also a war between two classes, where the "national democratic revolution" that was needed was a revolution from below. Unsurprisingly, this narrative posed a threat to elite power by highlighting the fraught relationship between the elite and the "masses", and by labelling existing state institutions and the existing regime of government as illegitimate and anti-democratic, based on their foreign construction and the continuing undermining of national autonomy they accommodated. But the narrative was also isolating to a middle-class public, who neither identified, as the nationalist intellectuals did, with the cause of the "masses", nor saw themselves as aligned with the corrupted elite political class. Their position, in this groundswell of popular nationalist sentiment, was an ambiguous one, making the most attractive alternative a compromise between the desire for a revolutionary break with the past, and the fear of a radical movement from below.

"Make the Philippines Great Again": Marcos and State-led Populist Nationalism

Just as Manuel Quezon had done in the late colonial period, the political leaders of the post-independence era took active steps to shape and direct the public debate over the nation's status and progress, especially in the face of popular nationalism. From the late 1950s, with the economy faltering, and both the Huk rebellion and popular President

Ramon Magsaysay dead, "top presidential aspirants like Carlos Garcia, Claro Recto, and José Laurel were searching for patriotic platforms and catchwords to sway the crowds to vote for them" (Ileto 1993: 65). The political elite took to using nationalist demands to appeal for power. In adopting the demands of the anti-imperialist movement for "true" sovereignty and a resurrected "people", the political elite of the time were staking claim to the resonant national imaginary to frame the legitimacy of their own political authority.

Diosdado Macapagal (active 1961–1965) was the first successful post-independent presidential candidate to bring the language of revolution to state discourse, declaring the 1896 Revolution "unfinished." But Macapagal would be outwitted by his successor Ferdinand Marcos, who would become master of a discourse of populist nationalism. In April 1965, on the eve of the close of Congress, President Macapagal had endorsed a request to send engineers and security forces to assist the South Vietnamese government. Marcos, who the same month had switched political parties, from Liberal Party head to Nacionalista presidential candidate, declared his opposition to Macapagal's decision: "This nation shall be great again", Marcos declared in opening his presidential campaign.

During a rule that spanned two decades (1965–1986), Marcos played a masterful rhetorical game, central to which was the conflation of nationalism, democracy, and class. As in the anti-state nationalist project referred to above, Marcos made the issue of a fragile Philippine sovereignty about the colonial project of the past, and the lawlessness and corruption of the present. Beginning with his inauguration speech, Marcos evoked the vision of a Philippines that had lost its way, overtaken by the greed and corruption of those in power; the Filipino subject, a brave hero of history, had been left without dignity and facing despair. Words had become cheap in the Philippines, he told his audience. But his mandate from "the people" was one of action. The sovereignty of "the people" was being mocked by the extravagant lifestyles and conspicuous consumption of the political class, by lawless elements and by "syndicated crime." People had lost "faith" in the government. It was time for the long-suffering citizens of the Philippines to stop bearing the burden. He called on the people to "join hands" with him so that he could bring change that was "bold" and "meaningful" and restore the Philippines as the democratic republic the nation's "forefathers" intended (Marcos 1965).

Marcos's orchestrated performance of populist nationalism didn't co-opt everyone. Far from it. In fact, opposition to Marcos appeared almost immediately. Within days of his inauguration, his hostile stance towards the United States was revealed as strategic bluster when he reneged on his campaign pledge to block Philippine involvement in the Vietnam War. Marcos knew full well that his Vietnam Aid bill put before the Philippine Senate was being noted with approval by the highest officials in the White House (Salonga 2001: 115). He was laying the groundwork for more financial and military assistance from United States President Lyndon Johnson. But students and young activists in the Philippines were enraged by Marcos's turnaround – even more so when he agreed to host a summit of Asian nations in 1966, convened by the US President, intended to express their support for American actions in Vietnam. On 24 October, about 2000 students gathered outside the US embassy and the Manila Hotel which was hosting the delegates, carrying placards and chanting slogans such as "Hey, hey, LBJ, how many kids did you kill today?" and "Yankee, go home!" (Totanes 2005: 4). The anti-summit demonstrations were a preview of the student activism that would mar Marcos's first term.[3] In late January 1969, an alliance of nationalist groups called the Movement for the Advancement of Nationalism (MAN), organized a demonstration with an even tougher anti-American stance calling for "the preservation of our national identity from the powerful onslaughts of American cultural imperialism", and demanding the repeal of the Military Bases Agreement and Mutual Defense Treaty between the United States and the Philippines (Totanes 2005: 6).

Only a few months earlier, in December 1968, José Maria Sison, along with 10 other revolutionaries who were mostly from the University of the Philippines, had formally established the Communist Party of the Philippines (CPP). Greatly inspired by Chinese Chairman Mao Zedong, the purpose of the new party, as declared by its founders, was to work for "the overthrow of U.S. imperialism, feudalism and bureaucratic capitalism, [and] the seizure of political power and its consolidation" (Guerrero 1970: 135).[4] The formation of the New People's Army (NPA), to wage a "protracted people's war" in the countryside, followed in March 1969. It was Marcos's brazen corruption and repressiveness, along with the violent and fraudulent elections of 1967 and 1969, that had "encouraged the formation and growth of the NPA, enabling it to draw support from the youth in the various schools, and colleges in Manila and other urban centres" (Salonga 2001: 206). Ironically, the NPA rebellion in the north would become one of the reasons cited by Marcos for imposition of martial law.

The 1969 election was labelled by international media including *Newsweek* and *Time* as the "dirtiest", "most violent", "most corrupt election" in modern Philippine history.[5] To fund the win, Marcos depleted the National Treasury, leaving insufficient funds to cover the mounting foreign debt and trade deficit, sparking the financial crisis of 1970. However, with his team of propagandists, Marcos hailed the landslide victory as "an overwhelming expression of the national will" (in Salonga 2001: 140). New "national habits" – a new "social and official morality" – were being developed, Marcos declared in his second inauguration speech. A "revolutionary reformation" was under way. But the building of the nation had only just begun. "Together", he declared, "we shall exile humiliation, we shall banish shame from this land" (Marcos 1969). It wouldn't come without sacrifice, he remarked, and such sacrifice and dedication he demanded first and foremost from himself. On 1 January 1970, he declared he had decided to give all his worldly possessions away to the Filipino people (Salonga 2001: 144).

But by early 1972, the country felt itself again in the grip of a crisis. Inflation saw the price of gas and other basic commodities increase. Crime escalated, and the student resistance led by the communists, with the Muslim insurgency in the South, inflamed the sense of fear, along with a feeling that the democratic order had reached the point of paralysis (Magadia S. J. 2005). In the face of crisis, the official political system seemed impotent and utterly inept, and Congress immobile, crippled by the blatant jockeying for power that seemed to inhibit even the simplest of remedies to the nation's many problems (Magadia S. J. 2005: 207). As the rumblings of rebellion increased, there was a growing awareness, not only amongst the students and activists of the left but also the broader middle-class public, that "the revolutionary situation in the Philippines demanded a radical restructuring of the existing social, political, and economic order" (Totanes 2005: 8).

Martial Law: Radical Cure for a "Sick" Society

"President Marcos has a very deep sense of history", said nationalist Teodoro Agoncillo, about the political developments of the early 1970s. "He knows not only our history, he also knows when the people, even if they are not very vocal about it, want a change. It was this feeling of President Marcos that the people wanted a change which gave him the courage to declare martial law" (Agoncillo 1974a: 12).

In his blueprint for national transformation, a short book entitled *Today's Revolution: Democracy* ([1971] 1974), Marcos used the same revolutionary anti-imperialist discourse, of the need to liberate the nation and finish the 1896 revolution, as the anti-state nationalists who opposed him. Knowing he needed to position himself against the colonial, or "alien", other, Marcos claimed that the real foreign manipulators were the students and the communists, whose sources of inspiration, being the ideas of Marx, Lenin, Stalin and Mao, were "alien and external to Philippine society and history" (Ileto 1993: 77). Having transferred the enemy to a section of the population within, Marcos was able to position himself within the historical struggle for democracy and self-determination. He described the "old society", the status quo, as the sick society of privilege and irresponsibility whose excesses and inequities spawned the unrest and the violence that threatened the political order. It was a society which, in its injustice and unresponsiveness to the needs of the greater number, had lost the right to exist (Marcos 1973b).

At the same time, he was creating the foundation for his claim of the need for exceptional powers. On the evening of 23 September 1972, having jailed his rivals, key opponents, and critics in the media, Marcos made the proclamation of martial law. "I Ferdinand E. Marcos", declared General Order No. 1, "Commander-in-Chief of the Armed Forces, do hereby assume all powers of Government and place all agencies and instrumentalities of the Government under my direction and control." No other recourse remained, the President claimed, in order "to save the Republic and reform society." For the old society was "sick", and a "new society" had to be built (Salonga 2001: 205). Through a radio station controlled by a close associate, Marcos declared: "The proclamation of martial law is not a military takeover." It was being done, he said:

> [...] to protect the Philippines and our democracy . . . . The Government of the Republic of the Philippines which was established by our people in 1946 continues. Again, I repeat. This is the same Government that you and the people established in 1946 under the Constitution of the Philippines. I have had to use this constitutional power in order that we may not completely lose the civil rights and freedom which we cherish . . . If there were any other solution at our disposal and within our capability which we could utilize to solve the present problem, I would choose it. But there is none. (in Salonga 2001: 205)

It was a governing logic based on arbitrary power imposed in the name of democracy – a twisted logic the country knew all too well from the history of American colonialism. The only democratic aspirations acceptable were those quiescent to the regime. Marcos claimed to be resolving the colonial condition by imposing the very constraints that were central to it.

It took less than a day for the republic Marcos claimed to have been saving to effectively disappear. All media platforms, newspapers, radio and television stations, were seized, except those few run by Marcos's close allies. All mass actions were prohibited, a curfew was imposed upon the entire population, and the legislative building housing the Philippine Congress was padlocked. The independent judiciary was effectively crippled when all judges below Supreme Court justices were required by Marcos to submit undated resignations, which he could accept at any time (Salonga 2001: 207).

Propaganda about the administration's achievements was broadcast on the allied television and radio stations, announcing the successes of the Marcos crusade "for good, efficient and honest government" following the imposition of martial law (Salonga 2001: 213). One year after the declaration of martial law, in his eighth State of the Nation Address, Marcos listed at length the social, economic and political transformations already achieved:

> At the root of all these, [he declared], is a new sense of vitality and discipline, a new sense of pride that has taken hold of our people. Here at least is a people who will obey the law not because they fear punishment but rather because they know that by supporting order and government, they are building with their own hands the future that they want. It makes one proud to be with them, and to see what they have become. (Marcos 1973a)

By mid-1973, Marcos proudly stated: "There is no real emergency in the country today." And yet martial law would be maintained for another seven and a half years (Salonga 2001: 223).

The imposition of martial law only deepened existing ideological and physical divisions between his opponents. Overt political activism and resistance needed to go underground. This more radical option became the domain of the emergent national democratic movement, led by the CPP and the NPA. During the years of martial law, this organized left movement known as the National Democrats (or "Natdems"), would grow to be the largest revolutionary movement in the world (Hedman 2001). For those who did not want to go underground, the challenge became how to respond to the injustices occurring without openly challenging the regime. The Social Democrats, or "Socdems", as the alternative activist opposition would become known, were also against US military bases and foreign domination in all forms; like the national democrats, they attacked the elitist nature of the political and economic system, and advocated for radical land redistribution in response to the chronic landlessness of peasants and farmers. What is more, they rejected Marcos's idea of "revolution from the top." But despite the fact that the two groups shared similar interpretations of what was wrong with Philippine society and espoused similar visions for its transformation, the predominantly middle-class social democrats were against violence as a means to achieve the ends, and they were also vehemently anti-communist, rejecting the dichotomy in the choice being presented between Marcos's "New Society" or the CPP's vanguard revolution. They argued for a "third way" – a radical but democratic way of achieving social change. But the Socdems found themselves pejoratively labelled "moderate" by the national democrats. Given many of their leaders emerged from Jesuit institutions such as Ateneo de Manila University, the Natdems devised the term "clerico-fascist" and claimed the Socdems were using religion as an opiate to deceive and exploit the masses, and lead them away from revolution (Salonga 2001: 151).

Middle Class Acquiescence to Authoritarianism

Despite the divided but vocal opposition, Marcos's ideology won substantial support amongst broad sections of the middle class. He received strong backing from highly educated technocrats in particular, as well as sections of the academe (Pinches 1996: 111). How can sense be made of this appeal? Undoubtedly, his legitimacy was supported by the fact that 1973 and 1974 were boom years for the export of Philippine commodities. The trade deficit was turned into surplus by a favourable world market. But penetrating more deeply was the way the President played on the lingering frustrations and anxieties that nurtured the middle class' ambivalence about democracy.

The democratic impasse in the country seemed terminal. So impenetrable had the oligarchic political state become that, perhaps with the exception of Ramon Magsaysay, governments of the day seemed unable, or unwilling, to absorb the democratic demands of citizens. The resulting accumulation of unfulfilled aspirations meant that the only hope for change, it seemed, was through radical measures.

It wasn't only the chronic misbehaviour of the political elite that was cause for anxiety. The sense of crime, lawlessness and disorder, including the increasing revolt of Marcos's opponents, once again increased anxiety among a broad middle class about the Filipinos' innate propensity for vice, and the capacity of Filipino citizens to behave in a way befitting a democracy. Marcos, people believed, was the strong hand of discipline needed to bring both those above and those below into order. Similar to the way Quezon's Theory of

Partyless Democracy had positioned the government as the neutral actor at the centre – capable of resolving disputes between capital and labour, propelling the country to economic prosperity, and overcoming the messiness of politics – Marcos's "democratic" regime promised to defeat the power base of the entrenched landed interests through his benevolent authority. A "revolution from the centre" by which redistributive policies and democratic reforms could, at last, be implemented, the "Democratic Revolution" also promised to bring discipline to the Filipino people more broadly, and to "eradicate their inherited 'colonial vices'" (Ileto 1993: 71). In the executive proclamation of martial law in 1972, Marcos presented the restoration of the Philippines as possible "only through strong leadership under the code of discipline" (McCallus 1989: 137).

At the same time, Marcos's propaganda promised to restore the once grand and dignified Filipino subject who had been compromised by a colonial past, addressing the indignity and shame attached to the nation's history. His plan for the "New Society" was positioned as a revolutionary remedy to see the Filipino reborn, and to establish a new founding legitimacy for Philippine "democracy." Feeding off notions of the "true" versus "false" Filipino that had been circulating since the start of the century, Marcos claimed he would build consensus around a "true Filipino ideology", under a new "Filipino" regime of Isang Bansa, Isang Diwa (One Nation, One Spirit).[6] He called on the people to "join hands" with him so that he could bring change that was "bold" and "meaningful", and restore the Philippines to the democratic republic the nation's "forefathers" intended: "This is a vision of our people rising above the routine to face formidable challenges and overcome them [...] It is our people bravely determining their own future" (Marcos 1965).

Significant to note, however, is the fact that middle-class support for Marcos's imposition of martial law, or at least their acquiescence to it, was in many cases a negotiated response – mediating deeply valued democratic aspirations, and the experiences of everyday life. As Jovito Salonga recalled of the time:

> [...] the bombings in the Greater Manila area suddenly stopped. Peace and order promptly descended upon Manila and its environs, to the satisfaction of the citizenry. There were no people in the streets at night because of the curfew. Mothers and housewives obviously welcomed martial law. In a matter of a few days, the streets were cleaner, and scores of young men who had been arrested for one misdemeanor or another were made to do some kind of community service. Such slogans as 'Martial Law, Philippine style' and 'Sa ikau-

unlad ng bayan, disiplina ang kailangan' (For the people to prosper, discipline is necessary) materialized almost everywhere. (Salonga 2001: 208)

Salonga, who was the legal counsel for Marcos's opponent Benigno Aquino, had at the time debated the merits of martial law with a close friend, the head of a big firm in Makati and a key leader of the Makati business community. He said of his friend:

> He was all out for its imposition. The nation needed discipline, he said; Western-style democracy wouldn't do. I argued that the aim of Marcos, a corrupt and repressive leader, was to perpetuate himself in power. Martial law was not the solution to the many problems of Philippine society, particularly social injustice, massive poverty, and rampant corruption. But in my friend's view, which was typical of the thinking of many Filipino business leaders at the time, Marcos was right in imposing martial law whatever his motivation might be. Perpetuating himself was not that important, as far as he was concerned. The economy had to grow, otherwise poverty would become worse. (2001: 209)

For many of the middle class, Marcos's proposals appeared "a useful compromise", as Ileto describes – "a means of getting on with their careers while still contributing to a 'revolution'" (1993: 78). If radical change was what was needed, Marcos's plan provided an alternative to the proposals of the Communists, in which the position of the middle class was not only ambiguous, but under threat.

It wasn't only technocrats and business leaders who lent their support to Marcos's regime. Members of the academic community willingly proffered intellectual rationalizations for the need to adapt abstract democratic principles to conditions in the Philippines. In late June 1976, at the Second National Conference of the Philippine Political Science Association at the University of the Philippines Diliman, several of the country's pre-eminent political scientists presented defences of Marcos's "New Society" and the introduction of martial law. In doing so, they too exhibited a position of ambivalence towards democracy.

The "problem", said Dean José Almonte,

> is the one we have inherited from historical antecedents, something that we cannot do anything about [...] we can't even see our own problems with our own eyes . . . in seeing our problems with the eyes of a Westerner, proposing a scheme of solution also devised by them,

and using the principles that they have formulated with their own experience, we are doing a great injustice to our 42 million people. (in Lopez 1976: 88–9)

Any attempt to come to grips with current Philippine politics, these scholars believed, must consider the applicability of these foreign political concepts, particularly the contradiction between the guarantee of individual liberties on the one hand, and the authority of government on the other. A constitution "is supposed to be a charter of liberty, a fundamental document establishing and guaranteeing individual rights against coercive authority", argued UP Professor of Political Science, Emerenciana Arcellana. And yet, "the same constitution that establishes individual rights likewise recognises the authority of the governing power to rule as the situation demands." When the situation calls "for stronger government, stricter discipline, and more restraint on individual rights", as it did in the Philippines at the current time, "even the world's most reputable democracies assume more authoritarian tones" for such emergencies, even if temporarily, "as a matter of self-preservation." Such a "crisis government", he continued, "may still be constitutional though de facto authoritarian." Hence the term for Marcos's government as "constitutional authoritarianism" (Arcellana 1976: 65–7).

Arcellana didn't stop there. For not only was Marcos's constitutional authoritarianism in line with the "state of exception" principle applied elsewhere; it was a particularly appropriate solution to circumstances in the Philippines given its consistency with the nature and preferences of the "Filipino people":

The Filipino people by and large are an uncomplaining lot, living simple, God-fearing lives. By nature trusting, friendly, and charming, these are people whom centuries of colonial subjection have rendered reticent, shy, self-defensive, and docile [...] Here are a people going about their daily tasks with scarcely a thought about the meaning of politics and how this may affect their lives. Even those who are drawn to participate in community affairs are more social beings than political animals in the Aristotelian sense.

How are such people, Arcellana asks, to govern themselves in the way democracy insinuates? What if they cannot, or will not, govern themselves? What constitutes meaningful participation for Filipinos?

It may be safe to assume that on the whole Filipinos do wish to develop into a modern and more prosperous nation. They will follow a resolute leader who can show them the way. They are disposed to obey authority and inclined to peaceable occupation. They are grateful for favours done for them. They appreciate strong but compassionate father/mother figures [...] Perhaps their experience with Western-type democracy in the post-World War II period has not been the happiest ... The Filipino people it seemed have had a surfeit of politics – noisy, Machiavellian, and corrupt. They rather welcomed the discipline of a new order, yes, a 'New Society', if that is possible. (Arcellana 1976: 68)

With this, Arcellana effectively revisited and reaffirmed the colonial metaphor of the Philippine nation as a child. "Growing up", he reflected, "is a painful, tedious process, but growth is possible, maturity being the goal of all development" (1976: 69).

Washington's Endorsement

Marcos's deployment of a democratic discourse to justify his exceptional powers not only resonated with a wider Philippine middle class; it also suited those in the White House who were concerned about the threats of popular democracy. Against a backdrop of increasingly heated international politics and the "communist threat" of the Cold War era, American policy directives were based on the premise that "democratization" in newly labelled "Third World" countries was at risk of throwing up certain geostrategic problems for proponents of the liberal political regime. Academic studies of the time supported the position that holding elections and the phenomenon of mass-mobilization in non-western countries, especially those in the decolonizing stage, were "risky processes", since they might lead to the emergence of political regimes that were "not very friendly to the 'free world'." Liberal democracy, it was claimed, "should be implemented in these countries with great care and trepidation" (Usul 2011: 1694). Theorists and practitioners of political development "sought to devise appropriate policies to contain and control the upsurge of participation which they thought was inevitable" (Cammack 1994: 355).[7]

It wasn't only that Marcos's imposition of martial law allowed for the eradication of the popular nationalist threat in the Philippines. When South Korea's Park Chung Hee declared martial law in late 1972, the US government immediately criticized the Korean leader. A month earlier, however, when Marcos's executive secretary travelled to Washington at the time martial law was pronounced to ensure all would go smoothly with the United States, he was warmly received.

"That's the best thing for the Philippines", Admiral Thomas Moorer, chairman of the Joint Chiefs of Staff, told aides after a meeting with Marcos's executive secretary, Alejandro Melchor (Salonga 2001: 211–12). Marcos, shrewd as he was, knew how to play his cards with the deeply self-interested former colonizer.

As Ray Bonner described in his 1987 book *Waltzing with a Dictator*, "[t]he reaction was universal. There was no opposition to what Marcos had done. No one was even concerned enough to ask how long martial law would be in effect. The only probing question was whether martial law would affect American business interests" (1987: 108–9). To alleviate this fear, Marcos had appointed US-trained technocrats to his cabinet. The US Chamber of Commerce in the Philippines had been amongst the first to congratulate Marcos upon his declaration of martial law (Salonga 2001: 211). Director of the World Bank, Robert McNamara, promised that if Marcos would use his exceptional powers to carry out development, the Bank would double its loans. World Bank loans in fact quadrupled.

Meanwhile, the growing opposition to the Marcos regime was ignored. The Interim Batasang Pambansa election of 1978 had been shamelessly fraudulent. Before the commission on elections could even tally results, Marcos announced that his wife Imelda and the other Marcos-allied candidates had won a landslide victory (Salonga 2001: 271). Leaders of the opposition were imprisoned. Soon after, US Vice President Walter Mondale visited the Philippines, and although he had agreed to hold a meeting with three political opponents, Macapagal, Roxas, and Lopez, no statement was issued and the meeting was not mentioned in any of the press briefings. Regardless of the fact that the Philippine people had just been defrauded by the dictatorship, with thorough TV, radio and print coverage Mondale and Marcos signed four aid agreements, and issued a joint communiqué announcing their agreement for continued US use of its military bases in the Philippines (Salonga 2001: 274).

By 1979, US-backed dictators elsewhere in the world were in trouble. The leaders of Iran, Nicaragua, and Korea had been toppled, and the US was anxious to stop this trend. The opposition in Manila watched these events closely, but American support for Marcos continued. It became increasingly evident that despite the rhetoric, when push came to shove, the United States was more interested in securing continued agreements with the Philippine government over its military bases in the archipelago than with the basic democratic rights of Filipinos. As committee hearing minutes later revealed, US Secretary of State Cyrus Vance had made the candid admission that "for as long as the military bases were in the Philippines, the human rights of Filipinos would have to 'yield to overriding U.S. security considerations'" (Salonga 2001: 274–5).

The ultimate insult came in 1981. In April that year, Marcos called a "national plebiscite" in order to amend his 1973 martial-law Constitution. Supposedly approved by 82 per cent of voters, the amendment changed the minimum age for running as President to 50, so that his 48-year-old opponent Benigno Aquino would be ineligible. It also approved the 63-year-old to run for another six-year term, with no limit on his re-election, granted himself and his allies lifetime immunity from prosecution, and affirmed the President's emergency powers to "close down media, indefinitely jail without formal charges any alleged subversive, and to declare martial law" (Salonga 2001: 324). Following the amendments, on 16 June 1981, the first presidential election in 12 years was held. The opposition had decided to boycott it, and Marcos claimed victory with 87 per cent of the vote. "I remember watching the TV news in Hawaii a day or two later", Salonga recalls. "I couldn't believe what I saw. There was Vice President George Bush, a Yale man, who had been sent by President Reagan to represent him in the Marcos inauguration in Manila, toasting Marcos in words that shocked me: 'We stand with the Philippines. We stand with you, sir. We love your adherence to democratic principles and to democratic processes'" (Salonga 2001: 325).

Limits to Authoritarianism

By the early 1980s, mounting foreign debt and a deteriorating trade balance had brought the domestic economy to a state of paralysis (Pinches 1996: 114). No doubt, awareness of a crippled economy was in part behind the turnaround in middle-class attitudes to the Marcos regime. But it was the political events of the early 1980s that provided the ultimate tipping point. Marcos's chief political opponent, Benigno (Ninoy) Aquino, leader of the Liberal Party, had been imprisoned by Marcos immediately following proclamation of martial law in 1971. Aquino's health deteriorated during his long internment, and in a rare concession in 1980, Marcos permitted his rival to travel for treatment to the United States, where he remained for three years, denouncing martial law and building an expatriate network that actively opposed the regime. Despite warnings about his safety, Aquino was determined to return to Manila in 1983. Landing at Manila international airport on 21 August, he would not even reach his native soil alive, shot in the head on the gangway before reaching the tarmac. The image of Aquino's body lying on the bitumen in broad daylight was broadcast around the country, despite the media censorship (Kusaka 2017b: 84).

The news also travelled fast to the United States, where the assassination became the no. 1 story.

It would prove the pivotal moment for the anti-dictatorship movement. More than any other event, it laid bare the brutality of the regime for all to see. "If an important member of the Philippine Senate, a former award-winning journalist and part of the scion of the landed class in Central Luzon could be cut down with such impunity", Segovia commented, "no one else (in the elite or those aspiring to be part of it) was safe" (2008: 92).

The assassination sent shockwaves through the middle class in particular. As one columnist reflected a few months later:

> Now it is entirely different. The people of the upper and middle classes in our society, those who kept quiet and were willing to give to the present leadership 'the benefit of the doubt' when it imposed martial law – have suddenly been awakened by the assassination of Ninoy Aquino, and are now moved to express their pent-up anger and frustrations against the decade-long suppression of their democratic rights, especially their right to know the truth. (in Villegas and Yang 2013: 348)

One month after the assassination, on 21 September 1983, an estimated half-million people took to the streets of Manila to rally against the President. Even in the financial district of Makati, streets were filled with smoke and confetti as people called for an end to Marcos's 18-year rule. The events provoked a rare (and temporary) moment of convergence between the Natdems, the Socdems, and other groups that had become openly critical of the President. Clad in black, addressing the protestors on a makeshift stage, the widowed Corazon Aquino read a jointly signed Manifesto of Freedom, Democracy, and Sovereignty that declared:

> The time has come to speak with one voice and act with one will [...] The Filipino people will no longer tolerate the loss of their liberties, the exploitation of their labor, the plunder of their natural resources, the shameless looting of public funds, the arbitrary arrests, brutal torture and ruthless murders of their children and their leaders, the arrogant presence of alien military bases on their land, the mockery of elections, and the denigration of their sovereignty – all perpetuated by a government that has forcibly imposed itself upon them with the support of the U.S. government [...] We shall not cease our struggle until our people are truly free and sovereign, and our country is truly democratic and independent.[8]

Up to this point, it had been the radical left that had played a decisive role in politicizing and mobilizing a popular movement against the Marcos regime, but over the next two-and-a-half years, the anti-dictatorship movement "increasingly came to be dominated by more moderate, liberal leadership that not only rejected Marcos, but also the Communist Party" (Pinches 1996: 113). The legitimacy of the movement was boosted when the Catholic Church, corporate executives including the Makati Business Club, and increasing critical voices from the United States joined in. Now, it seemed, the middle class had found the "Kairos" moment to come into their own.

Summary

That the Philippines was not captive to the same enduring authoritarianism as many of its regional neighbours was one of the most striking lessons of the Marcos era (Pinches 1997). And it confirmed the ongoing presence of an ambivalence towards power-sharing government. For the same two-sided response to democracy that led large segments of the middle class to support, or at least acquiesce to Marcos's exceptional powers, was also at the root of their determination, just over a decade later, to cut the dictator's authority off at the knees and restore a democratic mode of rule. Moreover, rather than signalling a reconciliation of the ambivalent forces that had inhabited the middle-class democratic imaginary, the events of February 1986 and decades that followed would demonstrate that the antagonism at its core - between the desire for freedom and the perceived need for restraint - would remain incendiary; that imperial recursions would remain the close companion of democratic aspiration. Indeed, the governing logic of Marcos - that the "old society" must first be overcome before democracy can reign; and that the transformation of society requires "law and order" which, in turn, legitimates the elimination of dissent – would continue to rear its head.

CHAPTER

5

"People Power", Populism and Ambivalence

"If all these childish claims to popularity on both sides have to be settled, I think we'd better settle it by calling an election right now, or say give everybody 60 days to campaign and to bring the issues to the people...I'm ready, I'm ready."[1] In late 1985, while being interviewed by satellite on US television, Marcos called a snap election. It was the middle of the night, Manila time.

What had become a broad and mainstream anti-dictatorship movement had been calling for an election since the volcanic events of 1983. With the election called, all but the CPP and the far left agreed to support the recently widowed Corazon Aquino as the Liberal Party candidate to oppose Marcos. "Cory", as she was affectionately known, had agreed to run for President after being presented with a staggering 1.2 million signatures. The Natdems remained in boycott mode, their leadership claiming that the election "would merely be 'a noisy and empty political battle' between factions of the ruling classes" and "would be rigged by the 'U.S.-Marcos dictatorship' while being 'meaningless to the broad masses'" (Quimpo 2008: 135).

On election day, 7 February, Marcos did indeed try to steal the vote. Taking the left by surprise, however, hundreds of thousands of "ordinary people" gathered at EDSA, the main arterial road of Metro Manila. Over three days of protest, between 22 and 25 February, they formed a human shield between defecting members of the army who were held up in the barracks, and the regime's military tanks. "Casual grit", author Melba Maggay had written in her diary at the time, "[t]hat was what it was the afternoon the tanks came charging. The engines began to roar, but the people refused to move, a defenseless but determined wall of restraint against the tidal lust for bloodshed" (Maggay 2011c). At the same time, leading figures in the Reagan administration were meeting in Washington to discuss how to dump Marcos. Two days later, he and his family were flown to Hawaii aboard a US aircraft.

From the outside, the massive street protest that brought about the end of a dictatorship was viewed as a kind of "end of history" moment. Vowing to reinstate democracy in the Philippines, Corazon Aquino was named *Time Magazine*'s Person of the Year in 1986, with the international community claiming her as an "icon" of freedom. It is not difficult to see why this widowed housewife-turned-presidential candidate captured the imagination of the world. As the end of the Cold War drew near and murmurs of revolt were reported within Communist Europe, Cory represented the triumph of democracy in the tradition of the West: not only triumph over a military-backed dictator, but also over a communist alternative. As Francis Fukuyama famously suggested soon after, "what we may be witnessing is . . . the end point of mankind's ideological evolution . . . and the universalization of Western liberal democracy as a final form of human government" (Fukuyama 1989: 4). Democratization scholars at the time also made much of the fact that the events surrounding the 1986 EDSA Revolution represented the rise to political prominence of a previously docile Philippine middle class. The Philippines seemed a prized case study, a tangible expression of the so-called "third wave" sweeping the developing world. The mass mobilizations, Hedman recalled, appeared as "classic instances of what Tocquevillean literature on transitions from authoritarian rule has referred to as a resurrected [middle class] civil society, fighting the good fight on behalf of democracy" (2006: 9).

American official and public discourse also heralded the moment as another step in helping the Filipinos to democratically come of age.[2] "Redemocratization", and the return of civilian governments in the Philippines and other countries such as Brazil and Argentina, were framed as affirmation of the US's democratizing global hegemony (Stauffer 1990: 8). America, capitalism and liberal democracy were the winners, it seemed, staging a victory dance on communism's grave.

Yet these teleological discourses from outside failed to understand the complexity of the moment – that it was embedded in a long history that wasn't defined by its singular coherence towards the moment of democratic transition, but by its oscillations towards and away from democracy. The spectacular events of 1986 would ultimately fail to purge government of elite control and fail to produce substantive measures to address the economic and social problems that had fuelled the mass struggles of the past. What was more, rather than signal the success of America's "colonial democracy" project, the events of February 1986 had thrown into stark relief the entangled web of American imperialism that remained in postcolonial Philippines. "The American hand in the outcome of EDSA", writes Stauffer, "surfaced for all to see in the order to Marcos not to use force to fight off the coup attempt and the People Power demonstration" (1990: 16). It was US Air Force helicopters that eventually "rescued" Marcos and his entourage from the presidential palace, taking them to Clark Field, then on to Hawaii, where the Reagan administration had promised asylum (Karnow 1989: 442).

At the same time, alongside the continuities, things did change. While the post-Marcos administration made opportunistic use of the new "people power" discourse to frame their own claims for political legitimacy, there was no doubt that the uprising of 1986 forced political elites to "give greater recognition to popular political agency" (Pinches 1997: 115). Genuine attempts were made to reorganize the political system and for electoral rules to allow more popular participation. The new local government code of 1991, for example, provided for the incorporation of non-government organizations in local decision-making processes (Pinches 1997: 116), and the new 1987 Constitution created the party list system, intended to ensure seats in the House of Representatives for under-represented community sectors and groups. The Constitution also included an anti-dynasty provision – a reaction to the nature of politics before and during the Marcos era. The provision remained toothless, however, without the passing of the necessary enabling legislation.

Parallel to such institutional changes went the shifting of non-institutional dynamics. Weakening of networks of traditional patronage politics and the rise of populist politics meant national elite, especially presidential candidates, needed to directly court the poorer classes, who made up the majority of voters. At the same time, the intensification of mediation of the political environment – not only through radio and television, but also the burgeoning of new communication technologies, in particular mobile phones – would magnify these effects (Rafael 2003).

But it was the middle class for whom the events of 1986 seemed to signal the greatest rise in political efficacy. One of the most striking effects of the EDSA protest was the way the middle class, enthused by its own ability to alter political events, became the principal protagonist in the narrative of national liberty and restoration. In the days, weeks, months and years afterwards, the phenomenon of February 1986 became memorialized as a middle class-led revolt. "[T]heir faces, their bravery, their stories and reflections", writes Pinches, "celebrated in the mass media both locally and internationally" have become synonymous with the event itself (Pinches 2010: 289). A narrative of an "enlightened" and "moderate" middle class as the vanguard of democracy not only became the orthodox account of the EDSA uprising (Villegas and Yang 2013: 355; Pinches 2010: 289), it developed into a "people power" motif that became central to middle-class political discourse. Hence the presumption by many observers that the events of 1986 marked the beginning of a coherent middle-class identity and ideology (Kimura 2003; Kusaka 2017b).

What requires emphasis, however, is that though the language of "people power" may have been new, the convictions behind it were not. Embedded within and emerging from a long history of the indigenization of democracy, the mythology constructed around the events of those three days in February invoked the same constituent and contradictory tensions that had characterized middle-class political consciousness for decades. The EDSA revolution, and the "people power" trope that emerged from it, had (and continues to have) such wide resonance and political efficacy amongst the middle class, not because it signalled the end of democratic ambivalence, but because it accommodated it. This is evidenced by the fact that in the post-EDSA political landscape, rather than proving inhibiting of pre-1986 dynamics, the "people power" narrative has enabled the reining in of popular democracy, and the legitimation of exclusionary and exceptional forms of authority in the name of preserving democracy.

The Janus Face of "People Power"

"It is a mistake", author Melba Maggay reflected on the events years later, "to appropriate 'people power' as an instrument of a re-assertive civil society fighting for democracy as elaborated by western liberalism with its highly developed language of 'rights'." She continued: "What we were fighting for was more fundamental – the right to breathe the air of freedom. It was the primal instinct to be rid of a repressive regime that prompted such massive droves of our people to seize a historic opportunity to take direct action [...] It was a fresh and simple response to the hard intransigence of a long-entrenched authoritarianism" (Maggay 2011b).

Most obviously, EDSA symbolized liberation of the nation from the indignity of suffering under oppressive power. Crowded together on EDSA, the "people" repeatedly sang together Bayan Ko ("My Country"), a song "that calls for the liberation of an oppressed homeland" (Kusaka 2017b: 87). Marcos, his iron fist rule and economic malfeasance, had become "the cause of a collective suffering" from which the Philippines ultimately needed to be delivered (Claudio 2013: 4). There is no doubt from amongst the narratives of my middle-class interviewees, that the events of 1986 represented much more than a moment of regime transition in the nation's political history. EDSA had become essentialized in the national identity. It had seemed a pinnacle in the century-long search for national dignity and "true" sovereignty.

Alongside the theme of national redemption was the redemption of the inferior Filipino subject which, spearheaded by an enlightened middle-class leadership, had finally proven itself worthy of democracy. The humiliating image of the Filipino subject of dubious democratic character and prone to vice had been displaced by the new image of a righteous "people" against a corrupt, dictatorial regime (Pinches 2010: 289). But viewing the events through the frame of morality failed to resolve the anxiety about the Filipino subject's susceptibility to vice. To the contrary, it made way for the proposition that the dark past of the Marcos years was the result of the Filipino subject's moral ineptitude.

A Lackey No Longer

The EDSA liberation experience freshly imbued a middle-class public with a taste for the symbolism of this defining moment to demonstrate the nation's dignity and independence from its colonial past. One of the outcomes of the left's slow collapse in the early years following the Marcos dictatorship[3] was that anti-US sentiments became more mainstream. In the early post-EDSA period, political, academic and journalistic factions of the middle class were determined to assert Filipino nationalism through a tougher stance towards the United States. The issue of American interference in the Philippines would soon rise to the surface, demonstrating the extent to which notions of "independence" and "sovereignty" remained incendiary, evidenced through their continued resonance in public sentiment and their strategic deployment by the political elite.

The US military bases in the Philippines had come to symbolize the lingering contradictions of the country's colonial history with America. On the one hand, the bases reflected the "special relationship" between the US and the Philippines dating back to the turn of the century. On the other, their continued presence, as Salonga put it, was "an affront to Philippine national pride and a symbol of imperfect independence and continuing dependence" (Salonga 2001: 470). The bases seemed all the more compromising in the aftermath of EDSA because the US had demonstrated, through its support of the Marcos regime, that its own strategic interests took priority over securing the rights of Filipinos. What was more, by now it was common knowledge that American bases were used to store nuclear weapons. Thanks to successful coalition building around a nuclear-free Philippines which had begun as early as 1980, the Philippines had voted in the United Nations General Assembly, and in a number of other international declarations, in favour of nuclear disarmament. This anti-nuclear position was enshrined in the new 1987 Constitution, which banned such weapons from entering the country.[4]

Despite its early utterances, the new Aquino administration soon revealed its anti-imperial rhetoric was more symbolic than genuine. Foreign secretary Raul Manglapus had previously argued that "the time had come to end the residual colonial relationship" with the US, and that "America's presence in the archipelago was a violation of national sovereignty." But after seven months of negotiations, the Aquino administration had signed an agreement with Washington in return for an aid package of $481 million a year, ensuring the operation of the American bases in the Philippines until 1991, when a longer-term pact would have to be made. The compromise, as Karnow writes, was "an indirect admission that [Aquino] could not afford to run the risk of losing American assistance, however much her nationalist foes derided her as servile to the United States" (1989: 432).[5]

In June 1991, the devastating eruption of Mount Pinatubo sent shockwaves through the country, with the scale of the explosion affecting the livelihoods of around two million people. Nearby Clark Air Base was abandoned by the US, leaving the American Naval Base at Subic Bay at the centre of the military base negotiation that was about to take place.[6]

Aquino's advisor, Raul Manglapus, together with US negotiator Mr Richard Armitage, announced publicly that the new Bases Agreement between the two countries had been reached, although a draft of the proposed treaty, cannily entitled "A Treaty of Friendship, Cooperation and Security", had not yet been debated by the Philippines' elected senators.[7] Over five days in early September, public hearings were held before the Senate Committee on Foreign Relations, morning and afternoon, to collect views, opinions, and expertise on the future of the US–Philippine military agreement. Those presenting included official government resource staff, members of cabinet, academics, and representatives of NGOs, churches, labour unions and other people's organizations. This was followed by a week-long closed-door committee debate. In the final days, President Aquino herself tried to lobby the Senate members to approve the bases treaty. But on its last meeting day, the Committee voted to approve a resolution of non-concurrence with the proposed bases agreement. The definitive Senate vote on the matter was due to take place the following day, on 16 September.

As more than 150,000 people assembled in heavy rain outside the chamber, speeches and deliberations inside began at 9 a.m. The eleven arguments in support of the US–Philippine bases Treaty bore a strong similarity to sentiments expressed in the immediate post-war period. Senator Lina, for example, explained he was voting in favour, not from fear of the economic repercussions of forgoing President Bush's promised benefits, but because of the "friendship that binds the Filipino people and the American people." "To quibble over money matters", he said, was to "reduce our relationship to a business transaction" and to degrade the national honour. Any concerns over onerous provisions could be ironed out, "because we can trust in the sense of decency, fairness, and justice of the American people" (in Salonga 2001: 458). "What has America done", asked Senator Tamano, "to deserve the shabby treatment we are giving her in the Senate. I believe in the altruism and goodness of the American people" (in Salonga 2001: 465).

For Senators Paterno and Rasul, the transition to independence from the United States was still occurring, despite the half century separating formal independence from the present. "Ratification would mean we opt for an orderly transition to a new relationship with the US – away from dependence to a new framework that will help our nation achieve full potential and economic sovereignty." Senator Rasul's rationale could easily be mistaken for statements made in 1946: "The reality is this: the only sources of aid, trade access and investment of the developing countries are the U.S. and her allies [...] We cannot afford to become self-reliant and free by ourselves" (in Salonga 2001: 461–2).

But perhaps more significantly, arguments against the treaty heard in the Senate chamber that day became an illuminating testament to the nationalist narratives that the politicians knew to hold currency in the post-1986 era of "people power." The senators who voted against the US–Philippines bases treaty presented themselves as standing at a critical moment in the nation's history, with a duty to return the Philippines' dignity and the control of its destiny to the Filipino people. And indeed, almost a quarter of a century later, standing amongst a crowd of anti-imperial protesters on Independence Day, I would hear multiple speakers rally the crowd by invoking the memory of what the 12 senators opposed had stood for that day.

"I cannot believe", said Senator Juan Enrile, former Marcos protégé who became the leader of dissident armed forces in 1986, "that the vitality of this country will be extinguished when the last bar girl in Olongapo turns off the light in the last cabaret. I have a higher vision of this country's destiny than as a depot of diminishing importance of a foreign power" (in Salonga 2001: 455). Friendship and cooperation with America was desirable, said Senator Guingona, "[b]ut we do not want servitude. We do not want an agreement that debases us as a nation. We do not want terms that degrade our dignity as a people" (in Salonga 2001: 457). Senator Pimental argued that the type of agreement being proposed between the US and the Philippines was not how sovereign nations dealt with each other. "That is the way an elephant deals with a flea", he said, calling out the asymmetry of the relationship:

> There is no question that the US is the sole superpower in the world today and we are just a flea floating in the Pacific Ocean and a former colony to boot. That is probably why the US is treating us as a subaltern, a subordinate and a lackey, who is expected to do whatever the master bids us to do. (in Salonga 2001: 462)

Seven years later, during Joseph Estrada's presidency, the Senate would ratify a "Visiting Forces Agreement" with the US – but in 1991, the senator knew how to ride out the zeitgeist:

> We have a divided past which we must now redeem. We have been exploited and made to quarrel among ourselves [...] They [the Americans] humiliate us when they think our independence can be bought and negotiated. We have become so dependent on the Americans we have never learned to be self-sufficient, we have lost the will and the initiative to live in freedom. It is not this chamber that is on trial, but rather our will and destiny as an independent and sovereign nation. In the community of nations, our country has been seen as a nation of beggars, a nation of prostitutes, a nation of cheaters, a nation of domestic helpers. If we do not assert ourselves today, we will also be known as a nation of cowards [...] Our forebears fought to become free, despite lack of arms and lack of means. They offered their lives in that struggle. We must now complete the unfinished task, our unfinished revolution, not with bloodshed as our forebears did, but with the stroke of a pen. (in Salonga 2001: 455–6)

With the vote locked at 11 for and 11 against, Senate President Jovito Salonga cast the deciding vote. He did not let the opportunity pass to make a determined point. Despite the fact the Philippines was time and again assured by high American officials that the military bases were "for the defense of our democratic way of life", he said, for almost 14 years these same bases were the reason the United States acquiesced to the Marcos dictatorship. This decision was about more than the bases themselves, said Salonga. It was part of the "search for our soul of the nation", a "quest for the best in the Filipino character", and a "search for the true Filipino spirit":

> We summon the memories of those we honor – from José Rizal to Andres Bonifacio, from Abad Santos to Ninoy Aquino. Their collective message, even on the eve of their death, was one of hope, not of fear, of faith, not of doubt; of confidence in the capacity of the Filipino to suffer and overcome, not of his willingness to stand the rigors of freedom and independence. (Salonga 2001: 469)

Today, Salonga pronounced, "we have finally summoned the political will to stand up and end 470 years of foreign military presence in the Philippines" (2001: 468). 16 September 1991 would join other times in the history of the nation – the Revolution of 1897, the battle for liberation against Japan from 1942 to 1945, and the most recent struggle against the darkness of martial law culminating in events of 1986 – "when we took our destiny in our own hands and faced the uncertain future with boldness and hope and faith." It was the day, Salonga declared, when the Senate had "found the soul, the true spirit of [the] nation" (2001: 472).

After 8pm, when the outcome was finally announced, jubilation erupted among anti-base advocates still waiting outside. Inside the Senate Chamber, 12 senators, who would become known as the "Magnificent 12", had successfully introduced and passed a resolution that sealed the treaty's fate. The outcome was even more remarkable given the Philippine Senate had long been considered a conservative and pro-US institution. What was more, it was chiefly traditional politicians, or *trapos*, who had rejected the long-standing subservient relationship between the Philippines and the US. "On that historic day", reflected Roland Simbulan, an insider in the Senate at the time, "the Philippine Senate became the beacon of Philippine sovereignty. By its action, it gave substance to the country's independence and taught Filipinos how to live out the spirit of sovereignty" (2018: 14–15). But "[t]he real moving spirit behind the 12 senators", he emphasized, "was the broad and unified people's movement outside the Senate. In the end, it was the power of the people that ended the most visible symbols of our colonial legacy and the Cold War in the Philippines" (2018: 12).

Closure of American military bases in 1992 and the subsequent cuts to American aid did reduce both the influence and profile of the United States in the Philippines (Pinches 1996: 115). One of the consequences would be a weakening of the ideological basis for the Philippine revolutionary movement, as the evils of US imperialism became a less persuasive rallying cry. And yet, as was to become evident in the era of President Rodrigo Duterte, the event would not put an end to the politically resonant narrative of the battle for national dignity, which remained just beneath the surface.

The Ongoing Project of Moral Restoration

"If my people ... shall humble themselves and pray, and seek my presence, and turn from their evil ways, I will forgive them their sins, and I will revive their land." (2 Chr 7: 14). These are the words inscribed on the wall of the EDSA Shrine, a small Catholic church built in 1989 to immortalize the peaceful demonstrations that took place on that site in 1986. For many members of the middle class, "people power" was not only a stand against entrenched oppression, it was also a profoundly religious experience. Staring down the regime's tanks, Cristina Montiel explained, with "nothing but prayers and whispered calls to their Mother Mary to protect them from harm", was the ultimate act of faith:

> At EDSA, the power of faith shone for all to marvel at. It was the inner dynamism that emboldened us to pit ourselves against arms and tanks, fearlessly to risk our lives believing that being for God and country was worth it all. From a shamed and humiliated people, we rose to be the light of God to all nations. (1994: 116)

The willingness of people to risk their own lives "for God and people" at EDSA was deemed a turning point for the nation – a symbol of the redemptive possibilities for the Philippines. Yet framing EDSA as a "miracle" from God (Claudio 2013), and as a deliverance by "divine intervention" (Wurfel 1990), as became embedded in the popular narrative of the middle class, only confirmed the belief in a fragile and contingent relationship between politics and morality.

While the events of February 1986 had demonstrated the potential of the Filipino subject, it was, according to Dy Jr and others, just a beginning. "[T]he root of the crisis facing the Filipinos in the last two or three decades", wrote Manuel B. Dy Jr of Ateneo de Manila University, was "moral in nature" (1994b: vii). "The February revolution may be considered a 'founding event' that sets the pace of national reconstruction: economic, political, and social", wrote Dy Jr. "What must not be left out, though, is the moral reconstruction of the Filipino character, for a nation is only as good as the people who compose it."

"One cannot emphasize sufficiently", wrote a colleague of Dy Jr's from the University, "the need for moral formation in the Philippines today; it is a most crucial and urgent task if we are to build from the ruins of a decadent past" (Astorga 1994: 125). The sentiment was echoed by newly elected officials, such as Senator Leticia Ramos-Shahani, who declared it was "the weakness and corruption of the moral foundations of [the] society" that were the cause of the nation's economic problems and political instability (Dy Jr 1994a: 19). To formalize the belief that something innate to the Filipino character lay at the bottom of the country's political and economic troubles, a Senate Resolution was passed on 7 September 1987 advocating for the institution of a national "Moral Recovery Program." Indeed, a taskforce was subsequently commissioned by the Committee on Education, Arts, and Culture to study the "strengths and weaknesses" of the Filipino, while the Department of Education, Culture and Sports (DECS) focused on "values development", producing a "Values for National Reconstruction" document that was designed for school teachers (Dy Jr 1994b: 54).

Concurrently, in the English-language newspapers and magazines circulating in the aftermath of EDSA, Marcos was being demonized as the epitome of the Philippines' moral corruption, while the face of the people power uprising, the newly inaugurated President, Corazon Aquino, was represented as the antipode of Marcos and the corrupt Filipino subject, symbolizing everything that was morally "good" (Kusaka 2017b: 87). The propagated sense of "the people" needing a "moral reconstruction" from the ineptitude of the past, along with the positioning of Aquino as the "saintly" (Thompson 2002) figurehead who could lead them out of the wilderness, was not only reminiscent of the early days of the Marcos presidency, but reflected the good/bad binary by which the Filipino subject had been characterized in the discourse of the post-war public sphere.

As had happened time and again, post-EDSA political elites, beginning with Aquino, used the fragile interpellation of "the nation" and "democracy", and the unresolved tension between democratic aspirations and self-doubt, to grant themselves extraordinary powers, while limiting the space for meaningful democratic change.

Aquino and her allies immediately sought to "harness the imaginary of People Power" (Claudio 2013: 14). She too had a stake in maintaining the narrative of the EDSA "miracle." "I am not embarrassed to tell you that I believe in miracles", she told an audience in May of the same year. "It is faith that saved our nation. It was our reliance on power greater than history that plucked us from the edge of calamity and set us down in freedom at God's appointed time"

(Aquino 1986b: 12). She was careful not to point to systemic flaws in the political system, including the monopolization of politics by the elite, given she was one of them, nor to mention the legacies of a long history of colonialism. Instead, Aquino reflected on the dark days of Marcos as an aberration:

> In the fifties, we had the most vibrant growth rate in the region . . . Throughout this period we elected five responsible presidents, each of whom honoured our democracy and nurtured our remarkable economic growth. And then Marcos happened, and we stumbled into backwardness. What had the Filipinos done to deserve a Marcos? I honestly do not know. But what I can say is that the experience taught us humility, turned us to God, and drove home the valuable political lesson that liberty must be won every day. (Aquino 1986b: 30)

In the 1987 elections, all senatorial candidates endorsed by the President won seats. It didn't seem to matter that Aquino was herself, by birth, "a member of one of the wealthiest and most powerful dynasties within the Filipino oligarchy" (Anderson 1988), and that, despite the anti-dynasty provision in the new Constitution, Aquino had at least eight family members running in various positions, from Senate to congressional posts, in the first post-EDSA elections.

Under the guise of "people power", a mostly enamoured middle class endorsed political rhetoric on the path to transformation that was almost indistinguishable from that used in the past by both Marcos and Quezon. "Now the country is back in our hands. Another revolution is about to begin", Aquino told an audience of workers on Labor Day in 1986:

> The economic revolution that will lift us from poverty, underdevelopment, and economic injustice. And again, only the power of a united people can make it succeed [...] I made a promise to you during the campaign and I repeat that promise. I shall ask for no greater sacrifice than I myself am prepared to make. I shall impose no heavier burden on our people than they are willing to carry. But sacrifices and burdens there will be . . . I ask you to respond now as you responded when I called on you to defy Marcos and win our freedom – without fighting, without envy, and with shared purpose and sacrifice. People's power can put our economy back on its feet, put food on our tables, shirts on our backs, roofs over our heads, and pride in our hearts. (Aquino 1986a: 13)

Follow her lead, was the message, and the devastated Philippine economy that had seen three quarters of the population fall below the poverty line would be turned around. Paradoxically, in the same speech, Aquino assured the workers that the right to form organizations and unions, and the right to strike, would be restored, and Marcos's oppressive legislation repealed. "Under this government there will be justice for the workers under the laws, and the laws will be just", Aquino declared. "But", she added,

> we must cooperate to reduce the uncertainties that have paralyzed economic activity in our country [..] [I]n this period while the country is trying to recover from the tyranny and theft of the Marcos regime, [I appeal to you] to exercise restraints in exercising your right to strike. Use it as a last resort . . . Make me prouder, my workers, of this second revolution to make our country free . . . Make the world wonder again at how a country reduced to beggary by reckless debts and a people reduced to penury lifted themselves and their country from humiliation to the greatest pride. (Aquino 1986a: 32)

During the campaign for the snap February 1986 election, Aquino had pledged an end to the suppression and censorship that marred the Marcos years. In its place, she promised, would be a pluralistic society, with enough democratic space for the articulation of competing ideas (Constantino 1987). By the end of the year, under pressure from (amongst others) former military leader Minister Enrile, the Aquino government took a hard stance against the communist movement. Members of the radical left who believed the revolution was far from "finished" by the events of EDSA were increasingly labelled the enemies of democracy. By February 1988, several top Communist leaders had been arrested, including two members of the central committee. "In the short period between EDSA and today", lamented Renato Constantino in March 1987, "we have seen Marcos as enemy being replaced by the bogey man of communism. The witch hunt is on again" (Constantino 1987: 92). "The anti-subversion law has been reinstated", wrote Constantino in a June 1987 newspaper article, "and a moral consensus is being organized to label any move to alter the status quo as subversion" (1987: 184). It was a continuation of the patterns of the past. Anti-communism was being used to justify imperial recursions within the realms of democratic governance, including the legitimation of excessive authority against "the forces of change" (Constantino 1987: 94).

The idea of leadership by a "moral" civil society fitted well with American-dominated academic literature on "third world" democratization dominated by an educated, modernized and enlightened middle class achieving reform in a non-confrontational manner. Instead of activist organizations, apolitical initiatives engaged in non-government development burgeoned during this period as foreign funds, grants and other financial assistance poured in after 1986. Between 1984 and 1995, the number of registered NGOs in the country is estimated to have increased from 23,800 to 70,200 (Kusaka 2017b: 31). As Kusaka explains, "... members of the middle class that had spearheaded the democratization movement acquired new confidence as social reformers and formed NGOs that engaged in social action on issues such as fair elections, poverty, indigenous people, women and so on" (Kusaka 2017b: 30). These charitable activities, it was believed, were "imbued with the 'spirit of People Power'" (Claudio 2013: 17). There was no need to march in the streets demanding a more just social system in order to pursue a pro-people's agenda (Segovia 2008: 99). In fact, the face of the People Power Revolution alongside Cory Aquino, Catholic Archbishop of Manila Cardinal Sin, had issued a warning to priests and nuns involved in cause-oriented groups "to rethink their positions or risk expulsion" (Constantino 1987: 92). "It was a difficult time to be an activist", reflected my interviewee, Belen, a university professor associated with the left. "Then, the academe was totally, totally anti-National Democrats."

Estrada vs. Duterte: Populists and the Role of Ambivalence

No one was more successful at leveraging the changing conditions in the post-EDSA environment than Joseph "Erap" Estrada. Still arguably the most quintessential populist candidate to emerge in Philippine political history, Estrada's bid for the presidency in 1998 attracted an unprecedented number of votes – almost 40 per cent, including a majority of the votes of the poor (Kusaka 2017b: 97). But the Estrada presidency would end abruptly in 2001, when he was forced from office by a street protest, this time labelled "People Power 2", that was orchestrated by the middle class.

The events of early 2001 would demonstrate just how contested, and constructed, the notion of "people power" really was. But the fate of Estrada's populist presidency, especially when viewed next to the success of the most recent populist President, Rodrigo Duterte, would also give important insights into the emotional economies of contemporary "people power" politics in the Philippines, and the underlying logic at play within the middle-class imaginary of democracy. First, it would confirm the extent to which the boundaries of legitimate democratic politics had become "home-grown." "Elections should not be the 'be-all and end-all'", one of my interviewees told me, reflecting on the events of 2001. "It's just a tool. It's just an enabler towards democratic ideals. You have to determine first, what are those ideals that you aspire for, adhere to, or believe in as a nation?" "It's not totally rejected what Western democracy is all about", he continued, "It's more assimilating, probably, that's the term [...] There are certain brands of western democracy, and there are certain 'home-grown' democratic practices." "We may not be accepted", he concluded, "but to us it's still democracy." Second, it would demonstrate the way the mobilizing success of a populist's discursive strategy depends on its ability to tap into historical narratives and unresolved emotions, especially around questions of identity. While the sources of a protracted democratic ambivalence would cause the middle class in vast proportions to turn against Estrada, a decade and a half later the same latent ambivalence would galvanize broad sections of the class in Duterte's favour.

People Power Without the People

Joseph Estrada began his political career in the late 1960s as mayor of San Juan. He moved to national politics by winning a Senate seat in the landmark elections of 1987, despite being in a pro-Marcos alliance and one of only two successful candidates who opposed Cory Aquino. As a Marcos loyalist, Estrada was "nowhere near EDSA during the four days of People Power that had precipitated the Marcos fall from power in February 1986" (Hedman 2001: 32). He was a beneficiary of the breakdown of the two-party system that took place after independence until martial law in 1972. A "Senate seat-warmer", as Lande describes him, Estrada would never have been chosen to lead either the Nacionalista or the Liberals. But in the post-Marcos era, popularity and money became the most important factors in building a presidential campaign (Lande 2001: 89). He was elected Vice President in 1992, and six years later he won the top job.

Estrada himself was hugely popular. From an upper-middle class family, he dropped out of an elite college in the 1960s to become an actor, starring in many blockbuster films. Unlike Corazon Aquino, who traded on "saintly charisma", Estrada brought his cinematic portrayals of a compassionate gangster into the public sphere. Wataru Kusaka (Kusaka 2017a) describes this as bandit-like morality, where compassion and violence co-exist under a patriarchal boss. Estrada's iconic role of Asiong Salonga – the Robin Hood of the slums of Manila – exposed vividly and emotionally the injustices of the impenetrable social hierarchies that defined everyday Philippine life.

The key to Estrada's victory was not only his celebrity star power,[8] but also the way he converted this popularity into chains of vertical loyalty between himself and the poor. A key feature of populist political discourse is the imbuing of the non-elites with dignity and legitimacy, the power of which lies in the stark contrast it offers to the signifiers of subordination in everyday life (Panizza 2005: 25). Amongst a population overwhelmingly living in poverty, Estrada's portrayal of the compassionate outlaw was extremely effective. Showpieces, such as sharing a meal with the poor and embracing the elderly, were crucial to his counter-narrative of solidarity and the politics of dignity. In his campaign for President, he spoke in Tagalog, criticizing elite rule and pledging to implement a "politics of the poor", wooing voters using words like *kabayan* ("countrymen") to "signify his solidarity and fraternity with the 'masses' (*masa*)" (Kusaka 2017b: 96).

Estrada was in fact backed by political and economic elites. The cash and organization behind his presidential campaign came from his alliance with the Marcos faction. Fellow supporters of the former President, including businessman Eduardo Conjuangco and former first lady Imelda Marcos, closed ranks behind Estrada's bid, forming a loose coalition known as Lapiang ng Masang Pilipino (meaning "struggle of the Filipino masses") (Lande 2001: 90).

Outwardly, however, Estrada attempted to transform his image from that of loyal Marcos ally to anti-American nationalist politician. In 1989, two years before he became one of the "Magnificent 12" senators who shut down US military bases, he starred in the film Sa Kuko ng Agila ("In the Claws of the Eagle"), playing a jeepney driver in the film who led the masses in a national movement against human rights abuses by US troops stationed in the Philippines (Kusaka 2017b: 96). Estrada even likened himself to the so-called "plebeian hero" of the armed struggle against the Spanish, Andres Bonifacio, claiming that his mission was "to complete the unfinished revolution and achieve a Philippines free of poverty and inequality" (Kusaka 2017b: 97). At the same time, in a deliberate demonstration to middle class-led NGOs that he was serious about poverty, Estrada appointed well known former social justice activists to the key portfolios of housing and agricultural reform. Along with appearing tough on crime, like Marcos he hired economists from the University of the Philippines and pledged to continue a program of economic reform in an effort to placate the fears that "pork-barrel largesse aimed at the poor would adversely impact the economy" (Kusaka 2017b: 97)

This time, however, such attempts to appeal to the middle class and business networks failed. Opinion amongst a majority of the middle and upper classes quickly turned against the President. Initially, it was the declining economic outlook and Estrada's blatant cronyism that soured the mood. Between 1997 and 2000, real GDP growth dropped 35 per cent, while the peso halved in value, and unemployment figures escalated. Although the Asian financial crisis of the late 1990s explained some of the losses, the Philippine economy failed to bounce back, despite not being hit as hard as neighbouring Indonesia or Thailand. Added to this, *The Financial Times* reported in 2000 that during the first two years of the Estrada administration, perceived corruption in the Philippines was the highest it had been in two decades (Lande 2001: 92). Matters reached a head when the governor of the province of Ilocos Sur, Luis Singson, implicated Estrada in a gaming scandal, accusing the President of acquiring as much as 400 million pesos (US$10 million) in winnings from the illegal lottery game *jueteng*. When the scandal broke, former President Aquino and Cardinal Sin, both of whom were considered by the middle class "the living symbols of People Power 1" and had already begun leading large protests against Estrada as early as August 1999, led a prayer rally calling for the President's resignation (Kusaka 2017b: 98).

There was more than economic mismanagement and corruption to the strong traction of demands for Estrada's resignation amongst the middle class. After all, Estrada's illicit gains were "small potatoes" in comparison to Marcos, and given he made no attempt at grabbing dictatorial power, his "sins against democracy" were much smaller too (Lande 2001: 99). Yet while Marcos doggedly held onto power for more than two decades, Estrada would be dislodged within two-and-a-half years. Although a "politics of dignity" had seen Estrada successfully mobilize almost wholesale support among the poorer population, it was another type of "politics of dignity" that drove anti-Estrada activism. With his broken English, his well-publicized bad habits of womanizing, gambling and drinking (habits associated with poor Filipino men), and his "aggressive flaunting of freedom from the established constraints of oligarchical democracy" (Hedman 2010: 108), Estrada embarrassed the middle classes, and offended their sense of national dignity. One of my interviewees, Victor, told me of "Erap":

> ... he was seen as an embarrassment ... [He] flaunted mistresses, [he] even used the proceeds of the gambling operations not only to amass wealth for himself but to distribute to his mistresses and house them in mansions [...] These images were counter-middle class. Still, even if let's say it's acceptable for some of the Filipino males to have this machismo etc., but when it comes to public, when it comes to their beliefs ... they don't flaunt it.

As anti-Estrada activism outside Congress gained momentum, a minority of members of the House of Representatives inside began preparing an impeachment complaint against the President. Hearings began on 6 December 2000. Daily events inside the House were for the first time being followed on radio and TV by Filipinos who sat transfixed in their homes and offices by the impeachment proceedings (Rafael 2003: 6). When senators allied with Estrada blocked the opening of a crucial envelope containing evidence of corruption, the trigger for a public uprising was pulled. On 16 January, Cardinal Sin and former President Aquino returned to the stage of the demonstrations in a re-enactment of People Power, calling on "civil" society to come back to the Parliament of the streets (Kusaka 2017b: 99). Over 200,000 demonstrators gathered in the same location as People Power 1, chanting and waving banners reading "Erap Resign!" and wearing black shirts to symbolize the "death of Philippine democracy" (Kusaka 2017b: 99). Mobilization efforts were helped significantly by the use of new communication technologies (Rafael 2003).

It took just days for the predominantly middle-class movement to unseat the President. By 20 January, four days after protests began, the chiefs of police and army stood before the crowd gathered at the EDSA Shrine to announce they were withdrawing their support for the administration (Kusaka 2017b: 101). On the same day, the Supreme Court unanimously declared the position of President as vacant, and Vice President Gloria Macapagal-Arroyo was sworn in as the Republic's new President.

Though there was much euphoria amongst Estrada's critics after his premature removal from office, it wasn't long before the international press and academics began asking questions about the extra-constitutional removal of a duly elected President. From the outside, the precedent that this set for Philippine democracy seemed concerning (Hedman 2010: 114). It was impossible to ignore the fact that unlike the events of 1986, it was not a President's unlawful retention of power through the abuse of democratic processes that was the centrepiece of the protest. This mass movement had in its sights an incumbent President whose election, as Hedman has argued, "by the broad mass of the Filipino people was established beyond a shadow of a doubt" (2010: 114). Yet by the middle classes who were involved, People Power 2 was extolled as a triumph of democracy and "civil society." As Kusaka explains, it was "an action undertaken by 'citizens' to guide the Philippines along the path of progress by returning a democracy warped by a corrupt leader to its proper state" (2017b: 105).

In unseating the popularly elected President through extra-constitutional means under the rubric of "morality" and "good governance", the middle classes themselves became the ones to differentiate and exclude a group of citizens from their right to participation in the name of saving democracy. Is this a limitation of popular democracy that desecrates the principle of political equity? Certainly. But this was the legitimation of a practice of power, in the name of democracy, that bore all the hallmarks of the Philippines' unjust historical experience.

Newly appointed President Gloria Macapagal-Arroyo immediately sought to position herself within the middle class's people power narrative. In her inaugural speech at the EDSA Shrine, she said that Filipinos "must improve moral standards in government and society in order to provide a strong foundation for good governance", setting herself apart from the transgressions of her predecessor. In an attempt to bolster the legitimacy of her appointment through extra-constitutional means, she stated, "People Power and the oneness of will and vision have made the new beginning possible." The reference to a "new beginning" sounded very familiar to inauguration speeches of the past. It included a pledge to deal with social and economic inequalities by completing "what Andres Bonifacio began" in 1896, finishing the "unfinished revolution." It also included a determination to move away from the "traditional" politics of the status quo, "based on patronage and personality." Cementing her place in the historical narrative, she declared to the crowds gathered:

> As we break from the past in our quest for a new Philippines, the unity, the Filipino's sense of history, and his unshakeable faith in the almighty that prevailed in EDSA '86 and EDSA 2001, will continue to guide and inspire us. I am certain that Filipinos of unborn generations will look back with pride to EDSA 2001, just as we look back with pride to Mactan, the Katipunan and other revolts, Bataan and Corregidor and EDSA "86."[9]

Demarcating the terms of permissible dissent. Events in the days following the People Power 2 demonstration would confirm not only the presence, but the functioning of the middle class's ambivalence with democratic politics in their condemnation of dissent. As soon as the anti-Erap street protest had begun, a counter-protest of pro-Erap supporters had also gathered in large numbers to defend the legitimacy of the administration, a show of support for Estrada's presidency of ten million citizens who voted for him. Anti-Erap demonstrations, the counter-demonstrators claimed, did not represent the Philippine people at all, but only a small, wealthy segment of the population (Kusaka 2017b: 100). Ultimately the momentum of People Power 2 proved too much for Estrada and his supporters to counter.

Three months after People Power 2, however, when Estrada was arrested for plunder, the conflict reached its peak. "The sight of Estrada treated as a common criminal", Rafael said, "infuriated his numerous supporters" who, having been ignored by politicians, the Catholic Church hierarchy, the middle class and the NGOs, "saw in Estrada a kind of patron who had given them hope" (Rafael 2003: 28–9). People Power 3 got under way at the symbolic and sacred EDSA Shrine. "[I]n a country where the poor are often seen by the middle class to be unsightly, spoken about and down to because deemed incapable of speaking up for themselves", Rafael wrote, "the masses became suddenly visible" (2003: 31). Politicians supporting Estrada provided transport, food and money for the demonstration at which an estimated 300,000 people gathered, more than the anti-Estrada demonstrations three months earlier. Yet despite the demonstrator numbers eclipsing People Power 2, the major television stations did not cover People Power 3, and the Catholic Church denounced the protest and forbade its members to join (which was mostly ignored).[10] When as many as 50,000 demonstrators stormed Malacanang Palace, they were met by police and soldiers, and during an intense night of conflict, four people died and over 100 were injured. In response, Arroyo declared a "state of rebellion" and "began rounding up and arresting opposition legislators, hoping to quell the crisis once and for all" (Kusaka 2017b: 104).

For a majority of the middle class, the two gatherings at EDSA that occurred within three months of each other in 2001 were fundamentally different events, with profoundly different crowds. Participants in People Power 3 were an ignorant and easily manipulated mob, "mobilized with handouts of money and food from opposition politicians" (Kusaka 2017b: 109). Dubbed "Poor People Power", its participants were "retrograde and reactionary" compared with the "technologically savvy and politically sophisticated" People Power 2 participants (Rafael 2003: 28–9), who acted in the country's best interests.

The events surrounding People Power 3 were perhaps the clearest confirmation since the emergence of the "people power" trope in 1986 that the middle classes associated the signifier of "the people" with themselves. It was the expression of their political will that fulfilled the people power narrative, even if, paradoxically, this involved overriding the volition of the majority of voters and dismissing their right to political equality.

Duterte, for Democracy's Sake

By 2006, just five years after the ousting of Estrada, a new term began circulating in middle-class and academic discourse: "people power fatigue." Twenty years since the downfall of the Marcos regime, and as Sheila Coronel captures it, "there was no joyous celebration, just weariness and disillusionment about the prospects for democracy" (2007: 175). Pride at the peaceful toppling of the dictator was replaced "by scepticism about the desirability – and long-term viability – of the elite democracy established after Marcos's fall." The attempt to oust Arroyo from the Presidency through a replication of the 1986 formula, though it had worked in 2001, failed almost before it had begun, with tanks, barbed wire, and battalions of heavily armed troops appearing alongside a "state of emergency" proclamation that recreated another pinnacle moment in the country's history – the Marcos declaration of martial law in 1972.

Once again, contemplation turned inwards. The deep dissatisfaction with the deficiency of the country's democracy turned into doubt about democratic capacity. The post-1986 period, rather than portraying the democratic fervour and virtue of the Filipino citizens, began to represent their ineptitude. It became defined as a period of abuse of freedom. "[A]fter EDSA, Cory Aquino", explained my interviewee Teddy, "they tried to restore freedom, and democracy. Now there's too much freedom." "There's too much", he went on to say, "because with freedom goes responsibility; freedom is not absolute." "We forgot that democracy was more than [freedom]", said another one of my interviewees, Victor. "It's not just a case of changing the leader, we ourselves have to change – as an individual, as a community. It starts from within also . . . democracy is about exercising restraint also." "Sad to say", yet another interviewee Nathan told me, "we don't have that moral compass yet, we don't have that strict freedom in our hearts."

The middle class were given a boost in the lead up to the 2010 national elections, with the entry of Corazon and Benigno (Ninoy) Aquino's son, Benigno (Noynoy) Aquino III, into the presidential race. Following the widely lamented but politically fortuitous death in 2009 of the former President "Cory" and icon of the original People Power moment, the possibility of son Noynoy taking over the reins and restoring dignity and moral order was declared a "game changer" (Thompson 2010: 3). In common with his mother three decades earlier, Aquino's narrative of reform was tied to the promise that economic prosperity and nation building could go hand in hand with liberal democratic values – the protection of private property, of individual civil rights, and minimal government interference in the structure of society outside existing liberal institutions.

Following his successful election, Aquino's reformist government, from 2010 to 2016, produced an excellent economic scorecard, with GDP growth reaching its highest level in four decades. Major legislative victories were won, including the imposition of a tax on tobacco and a reproductive health law, despite the disapproval of the ever-powerful Catholic Church in the case of the latter. What is more, Aquino remained highly popular throughout his term, even as he left office, and the record of his administration appeared relatively clean. Yet this was no antidote to the deep underlying frustration and disillusionment with the way democracy in the Philippines worked. At least a quarter of the population remained in poverty, and the level of inequality remained an embarrassment and a stain. Added to this, despite paying high taxes, the urban-based middle class suffered the daily miseries of traffic congestion, rickety trains, and dilapidated airports. All the while, a seemingly greedy and tone-deaf Manila elite continued to prosper, benefitting from the country's weak institutions, including the corrupt justice system. It was the failure of democracy in these everyday realities that would give potency, once again, to a latent ambivalence about the transformative capacity of a "liberal" regime in the Philippines.

The thirtieth anniversary of the People Power Revolution of 1986 was celebrated two months before the 2016 national election. At the time of the commemorations, the upper and middle classes were firmly leading the charge in supporting the candidacy of Rodrigo Duterte for President (SWS 2019). By early May, the self-declared "dictator" and foul-mouthed provincial strongman from the South was declared the convincing victor in the presidential race, securing almost 40 per cent of the popular ballot, including the vote of more than half of the country's middle and upper class (ABS-CBN 2016). Although this time it wasn't a street demonstration to oust an overstaying autocrat, it was an "electoral insurgency" (Bello 2016) to instate one, to some the tangible energy and momentum for a radical shake up to the status-quo resembled the events of 1986, with the election even being labelled a People Power revolution again led by the middle class (Ota 2016).

Duterte enjoyed popularity across the country's class divides, but the point that needs emphasizing in the context of this book is that his success amongst so many of the middle class was not random, nor mystifying: it can be explained by his mobilization of a central antagonism that underlies Philippine politics – between a national solidarity that expresses itself in a collective aspiration for dignity, on the one hand, and an anxiety about misbehaviour and inadequacy that tolerates violence, exclusion and repression in the name of discipline and order on the other. The unmistakable reality was that Duterte had won middle-class support despite, or perhaps because of, his professed willingness to subvert democratic institutions and processes in order to redeem the Philippines.

Paradoxically, it was the existence of democratic aspirations that had brought many in the middle class to this point. Repeatedly, amongst the narratives of my middle-class respondents, the sentiment expressed was that the search for the fulfilment of democratic dreams that had culminated in the moment of 1986 had brought them to a critical reflection on the state within. Thirty years after EDSA, the collective identity of Filipinos as democratic and peace-loving felt under challenge. Weak institutions that only benefit a handful of elites, combined with a sense of lawlessness amongst the population, put the constitution of the nation itself in doubt. The interpellation of "the Filipino" and "the nation" seemed once again fragile and floating, a situation that only perpetuated the existential crisis that continued to lie just below the surface.

In the lead-up to the election, Duterte took advantage of the fact that the oligarchic political state in the Philippines remained seemingly impenetrable and unable to absorb the democratic demands of its citizens, even under an administration such as that of Benigno Aquino, which was dedicated to "reform." The accumulation of unfulfilled aspirations meant the only hope for democratic reform was through drastic change. In such a context, Duterte positioned himself as a redemptive leader, and called on "the people" to trust him to exercise exceptional power in order to deliver them out of the wilderness. What had felt like aimless wandering in the post-EDSA wilderness had gone on for too long.

Looking through a long, historical lens it is possible to see that while Estrada's populism of two decades earlier was class-based, with a clever performance of the bestowing of dignity on the working poor, Duterte's performance was a populist nationalism that belonged to the playbook of Marcos, and even of Manuel Quezon much earlier. Duterte's persuasiveness for a middle-class audience derived from the fact that he gave voice to the ghosts of Philippine democracy, those outside and those within. He ignited the two opposing impulses that for decades had lain just below the surface. On the one hand, Duterte embodied the Filipino's defiance of an unresolved history of colonial subjugation. The resonance of this appeal was vividly captured in September 2016, when President Duterte "cursed" US President Barack Obama. During the press conference at Davao International Airport, at which the President (in)famously rejected the right of the United States to interfere in the Philippines' business, he stated:

> I am a president of a sovereign state. And we have long ceased to be a colony. I do not have any master but the Filipino people. (Rappler.com 2016)

It came as part of a lengthy and irritated monologue during which the President not only granted himself the status of both spokesman and defender of "the people", but also claimed that given the historical record of the United States in the Philippines, President Obama had no credibility in holding him to account, and that past actions of American governments towards the Filipino people belie any feigned concern about human rights in the present.

In cursing Obama, and telling him to mind his own business, Duterte behaved badly, but in this very unruliness lay his appeal. The more his non-conformist and undisciplined behaviour drew international disapproval, the more compelling to many was his leadership. Why? Because he embodied the scrutinized Filipino "native" subject of history, looked down upon by the "foreign" outsider; in standing up for "the people", he signified a refusal to continue to indulge the injuries of the past. Tapping into the Philippines' continuing search for a revolutionary break with the past, Duterte called to an end, once and for all, the undermining and diminishing of the nation's sovereignty, and promised a restoration of dignity. To an audience in October 2016 he said:

> I can lose the presidency anytime. If Congress would oust me, fine. That is part of the destiny of my presidency because I won without money and machinery. If I lose my life, that's part of the territory of being president. But I would never allow our dignity and honor to be just like a doormat before the international public [...] If there is one thing I would like to prove to America and to everybody is that there is such a thing as the dignity of the Filipino people. (Duterte 2016)

Alongside promises to stand up for genuine sovereignty and national dignity, to finally unshackle the Philippines from its history of imperial authority, Duterte made the seemingly contradictory promise to impose discipline on the nation via an arbitrary authority that would offer little to no tolerance of dissent. "It's going to be a dictatorship", he warned. "The police and the military will be the backbone" (Duterte 2015). Duterte gave a voice to the latent anxiety that Filipinos could not be trusted with too much freedom. He presented himself as the disciplinarian and strong hand the country needed. This was a man who, after a 20-year reign in what was once the murder capital of the Philippines, according to the popular narrative left Davao City as a peace and order paradise where virtuous citizens could live. It was the "tough love" of a patriarch whose source of legitimacy lay beyond the rule of law, which itself was just an instrument of abuse of power (Kusaka 2017b: 264). In the ultimate paradox, it bore striking similarity to the US colonial project of benign authoritarianism, based on a logic of attaining liberty through its denial.

"Many people [at the moment] are abusing their freedom and doing things which are not good", said my interviewee Garrett. "[B]ut we have this one politician, Duterte, [whose] type of leadership is like Marcos. And many people like that. And if you see Davao right now, it is one of the safest places in the Philippines. For me, if that type of leadership is implemented again, I think it's much better." For Garrett and others, the exercise of strong political authority, even if that authority oversteps the boundaries of individual freedoms and liberties, was deemed necessary and acceptable for the conditions in which democracy operates in the Philippines. Given the weakness of disciplining institutions, only a presidential figure with the power to impose arbitrary restrictions could do what is necessary. If the Philippines as a nation needed discipline, then an exercise of power that infringes on people's full liberal rights is deemed not only legitimate, but central to democratic renewal.

Contradictory? Yes. But it confirms the presence and the potency of the deeply embedded ambivalence within the democratic imaginary of the middle class. It allows, as I discovered in my interviews, even the most educated of people to express something that is assuredly ambivalent – that the Philippines needs a strong leader like Duterte, for democracy's sake. At a glance, it may seem to the observer a deficient form of democratic agency, or a misunderstanding of democratic principles. But the resonance of Duterte's narratives and the perceived legitimacy of his leadership, speaks to a number of lessons that have been raised in this book. Ambivalence is not a failure of democratic agency or a pathological form of democratic practice. It is a situated, negotiated and volitional response. The democratic ambivalence that was exercised by broad sections of the middle class in the election of Duterte, reflects an enlivening of political esteem and efficacy among frustrated citizens – citizens who could choose to exit the race altogether and give up on their democratic dreams, but who instead attempted to reclaim the public sphere away from the circus of electoral politics, which not only fails to transform society and to give voice to unutterable miseries, but inoculates the worst of hypocrites from facing judgement.

I expressed my uncertainty and concern to a middle-class friend in Manila at the time, about what may unfold in the coming years under such an administration. His expression in response poignantly captured the mood: "I would take a rollercoaster any day over six more years of the same merry-go-round."

Conclusion

Towards the end of one of my interviews, a respondent now aged in her late thirties recalled a memory from high school. She had written a poem about America's involvement in the Philippines, and about the idea of being free:

> I think what I essentially wrote was, Are we really free? They say they're giving us freedom, but are we really free from what they want us to be? [...] I still feel this way, like, it's not really true democracy . . . Okay, they educated us, but they said, 'This is how we want you to be.' It wasn't, 'Okay, this is how we want to govern ourselves, how we want to live our own lives.'

I began this research some eight years ago, dissatisfied and irritated by the pejorative language so often used in the democracy literature to characterize the trajectory of Philippine politics. Not only did it seem far removed from an understanding of the lived experience, it came from a place of denialism, it seemed to me, about the fact that the Philippine story was not simply an aberration to the narrative of liberal democracy's global advance. It was a kind of looking glass. What is more, most studies of contemporary Philippine politics presented, it appeared to me, what Stoler brilliantly terms a "historically truncated optic" (2016: 336), constricting both the temporal and geopolitical view of how the politics of today has emerged. Most particularly, where was the serious discussion in the mainstream democratization literature, about the "durable damages" of imperial relations on postcolonial democratic terrains? I return to these kindling discomforts as I try to bring the project full circle, hoping that the findings of this book offer some acuity to the Philippine story, and elucidate what the story has to tell us about the fate of democracy more broadly. In this final chapter, I first turn to the empirical findings of the research and summarize the new insights offered to Philippine studies. Then, I revisit the theme of the middle class and democracy, reiterating the methodological and theoretical challenges that an embedded historical study of middle-class political subjectivity presents to prevailing assumptions about the relationship. Finally, I return to the concept of democratic ambivalence, extending the empirical and theoretical case for ambivalence as inevitable and innate in democratic life, to make the normative proposition that the presence of ambivalence is a desirable and necessary feature of a functioning democracy.

The Philippines' long journey to ambivalence. Benedict Anderson concluded his seminal essay titled "Cacique Democracy and the Philippines: Origins and Dreams" with a provocation: that the Filipino population are tricked by electoral politics as in a casino, believing they can win, time and again, therefore continuing to play, when actually they are never even in the game. Anderson was writing his essay in the wake of the disappointments and dynasticism of the first post-EDSA elections. He described the "giddy exhilaration" that fed the hope amongst the middle class that the resumption of elections would not only give them power, but also deliver the legislative reforms they desired (1998: 218). By 1987, Anderson concludes, these middle class "illusions" had been dashed. Duped into oligarchical politics once again, it would seem, by the chicanery of the political elite.

Though Anderson's intention was to emphasize the hegemony of the country's political oligarchy, the analysis attributes to those beneath a democratic pathology characterized by naivety and gullibility. It renders citizens as deficient in their democratic agency, while at the same time papering over the normative effects of a history of exclusion, contradiction, and oppression in the name of democracy. Anderson is unequivocal about the role of historical, societal and structural factors in constructing the seemingly impervious elite-dominated politics found in the contemporary period. Yet he does not extend the same logic of contingency to the way citizens, and middle-class citizens in particular, imagine democracy – the meanings, values, and expectations they attach to it.

Given so much experience of the yawning gap between the democratic ideal and the reality of democratic politics, why should it be assumed the middle class were naively expecting heaven on earth? An alternative reading, as the one I have attempted in this book, would suggest that rather than capricious and green when it comes to the workings of democracy, the contemporary middle class in the Philippines derives its outlook on democratic politics from a conciliation of the democratic ideal with the lived experience of its practice – an outlook, shaped by historical experience, that deems democracy to be both the ultimate goal of the Filipino people, and a danger to their hopes of prosperity. It is this deep-seated and historically rooted ambivalence about democracy, not naivety or mischief, that best explains the middle class's simultaneous support for self-government and their intermittent tolerance of top-down rule.

The study began, in Chapter 1, by illuminating the central paradox of the United States' "democratizing" mission in the Pacific Archipelago, in the fact that the colonial program gave lie to the idea of the citizenry as the "constitutional creators" of democracy. The ideal of democracy, it argued, was undermined by the humiliating and infantilizing practices of power deployed in its name. What is more, notions of democracy and national sovereignty were continually conflated. Only when the Philippines showed itself capable of supervised democratic governance would the country earn the right to be sovereign.

Rather than remaining in the colonial story of the past, the second part of the book, Chapters 2 and 3, traced the ways this imperial duress shaped the subjectivities and meanings constructed by the middle class, such that the ghosts of that democratic betrayal continued to haunt the democratic imaginary of the postcolonial Philippines. It wasn't only that the fusion between democracy and independence remained a consistent feature of the postcolonial democratic imaginings. The implicit practice of power of the United States over the Philippines established under colonial rule through the politics of representation continued to shape politics in the postcolonial Philippines through the reified binary between the benevolent American and the Filipino who was of doubtful self-governing capacity. Four decades under foreign gaze left an anxiety within many in the Philippines about the capacity to correctly inhabit this democratic freedom. The "colonial present" manifested itself in an imperative to chase freedom that simultaneously shunned and embraced the need for arbitrary power. I used the term democratic ambivalence to capture this double-sided response of the middle class to democratic politics. The postcolonial perceptions of "self" served to legitimize the continued direct interference of the United States in the Philippines' sovereignty, and to compromise postcolonial nation building.

The presence of an underlying ambivalence towards democracy, Chapters 4 and 5 argued, makes sense of the middle class's seemingly incongruent role in the politics of an independent Philippines, from their support of Ferdinand Marcos and his constitutional authoritarianism, to their role in his spectacular deposing in 1986, through to the endorsement of the firebrand strong-man Rodrigo Duterte three decades later. Via this lens, the politics of the present is not only revealed as more complex than is supposed by pejorative theses of political unsophistication, false consciousness or "authoritarian nostalgia." It is connected to a largely intangible yet durable legacy of the encounter with American imperialism. Fluctuations between a politics of national solidarity (evidenced by People Power 1), and a politics of moral exclusion (culminating in the events of People Power 2 and 3), are best understood as evidence of the middle class's deep-seated and protracted ambivalence towards democracy – a defining characteristic of a postcolonial society still negotiating the paradoxes of democracy, including the legacies of the collective experience of learning democracy under conditions of duress.

In retelling the story of the Philippine's journey with democracy through a colonial genealogy of middle-class ambivalence, this research has offered a fresh take on the seemingly perplexing fluctuations in middle-class politics and on the epistemic legacies of American imperialism in the Islands. By synthesizing a broad scope of the existing literature by both historians and social scientists, and by reinterpreting these diverse writings to draw insights into middle-class views, the book has created linkages across otherwise disparate fields of inquiry. Moreover, by connecting recent historical works of the late nineteenth century, which confirm the important political and ideational role played by members of a nascent middle class during those revolutionary times (Cullinane 2004, 2014; Richardson 2013; Mojares 2006), to the longer story of political development in modern twentieth century Philippines, the findings propose a number of specific adjustments to the existing literature on Philippine studies. Most obviously, the research rebuts the conventional narrative about a historically quiescent middle class, demonstrating that the starting point for studying the significance of middle-class political beliefs and behaviour lies much earlier than the existing literature posits. It also answers previously unexamined questions about the impact of America's contradictory imperial policy of "democratic tutelage" on the development of middle-class beliefs, finding that the roots of a middle-class moral discourse, that divides "the people" into dutiful citizens versus ignorant masses, lie much deeper than the episode of 1986 and the era of neoliberalism (Kusaka 2017b).

What to make of an ambivalent middle class. Beyond the specifics of the Philippine case, the book has raised questions about the analytical framework conventionally used to understand the qualitative relationship between the middle classes and democracy. The middle classes will not always be shock-absorbers against all forms of despotism. To the contrary, in many parts of the world, not least in China and Russia, the middle classes are the stabilizing forces that enable non-democratic regimes to maintain power (Keane 2020: 73). Even in places where the middle class prefers self-government and the rotation of representatives that elections provide, such as in the Philippines, this doesn't negate feelings of frustration and despondency with democracy's capacity to deliver the lives they desire. Nor does it guarantee their silence when corruption and abuse of power masquerade behind democratic rhetoric. From time to time, the gap between the promises of power-sharing government and the realities of life on the ground will be too much, and the taste for tough leadership and top-down rule too strong. Even Tocqueville warned that the middle classes could become supporters of authoritarian rulers, putting regime stability and personal interests above democratic idealism (Keane 2020: 68). To continue to frame this simply as a flaw in middle-class agency, and as a deviation from the middle class's "true" political character, is to continue the fairy tale that the Atlantic-region middle class of the nineteenth century, embroiled though they were in the spoils of an imperial global economy, remain a universal benchmark. What is more, it risks papering over the seriousness of deficiencies in democratic regimes that prompt middle classes to "act out" in the first place. It serves to protect those who would pretend all is well, when clearly it is not.

In contrast, the emphasis in this study has been on the mediated and negotiated nature of middle-class political subjectivity – shifting from normative assumptions about how a middle class should value democracy, and the meanings they should attach to it, to exploratory questions of how they do value it, and from where their evaluative frames derive. It demonstrates that the formation of a middle-class political consciousness is a complex and protracted process, shaped as much if not more by the context of its own political transition, and by local struggles over symbols, meanings and ideologies, as it is by an abstract model of "enlightened" middle-class thought. Moreover, the Philippine story demonstrates the need to put studies of middle classes in a geopolitical frame, in order to bring to light the way that unequal power relations, and imperial practices of exclusion and inclusion, traverse the boundaries we may conveniently use to categorize the past.

To be, or not to be, ambivalent about democracy. The third, and perhaps most significant outcome of the book, is the development of the concept of democratic ambivalence. Empirically, the book demonstrated the way that a deep-seated and stable ambivalence towards democracy in the Philippines is the result of a protracted abuse of power, veiled behind democratic rhetoric. To be ambivalent is to withhold permanent allegiance. In the context of a democracy which has failed to deliver on its promises, and failed to absorb the democratic aspirations of its citizens and channel their disappointments and despondency through meaningful rotations of power, ambivalence towards democracy is a rational, deliberate and non-silent expression of constitutional power. Ambivalence has enabled citizens to recognize that what has been labelled as democracy, whether by a colonial authority or a political elite, is in fact a lullaby, mere rhetoric that inoculates the worst of hypocrites and crooks from justice, and that to be silent in the face of this fact would only serve the interests of those who would continue to paper over it.

But the applicability of the concept of democratic ambivalence extends well beyond the Philippine case. It offers a lesson of global importance to the study of democracy. The geographically vast detection of ambivalence, especially amongst middle-class publics, should force us to rethink the way we frame the disillusionments, disappointments and misgivings of citizens with their existing democracies. How do we habituate our studies of democratic attitudes and beliefs to the permanent gap that exists between political aspirations, visions and promises propagated by an ideal on the one hand, and the actual real-world constraints of the practice of democracy on the other? The theoretical proposition offered by this book is that ambivalence, rather than a pathology or flaw, is in fact one of democracy's innate qualities. Democracy cautions people against expecting paradise on earth. It sensitizes them to the temporality of the power relations in which they live. The disappointments, frustrations and unmet aspirations which democracy institutionally accommodates, through the continual possibility of change, are the very features of democratic life that in fact nurture a sense of ambivalence.

If living in a democracy means embracing the ongoing presence of choice, and by extension, learning to live with the permanent antagonism between accepting what is and striving for what could be, then ambivalence is not only a mediated response to democracy, but a necessary one. Here, finally, is where the normative case for democratic ambivalence is made. Ambivalence is, I argue, one of democracy's internal safeguards. First, by warning against idealizations of democracy that promise paradise on earth, ambivalence enables citizens to deal with the permanent presence of disappointment and failure without withdrawing altogether, and without turning to fanaticism to resolve inconsistencies. Second, in being against certainty, ambivalence warns of the danger that comes from totalizing ideologies – grand narratives by which a group tries to seize power, or as Claude Lefort describes it, when "the process of occultation of the institution of social reality seeks to complete itself" (1991: 70) by denying all opposition between civil society and the state. Ambivalence resists the certainty that may lead to fanaticism and serves as a weapon against concentrated power clothed as "truth." To borrow from Leszek Kolakowski, it allows people to "[believe] in God and the superiority of eternal salvation over temporal well-being, yet does not demand that heretics be converted at the stake" (1961: 202). Last, in rejecting passivity, certainty and objectivity, in favour of a permanent state of contemplation, ambivalence contributes to a continual denaturing of existing structures of authority. "The world is ambivalent", wrote Zygmunt Bauman, "though its colonizers and rulers do not like it to be such and by hook or by crook try to pass it off for one that is not" (1991: 179). Or consider the way Ernesto Laclau (1990) sees the political as a state of constant conflict, deriving from inherent identity claims in the struggle for dominance. While the collective identity of "the people" claims to accommodate difference, this is impossible, Laclau argues, without the "constitutive exclusion" of the "Other." If this is the case, democracy should stimulate our skepticism – about who is being excluded in the name of "the people", and who has managed to gain the power to constitute their particular identity as a unified whole (Panizza 2005: 16). Ambivalence prompts reflection on what can be done to preserve and to enrich democracy. It is this type of watchfulness and constant contemplation that a living democracy functionally requires.

But, of course, there is a necessary caveat. For ambivalence, by definition, has two sides. There is no doubt that opponents of democracy take advantage of ambivalence to flex their muscles. The Philippine story chronicles time and again the mobilization of ambivalence by political actors to weaken and even destroy power-sharing democracy. In particular, a discussion of ambivalence would not be complete without addressing the close relationship between ambivalence and populism. We need only think of the instances of populist actors everywhere provoking and mustering public ambivalence about democracy to garner power, through pronouncements of alternative visions and promises of social and political transformation.

There are those who argue that populism in the Philippines and elsewhere has a potential to deepen democracy, insofar as it gives prominence to a flawed system of politics, including corrupted institutions controlled by narrow elite interests, as well as to fundamental issues that seem to suffer from perpetual elite neglect, such as socioeconomic inequality (Kusaka 2017b; Curato 2016; Webb and Curato 2019). There is little doubt that populism is, in large part, a response to the limits and dysfunctions of existing democracies. It raises the question: within prevailing understandings of "liberal democracy", which narrowly focus on individual rights and citizens' electoral participation, how are people to imagine, for example, that changes in the social and economic structure of their societies can be achieved, if not through pinning their hopes on a populist's pledge? How, other than through what may be perceived as radical electoral behaviour, can citizens exercise their constituent and sovereign power to shape the norms and the rules that regulate the exercise of power? Accentuating these questions only highlights the Janus-face of populism – that it is guided by a logic that has the potential to attack democracy from within. In the name of restoring sovereignty to "the people", populism promotes hostility, even violence, towards a constructed "enemy." It privileges the leader and weakens power-constraining institutions while denying plurality. Both Duterte and Marcos declared an end to the arbitrary politics of the ruling oligarchy. Both then proceeded to attack the very monitory institutions – including independent journalism, human rights organizations and the judiciary – that constrain arbitrary power, governing instead by a kind of "self-styled machismo" resembling "a permanent coup d'état in slow motion" (Keane 2017). And they join a long list of populist actors, not least Trump, Orbán and Modi, who have done the same. Even so-called "left-wing populism" is built on friend-enemy dichotomies that sit uncomfortably with democracy.[1]

But it is in the dialectics of populism (Tormey 2018), in particular in the ambivalence upon which populism feeds, that we find potential for a reimagining of democracy. While populism is hostile to openness and contingency, instead operating on simplified and totalizing narratives, the ambivalence to which it gives voice can and often does strike back. This is to say that ambivalent voters are not mindlessly captive to the populist narrative. Democratic ambivalence is promiscuous. It resists certainty. It is restless, in search of a home, but with no fixed address. The same ambivalence that can lend support to populism can also prompt reflection on how to prevent democracy's degeneration. It is the reasoning capacity and the agency exhibited in middle-class ambivalence that also confirms its democratic potential. The Philippine middle class demonstrated this point dramatically by initially empowering then later deposing Marcos's dictatorial regime. Under the Duterte administration, democratic ambivalence has seen many amongst the middle class acquiesce to, or even endorse, a widespread punitive and violent denial of liberty. But the evidence from history, especially the Marcos era, suggests it will not be allowed to last. After all. ambivalence, although reflecting the contradictions and compromises of democracy in the past, also signals a desire for change.

It only remains to be asked: if the ambivalence mobilized by Duterte to win power in May 2016 is connected to the ambivalence detected in the Sakdalista movement as far back as the 1930s, is this a sad story of the middle class's failure to learn from experience? Even if the tail of middle-class ambivalence returns to reject Duterte's illiberalism, as it eventually did to Marcos, does the same cycle again await the Philippines in the future? It remains to be seen whether the ambivalence of the Philippine middle class can find a more down-to-earth, plain-speaking, humble iteration of democratic politics in which to take shelter. Whatever the future may hold for democracy in the Philippines, if making a defence of ambivalence, as I have done in this book, draws the ire of committed democrats, who feel uncomfortable with the very prospect of vindicating equivocation, let that outrage be directed at ambivalence's imperial roots, and spare its contemporary carriers yet more indignity and exasperation.

Notes

Preface

1 I learned in a subsequent interview with one of the key participants that the idea had initially emerged prior to the 2010 presidential election. But when Corazon and Benigno Aquino's son, "Noynoy", entered the presidential campaign in autumn 2009 in the wake of public grief at his mother's death, the group behind it decided to wait, as Noynoy already seemed the people's choice.

Introduction

1 Interviewees have been given alias names to provide anonymity.
2 The introduction to Heiman, Liechty and Freeman's book *The Global Middle Classes: Theorizing through Ethnography* (2012) provides a good discussion of the reasons for the underdeveloped literature on ethnography of middle classes.
3 Carl Lande (1965) was the first scholar to link informal structures, especially the influence of patron-client networks, to weak political parties and directionless national policy and legislation.
4 For example, see the introductory discussion on "the cognitively incapable" in Shin and Kim's 2017 article, "Liberal Democracy as the End of History: Western Theories versus Eastern Asian Realities"; also see the discussion of "equivocal and confused" citizens in Chang, Zhu, and Park's 2007 essay in the *Journal of Democracy*, "The Democracy Barometers (Part I): Authoritarian Nostalgia in Asia."
5 See www.worldvaluessurvey.org/wvs.jsp.
6 Perhaps the best illustration of this is the thesis of Eva Lotta Hedman in her book *In the Name of Civil Society* (2006). Hedman studies middle-class-led election watch campaigns from 1953 through to the middle-class-led mobilizations of 1986 and 2001. She argues that these mobilizations "in the name of civil society", which appear as classic instances of an enlightened middle class leading the charge for social change on behalf of democracy, are in fact better explained by a Gramscian process of "transformism" led by the "dominant bloc" (the United States, the Catholic Church, and the capitalist class) (2006: 9). Hedman argues that the dominant powers in the Philippines have consistently obtained the institutional and ideological support of middle-class publics for their continued rule by using liberal democratic discourse, producing "narratives and spectacles" that interpellated Filipinos as indi-

vidual citizens "with moral duties and inviolable rights" (2006: 13). By creating the illusion that members of middle-class civil society are democracy's vanguard, the "dominant bloc" not only gains consent for a continuation of the status quo (oligarchical democracy), but also staves off challenges to it, by rendering more radical ideas of social change and democratization invisible or illegitimate (2006: 143). Moments of spontaneous resurgence such as the "People Power Revolution" of 1986 are less an indication of middle-class civil society's democratizing potential than evidence of the ideological hegemony of the dominant forces, and the false consciousness that distracts people from their true identity as collective class agents. Although Hedman's study is persuasive, conspicuously absent from the account are the voices of middle-class actors themselves, and their own narrated rationalizations for participation at particular historical conjunctures. Hedman assumes critical mobilizations as evidence of a middle class under the spell of the ideological narratives of the dominant bloc, rather than analysing the actual language and idioms of participants. See Ramon Guillermo's review for a helpful discussion of the contributions and limitations of Hedman's book (2008).

7 The development of a stratification methodology by the highly influential independent opinion-polling body in the Philippines, the Social Weather Station (SWS), founded in 1985, was a strong impetus for the acknowledgement of a middle class in Philippine society. Where A and B were rich households, defined by consumption, and D and E were moderately and very poor respectively, Class C was defined as the middle class, thus enabling researchers to identify and measure "middle class" opinions and values as a distinct group (Turner 1995: 91). It was around the same time, during the last years of the Marcos dictatorship, that the term "middle class" became increasingly applied to political action.

8 Estimates suggest the middle class constitutes at most 12 per cent of the population (Rivera 2006). While not growing in numbers as dramatically as elsewhere in the region, the Philippine middle class is now more politically independent, economically prosperous, and visible (thanks to new, spacious high-class malls and condominiums) than at any time in history (Pinches 2010).

9 It was not until 1996, when a small number of boxes filled with Katipunan documents were uncovered in the Spanish military archives, that researchers could work out more accurately the details that were previously not clear, including the contentious issue of the Katipunan's class composition (Richardson 2013: xiii, 399).

10 Perhaps the best articulation of this theoretical model of causation is the "theory of democratic culture" by Ronald Inglehart and Christian Welzel (2009).

11 For an overview of the concept of *milieu* see Dariuš Ziforun's chapter, "The Diversity of Milieu in Diversity Studies", in the *Routledge International Handbook of Diversity Studies* (2015).

12 Doty (1996), Slater (2006) and others have argued that throughout the

twentieth century and into the twenty-first, democracy has been used as a discursive tool to justify a hierarchy of global power by constructing a "democratic" West versus a "democratizing" non-Western world, with important implications for power and agency in international politics. As Slater explains: "The imperative to 'democratise' ... creates ... an asymmetry between those announcing the imperative and those subjected to it, between those who 'democratise' and those who are 'democratised'" (2006: 1382).

13 It was in the late nineteenth century that Nietzsche labelled his works *Beyond Good and Evil* (1886) and *On the Genealogy of Morality* (1887) as "genealogy." See (Nietzsche 2001) and (Nietzsche 1994).

14 Almost a century later, Foucault evoked Nietzsche's philosophical work in positioning genealogy as a methodological antidote to the limitations of existing social studies, deploying it in his seminal work *Discipline and Punish*, published in 1975. In embracing genealogy, Foucault rejected his earlier reliance on the methods of "archaeology", which he came to see could not easily explain historical ruptures and transformations.

15 EDSA is the acronym commonly referring to Epifanio de los Santos Avenue, an arterial highway linking the south of Metro Manila to the north, and the gathering site of the majority of protesters during the February 1986 uprising against Marcos.

1 Bridling the Rise of Asia to Make Way for America's "Democratic" Empire

1 An estimated 4000 Americans lost their lives, through battle or other causes such as disease. Philippine military casualties alone were four times this number, and civilian deaths as high as a quarter of a million (Kramer 2006: 201 n140).

2 See http://malacanang.gov.ph/4071-jose-rizals-homage-to-luna-and-hidalgo/

3 When the Indonesian Revolution began in 1945, the Indonesian language Jakarta daily *Asia Raya* wrote, "Rizal is the hero of the Philippines, the hero of the Malays: so, also, the hero of Asia, for those who struggle to ennoble the native people." In another publication in Indonesia at the time, he was called "the hero of all countries under oppression fighting oppressors" (Nery 2011: 109).

4 Emilio Jacinto would go on to become a Filipino General during the Revolution against Spain.

5 Also see Reynaldo Ileto's discussion of the Tagalog meanings of freedom (1979: 107–8).

6 The first half of the nineteenth century saw many advances within the continent. As early as 1854, there was an attempted annexation of the Hawaiian Islands that ultimately failed, until 1887 when the Senate secured exclusive rights to the use of Pearl Harbor as a naval station. In the meantime, in 1878 American navy forces had acquired by force the

use of a harbour in the Samoan Islands. When, a decade later, the Germans threatened to encroach on this South Pacific territory, the American government demonstrated its intention to defend its claim of foreign territory with vehemence (Clyde and Beers 1991: 216).

7   José Rizal was more cautious. In an article published in *Solidaridad* in 1889-1890, Rizal reflected on the possibility of the United States becoming a player in international geopolitics:
"If the Philippines secures their independence after heroic and stubborn conflicts, they can rest assured that neither England, nor Germany, nor France and still less Holland, will dare to take up what Spain has been unable to hold . . . Perhaps the great American Republic, whose interests like in the Pacific . . . may some day dream of foreign possession. This is not impossible, for the example is contagious, covetousness and ambition are among the strongest vices . . . the European powers would not allow her to proceed . . . North America would be quite a troublesome rival, if she should once get into the business. Furthermore, this is contrary to her traditions" (in San Juan 2011: 153).

8   The Treaty of Paris was the agreement signed between the United States and Spain, which marked the latter's relinquishment of its empire, including Cuba, Puerto Rico, Guam, and the Philippines. For cessation of the Philippines, the United States made a payment to Spain of US$20 million.

9   As Hilfrich explains: "From the beginning, Puerto Rico and the Philippines were placed in two different categories. The US government insisted on retaining the former from the start, but left the future of the Philippines to negotiations. This difference, but also the archipelago's size and distance, ensured that the imperialism debate would concentrate on the Philippines" (2012: 17).

10 The campaign of those in favour of annexation was helped by the fact that just days before the vote, war had broken out in the Islands between American and Filipino forces. Immediately, propaganda was spread about the Filipinos unduly starting the conflict, and the question of what to do with the Philippines became one of defending national honour.

11 Amid criticism, Bryan justified his decision to support the Treaty by arguing the future of American imperial policy should be decided upon at the ballot box.

12 As Keane notes of America's nineteenth-century foray into imperialism: "The aspiring American democracy quietly occupied and claimed Baker Island and Howland Island and guano-rich Jarvis Island (1857), Johnston Island and Kingman Reef (1858), Midway Island (1867), Samoa Island (1889), Guam Island and Palmyra (1898)" (2009: 371).

13 As of 1913, for example, only the four out of 31 bureaus that were deemed least politically and administratively important – Weather, Archives, Patents, and Copyrights – were directed by Filipinos (Salamanca 1984: 59).

14 The Philippine Assembly served as the lower house in a bicameral

Philippine Legislature codified in the Philippine Organic Act of 1902. The Assembly consisted of representatives from the Filipino elite, following the first Assembly elections held on 30 July 1907. The second Philippine Commission, appointed by US President McKinley in 1900, and consisting of American officials, would operate as the Legislature's upper house until it was replaced by the Philippine Senate in 1916.

2 The Colonizer Outside: Living Democratically in a Paradox

1. Pardo de Tavera was himself a physician and scholar from a wealthy Manila family, who received his education from the most prestigious schools before finishing his medical training at the University of Paris where his family migrated. He returned to the Philippines in 1892, and when hostilities with Spain broke out four years later, he joined the resistance as a non-combatant, representing Cebu in the Malolos Congress. Though he had taken part in the framing and signing of the Constitution of the first Republic of the Philippines, when fighting between Americans and Filipinos began in early 1899, he soon began advocating the position that the political and cultural incoherence of the Philippines rendered it unfit for independence, and that attachment to the US provided the greatest hope of social progress. Unsurprisingly, this position endeared him to Governor-General Taft. Pardo de Tavera became Taft's right-hand man.
2. In late 1931, the Communist Party was declared by the Manila Court of First Instance an illegal organization.
3. Officially known as the Philippine Independence Act, the Tydings-McDuffie Act was the law establishing the process by which the Philippines would become independent. Enacted on 24 March 1934, the Act outlined the ten-year transition period, and the establishment during that time of the Commonwealth of the Philippines.
4. Despite efforts by Quezon and his Nacionalista Party colleagues to quell the threat to their establishment, extraordinary developments were occurring in the Central Luzon region. Not only did radical workers' politics begin to threaten the balance of power through electoral politics, the union movement also resonated loudly and began to challenge the landlord-dominated agricultural model. As American economist Kenneth Kurihara (1945: 64) wrote in 1945: "The government expected to see the class struggle greatly tempered. But organised labor was neither appeased nor pacified. On the contrary, it turned more and more to the 'left'. Social justice now became the battle cry of the organised workers and peasants in their struggle for economic security." In fact, one of the outcomes of Quezon's pro-labour policy was the revival of a vigorous communist movement from the mid-1930s. Together with the Socialist Party, formed a few years earlier, the two drew up plans for a resistance movement.

3 The Colonizer Within: Imperial Recursions in Imaginings of Democracy

1. In the final months of the Japanese occupation, Manuel Quezon, head of the Commonwealth Government since 1935 and the principal political leader in the first half of the century, died in exile in the United States. His long-time colleague and rival, Vice President Sergio Osmeña, succeeded Quezon and restored the Philippine Commonwealth government upon his own return from exile in late 1944. A national election was scheduled for April 1946 to appoint the President and Vice President of the soon-to-be-independent Philippine Republic. While Osmeña had refused to campaign, claiming that the Filipino people knew his 40-year record, the younger Manuel Roxas, a Nacionalista Party colleague of Osmeña since the 1930s, left the Party and founded the Liberal Party on 19 January 1946, and ran as Osmeña's rival. Both candidates for President were pro-American. Decades earlier, Osmeña and others had abandoned the position of indignation of the 1910 Nacionalista Party letter to the American President, and instead deployed the colonial narrative of history, no doubt to minimize disruption to their own positions of power. But it was Roxas who would, by only a small margin, emerge the winner.
2. Claude Albert Buss was an American diplomat in the Islands during the Second World War, and surrendered Manila on behalf of his government to the Japanese in January 1942. In the years immediately following the war, he was specialist consultant on Southeast Asia to the US Embassy in Japan.
3. The newspaper began life during the first decade of the American occupation, with the first issue published in January 1907, containing both English and Spanish languages. Though initially the paper had trouble finding private finance to keep it running, by 1925 it was doing good business and had established a regular and wide readership.
4. One student from Zamboanga wrote to the paper in 1950 to say that he was studying democracy and the Philippines' current social issues as part of a Social Studies course at secondary college. For the course assessment, students were required to research the "merits and demerits of democracy in the Philippines." Three quarters of the class had used the *Free Press* as their basic source. "To make the obvious conclusion", he wrote, "Locsin and the *Free Press* furnish the basic texts of democracy in the Philippines" (cited in Quimpan 1950: 51).
5. The Bill stated: ". . . whenever the President of the United States, after the investigation by the United States Tariff Commission . . . finds, with respect of any Philippines articles (other than those for which quotas are established . . .) that they are coming or likely to come into substantial competition with like articles which are the product of the United States, he shall so proclaim, and in his proclamation shall establish the total amount of such Philippine articles which may in each of specified periods

be entered, or withdrawn from warehouse, in the United States for consumption . . . " (in Jenkins 1954: 66).
6. In 1955, the Laurel–Langley Treaty would revise the Bell Trade Act of 1946, under pressure from Filipino nationalists who rejected the tying of the Philippine economy to the United States. Amongst other amendments to the original terms, the parity provision was made reciprocal. The treaty expired in 1974.
7. It wasn't always a simple story of heroic resistance, however. Towards the close of the war, Hukbalahap leaders had lost control over many of the guerrilla units. Without knowledge of the Military Committee, some units began to hold trials and even kill innocent people, some for being landlords, others for refusing to give food and clothing to Huk soldiers (Lopez 1951). But this was not typical of the movement as a whole.
8. As early as February 1945, 109 Hukbalahap guerillas were massacred in a single incident in Malolos, Bulucan, having first been detained before being forced by USAFFE forces to dig a mass grave (see Kerkvliet 2014: 128).
9. The United Front in wartime was preceded by a loose coalition of progressive forces established for the 1937 election, called the Popular Front, a political party designed to obtain the support of all groups left of centre, and to unite the peasant working class with the middle class, to challenge the concentration of wealth in the hands of a small elite (see Tan 1981).
10. "With all [the] abuses heaped on them through so many years, it is not surprising that the peasants have risen in arms", wrote Filemon V. Tutay, for example (Tutay 1946). Or the week after independence, in response to the pronouncement by Pampanga Governor Pablo Angeles David of a "mailed fist" policy against the Huks, Teodoro Locsin reminded readers that "The peasants rob and kill, it is angrily charged. But there is very little anger over their continuing poverty which as surely maims, stunts and kills as any gunshot" (Locsin 1946b). "Yes", wrote Vanetin Montes of Manila, "let us send missionaries with Bibles" to the Huks, "but not to pacify the dissatisfied masses but to right wrong and injustice in our economic, political and social order. Let the missionaries with Bibles go to the moneyed social classes, hacenderos and caciques . . ." (Montes 1947).

4 Searching for a Revolutionary Break with the Past

1. Personal correspondence, 21 August 2015.
2. A discourse of "unfinished revolution" had "existed for decades in the peripheries of the political system" (Ileto 1993: 66). It "flourished in the rhetoric of the labor movement from the first decade of [the twentieth] century, finding its way into various peasant movements in central Luzon in the 1920s and 1930s. The sign carries with it an interpretation of the Philippine Revolution as a mass movement initiated by Andres Bonifacio" and "a critique of the *ilustrado* betrayal of the cause" (Ileto 1993: 67).
3. Dubbed the "Diliman Commune", in 1971 parts of the University of the

Philippines campus were occupied by students. Organizers made direct links between the students' defiance of the Marcos administration and the 1896 "Cry of Balintawak", claiming the movement was a continuation of the "unfinished revolution" of the late nineteenth century (Ileto 1993: 74). It was not simply an event in the history books. It was being lived. They were continuing to champion its cause.

4 On its establishment, the CPP's founding chairman Jose Maria Sison condemned the old communist party, the PKP, for falling into "the counterrevolutionary practice of directly participating in the puppet elections" (Guerrero 1970: 44), and reminded party members of events of the past, including the illegalization of the movement in the early 1930s, and the exclusion of the Democratic Alliance from Congress (Quimpo 2008: 132). "Rebolusyon, hindi eleksyon" (Revolution, not election) became the rallying cry, and any suggestions from cadres within of taking a reformist approach, and of participating in Marcos's election on the premise it may open "democratic space" and lead to a mass movement, were swiftly condemned (Quimpo 2008: 133).

5 *Newsweek*, 24 November 1969, and 16 February 1970; *Time*, 16 February 1970.

6 In 1978 Marcos issued a presidential decree (No.1413) declaring "Isang Bansa, Isang Diwa" be adopted as the official national motto of the Philippines. The decree included an instruction that "this motto be made known to every Filipino so that he may take pride in this new symbol of nationhood" (see https://www.officialgazette.gov.ph/1978/06/09/presidential-decree-no-1413-s-1978).

7 Conservative or even negative approaches to democratization dominated the 1960s and 1970s. Samuel Huntington's seminal article, "Political Development and Political Decay", for example, proposed "institutionalization" as a prerequisite to the transition to liberal democracy. Huntington argued that "a hasty transition to democracy would produce large-scale 'mass mobilization' that might lead to political chaos" (in Usul 2011: 1695); and that the political turmoil caused by the over-politicization of the masses might lead to "pathological" regimes (such as socialism). Huntington argued that the establishment of political institutions – rule of law, an effective bureaucracy, and a strong judiciary – was necessary for producing a "viable democracy" (Huntington 1965).

8 The Manifesto, dated 21 September 1983, was jointly issued by the National Democrats, Social Democrats, Christian Democrats, and Liberal Democrats (see Filipiniana Collection, Rizal Library, Ateneo de Manila University).

5 "People Power", Populism and Ambivalence

1 Reported in the *New York Times*, 4 November 1985, "Marcos Declares He'll Call a Vote Early Next Year" by Seth Mydans.

2 For example, see Lewis (1986).

3 The National Democrats had decided to boycott the February 1986 elec-

tion, which turned out to be a tactical mistake. They contested the 1987 and 1988 local elections with poor results – the momentum had gone. Over the following years, the Natdems were split three ways on elections – some advocating "Rebolysyon, hindi eleksyon!" (Revolution, not elections!), some advocating participation in elections as a tool for propaganda and education, and a third group believing all-out participation was the only way forward (Quimpo 2008: 137). This would lead to a big debate and split in the broad left in 1992–1993.

4 Sec 7 Article II of the 1987 Constitution says: "The Philippines, consistent with the national interest, pursues, and adopts the policy of freedom from nuclear weapons."

5 The continuing entanglement of the Aquino administration with the United States was confirmed in November 1989. Confronted with 3,000 dissident soldiers staging the sixth and most serious coup attempt since she had taken office, this time involving the bombing of Malacanang Palace by rebel helicopter pilots, Aquino put in a call to Washington. President George Bush ordered US jets based at the Clark Air Base nearby to intervene, thwarting the coup until Aquino could declare a "state of emergency" (Karnow 1989: 433).

6 America's military involvement at Subic Bay dated back to 1901, when President Roosevelt issued an executive order designating the Bay and 70,000 acres of adjacent land, including the town of Olongapo, as a US-controlled military reservation (Salonga 2001: 445). After the Second World War, Subic became one of the US Navy's most strategic global support facilities, and the staging area for the majority of US activities in Southeast Asia and the Middle East.

7 In an unprecedented step, the 1987 Constitution had provided that the Senate must ratify any new agreement between the United States and the Philippine government, once the existing arrangement relating to the military bases expired in 1991. Aware that the pact would need the ratification of at least 16 of the 24 senators, Richard Armitage, with some pressure groups, had already begun targeting those senators known to be against (Salonga 2001: 447).

8 As Anna Cristina Pertierra (2017) observes, celebrities – from noontime show hosts to singers to the world's greatest pound-for-pound boxer of all time – are often the only candidates who can break the rule of deeply entrenched political dynasties.

9 See https://en.wikisource.org/wiki/Gloria_Macapagal_Arroyo%27s_First_Inaugural_Address.

10 Even Robinsons Galleria, the shopping mall opposite the EDSA Shrine that had opened its doors and offered the use of its facilities to People Power 2 participants, locked out the demonstrators of People Power 3 (Kusaka 2017b: 103).

Conclusion

1 See Keane (2017) for a rebuttal of Chantal Mouffe's argument for reclaiming populism for the left, as sketched in Enrique Krauze's book *Redeemers: Ideas and Power in Latin America* (2011).

References

ABS-CBN. 2016. "More Class ABC Voters Picked Duterte: Exit Poll." *ABS-CBN News* 11 May. http://news.abs-cbn.com/halalan2016/nation/05/11/16/more-class-abc-voters-picked-duterte-exit-poll. Accessed 26 November, 2017.

Abueva, Jose Veloso. 1976. "Filipino Democracy and the American Legacy." *The Annals of the American Academy of Political and Social Science* 428 (1): 114–33. doi: 10.1177/000271627642800111.

Agoncillo, Teodoro A. 1960. "The Retelling of Philippine History." *Progress*, 1169.

Agoncillo, Teodoro A. 1974a. "All Historians Are Controversial." *Archipelago*, 7 July, 11–13.

Agoncillo, Teodoro A. 1974b. "The Aristocrat of Philippine Politics: Manuel L. Quezon as Symbol and Reality Welded Filipinos." *Archipelago*, August, 8–13.

Alcid, Velasco. 1946. "One step Short of Communism." *Philippine Free Press*, April 27, 4, 22, 23.

Anderson, Benedict. 1983. *Imagined Communities: Reflections on the Origin and Spread of Nationalism*. London: Verso.

Anderson, Benedict. 1988. "Cacique Democracy in the Philippines: Origins and Dreams." *New Left Review* 169 (3): 3–31.

Angeles, Juan D. 1947. "'Know Nothings' and the Huks." *Philippine Free Press*, April 12, 16.

Anonymous. 1946. "The Huks Exposed." *Philippine Free Press*, June 15, 6,22.

Anonymous. 1947. "A Challenge to our Rights." *Philippine Free Press*, February 15, 16.

Anonymous. 1949. "A Citizen Writes to his President." *Philippine Free Press*, December 3, 50–1.

Apilado, Mariano Casuga. 1999. *Revolutionary Spirituality: A Study of the Protestant Role in the American Colonial Rule of the Philippines, 1898-1928*, Volume 1. Quezon City: New Day Publishers.

Appleman Williams, William. 1955. "The Frontier Thesis and American Foreign Policy." *Pacific Historical Review* 24 (November): 379–95.

Aquino, Corazon. 1986a. "Cory – To Labor." *Philippine Free Press*, May 31, 13, 32.

Aquino, Corazon. 1986b. "Cory – To the ADB." *Philippine Free Press*, May 31, 12, 30.

Aquino, Melchor. 1947. "The People's Own Doing." *Philippine Free Press*, November 1, 25.

Arcellana, Emerenciana Y. 1976. "A Theory of Philippine Politics and Its Implications for National Development." *Philippine Political Science Journal* (Special Issue: Second National Conference of the Philippine Political Science Association) 3 (3): 61–9.

Astorga, Ma. Christina A. 1994. "Christian Faith and Philippine Moral Transformation." In *Values in Philippine Culture and Education*, edited by Manuel B. Dy Jr, 121–9. Washington: The Council for Research in Values and Philosophy.

Baum, Bruce David, and Duchess Harris. 2009. *Racially Writing the Republic: Racists, Race Rebels, and Transformations of American Identity*. Durham: Duke University Press.

Bauman, Zygmunt. 1991. *Modernity and Ambivalence*. Cambridge, Cambridgeshire: Polity.

Bellin, Eva. 2000. "Contingent Democrats: Industrialists, Labor, and Democratization in Late-Developing Countries." *World Politics* 52 (2): 175–205. doi: 10.1017/S0043887100002598.

Bello, Walden. 2016. "Chronicling an Electoral Insurgency: 'Dutertismo' Captures the Philippines." www.tni.org/en/article/chronicling-an-electoral-insurgency-dutertismo-captures-the-philippines.

Birdsall, Nancy. 2016. "Middle-class Heroes: The Best Guarantee of Good Governance." *Foreign Affairs* 95 (2): 25–32.

Bonikowski, Bart. 2017. "Ethno nationalist Populism and the Mobilization of Collective Resentment." *The British Journal of Sociology* 68: S181–S213. doi: 10.1111/1468-4446.12325.

Bonner, Ray. 1987. *Waltzing with a Dictator: The Marcoses and the Making of American Policy*. New York: Times Books.

Borromeo, Danilo P. 1949. "Blame the People." *Philippine Free Press*, September 18, 59.

Brauer, Jerald C. 1966. *Protestantism in America: A Narrative History (Revised Edition)*. London: SCM Press.

Buss, Claude A. 1954. "Introduction: The Setting of American Economic Policy Toward the Philippines." In *American Economic Policy Toward the Philippines*, edited by Shirley Jenkins. California: Stanford University Press.

Calabang, Casiano T. 1946. "Given Square Deal." *Philippine Free Press*, June 1, 4, 21.

Calhoun, Craig. 2007. "Nationalism and Cultures of Democracy." *Public Culture* 19 (1): 151–73. doi: 10.1215/08992363-2006-028.

Calhoun, Craig. 2012. *The Roots of radicalism: Tradition, The Public Sphere, and Early Nineteenth-Century Social Movements*. Chicago: University of Chicago Press.

Cammack, Paul. 1994. "Political Development Theory and the Dissemination of Democracy." *Democratization* 1 (2): 353–74. doi: 10.1080/13510349408403398.

Capistrano, Samuel R. 1947. "Report on the Plebiscite " *Philippine Free Press*, April 5, 17.
Castoriadis, Cornelius. 1987. *The Imaginary Institution of Society*. Cambridge: Polity.
Castoriadis, Cornelius. 1993. "The Greek and the Modern Political Imaginary." *Salmagundi* (100): 102–29.
Castoriadis, Cornelius. 1997. *World in Fragments: Writings on Politics, Society, Psychoanalysis, and the Imagination*. California: Stanford University Press.
Castoriadis, Cornelius. 2007. *Figures of the Thinkable*. California: Stanford University Press.
Chavarria, Domingo. 1949. "Is Something Wrong with Our Democracy?" *Philippine Free Press*, September 17, 30.
Chang, Yu-tzung, Yunhan Zhu and Chong-min Park. 2007. "The Democracy Barometers (Part I): Authoritarian Nostalgia in Asia." *Journal of Democracy* 18 (3): 66-80.
Chen, Xiaomei. 2002. *Occidentialism: A Theory of Counter-discourse in Post-Mao China*. Lanham: Rowman & Littlefield.
Claudio, Lisandro E. 2013. *Taming People's Power: The EDSA Revolutions and their Contradictions*. Quezon City: Ateneo de Manila University Press.
Clyde, Paul Hibbert, and Burton F. Beers. 1991. *The Far East: A History of Western Impacts and Eastern Responses, 1830–1975*. 6th ed. Prospect Heights, Ill: Waveland Press.
Code, Lorraine. 1992. Taking Subjectivity into Account. In *Feminist Epistemologies*, edited by Linda Alcoff and Elizabeth Potter. London: Routledge, 15-48.
Connell, R. W. 1997. "Why Is Classical Theory Classical?" *American Journal of Sociology* 102 (6): 1511–57. doi: 10.1086/231125.
Constantino, Renato. 1969. *The Making of a Filipino: A Story of Philippine Colonial Politics*. Quezon City: Malaya Books.
Constantino, Renato. 1977. *Insight & Foresight*. Quezon City: Foundation for Nationalist Studies.
Constantino, Renato. 1986. *Vintage Retro: Memorable Speeches and Writings*. Quezon City: Foundation for Nationalist Studies.
Constantino, Renato. 1987. *The Aquino Watch*. Quezon City: Karrel, Inc.
Cornelio, Jayeel Serrano. 2016. *Being Catholic in the Contemporary Philippines: Young People Reinterpreting Religion*. Abingdon: Routledge.
Coronel, Sheila. 2007. "The Philippines in 2006: Democracy and its Discontents." *Asia Survey* 47 (1): 175–82.
Cotterell, Arthur. 2010. *Western Power in Asia: Its Slow Rise and Swift Fall, 1415–1999*. Hoboken, NJ: John Wiley & Sons (Asia).
Cullinane, Michael. 2004. *Ilustrado Politics: Filipino Elite Responses to American Rule, 1898–1908*. Quezon City: Ateneo de Manila University Press.
Cullinane, Michael. 2014. *Arenas of Conspiracy and Rebellion in Late*

Nineteenth-Century Philippines: The Case of the April 1898 Uprising in Cebu. Quezon City: Ateneo de Manila University Press.

Curaming, Rommel, and Lisandro Claudio. 2010. "A Historicised (Re)Assessment of EDSA 'People Power' (1986)." Asia Research Institute Working Paper No. 134.

Curato, Nicole. 2016. "Politics of Anxiety, Politics of Hope: Penal Populism and Duterte's Rise to Power." *Journal of Current Southeast Asian Affairs* 35 (3): 91–109.

David, Simon. 1948. "Mr. David's Letter." *Philippine Free Press*, March 13.

Dejung, Christof, David Motadel, and Jürgen Osterhammel. 2019. *The Global Bourgeoisie: The Rise of the Middle Classes in the Age of Empire*. Princeton: Princeton University Press.

Delmendo, Sharon. 2004. *The Star-entangled Banner: One Hundred Years of America in the Philippines*. New Brunswick: Rutgers University Press.

Dian, B. 1949. "Primer on Philippine Politics." *Philippine Free Press*, June 25, 58–9.

Dickinson, J.M. 1910. Special Report of J.M. Dickinson, Secretary of War, to the President on the Philippines. edited by War Department. Washington, Government Printing Office: [American Historical Collection, ADMU].

Doty, Roxanne Lynn. 1993. "Foreign Policy as Social Construction: A Post-Positivist Analysis of U.S. Counterinsurgency Policy in the Philippines." *International Studies Quarterly* 37 (3): 297–320. doi: 10.2307/2600810.

Doty, Roxanne Lynn. 1996. *Imperial Encounters: The Politics of Representation in North-South Relations*, Volume 5. Minneapolis: University of Minnesota Press.

Duterte, Rodrigo. 2015. *#TheLeaderIWant: Leadership, Duterte Style*, edited by Maria A. Ressa. Manila: Rappler.com.

Duterte, Rodrigo. 2016. Speech of President Duterte during the Philippine Economic Forum. 26 October. Presidential Communications Operations Office, Malacanang, Manila.

Dy Jr, Manuel B. 1994a. "Outline of a Project of Filipino Ethics." In *Values in Philippine Culture and Education*, edited by Manuel B. Dy Jr, 19–25. Washington: The Council for Research in Values and Philosophy.

Dy Jr, Manuel B. 1994b. *Values in Philippine Culture and Education, Philippine Philosophical Studies, I*. Washington: The Council for Research in Values and Philosophy.

Editorial. 1936. "The Agrarian Revolt." *Philippine Free Press*, November 21.

Editorial. 1946a. "And Now?" *Philippine Free Press*, September 21, Cover page.

Editorial. 1946b. "Congressional Fun." *Philippine Free Press*, May 18, Cover page.

Editorial. 1946c. "Cover Page." *Philippine Free Press*, February 23.

Editorial. 1946d. "Ominous Outlook." *Philippine Free Press*, April 6, 3.

Editorial. 1946e. "TARUC Prepares for Martydom." *Philippine Free Press*, July 13, 18.

Editorial. 1947a. "Free Press' Readers and Parity." *Philippine Free Press*, March 1, 38-39.
Editorial. 1947b. "Free Press' Readers React to 'Parity'." *Philippine Free Press*, January 11, 4–5.
Editorial. 1947c. "The Morning After." *Philippine Free Press*, November 15, Cover page.
Editorial. 1947d. "Not So Funny." *Philippine Free Press*, October 4, Cover Page.
Editorial. 1947e. "The One Year Old." *Philippine Free Press*, July 28, Cover page.
Editorial. 1947f. "Title." *Philippine Free Press*, February 15.
Editorial. 1948. "Huks Outlawed." *Philippine Free Press*, March 13, 15.
Editorial. 1949a. "Betrayed." *Philippine Free Press*, June 18, Cover page.
Editorial. 1949b. "Return." *Philippine Free Press*, August 20, Cover page.
Editorial. 1949c. "Shopworn Angels." *Philippine Free Press*, March 19, Cover page.
Editorial. 1949d. "Warm Welcome." *Philippine Free Press*, August 6, Cover page.
Editorial. 1950a. "Blood Transfusion – Can it Save Him?" *Philippine Free Press*, November 4, Cover page.
Editorial. 1950b. "Late Flashes from Huk Front." *Philippine Free Press*, April 1, 60.
Editorial. 1950c. "The News Headlines." *Philippine Free Press*, August 5, Cover page.
Editorial. 1959. "The Rise of the Middle Class Elite." *Mirror*, 7 November, 11–12.
Estabaya, Irene Ramos. 1947. "Fair Warning, to Filipinos Who Love Democracy." *Philippine Free Press*, November 19, 28.
Ezrahi, Yaron. 2012. *Imagined Democracies: Necessary Political Fictions*. Cambridge: Cambridge University Press.
Fernandez, Alejandro M. 1947. "The Road to Peace: A Reply." *Philippine Free Press*, 15 February, 18–19.
Fishkin, Shelley Fisher. 2010. "Reflections." *The Mark Twain Annual* 8 (1): 22–8.
Foucault, Michel. 1978. *The History of Sexuality*. 1st American ed. New York: Pantheon Books.
Foucault, Michel. 1979. *Discipline and Punish: The Birth of the Prison*. New York: Vintage Books.
Friend, Theodore. 1988. "The 'Yellow Revolution': Its Mixed Historical Legacy." *Philippine Studies* 36 (2): 166–82.
Frohnen, Bruce P., ed. 2009. *The American Nation: Primary Sources*. Indianapolis: Liberty Fund.
Fukuyama, Francis. 1989. "The End of History?" *The National Interest* 16: 3–18.
Gardner, William Howard. 1927. "The Philippine Muddle." First printed in Harper's Magazine, November 1926. Reprinted with permission.

Go, Julian. 2007. "The Provinciality of American Empire: 'Liber al Exceptionalism' and U.S. Colonial Rule, 1898–1912." *Comparative Studies in Society and History* 49 (1): 74–108.
doi: 10.1017/S0010417507000412.

Go, Julian. 2009. "The 'New' Sociology of Empire and Colonialism." *Sociology Compass* 3 (5): 775–88.
doi: 10.1111/j.1751-9020.2009.00232.x.

Grant, John. 2014. "On the Critique of Political Imaginaries." *European Journal of Political Theory* 23 (January): 1–19.
doi: 10.1177/1474885113519259.

Gregory, Derek. 2004. *The Colonial Present*. Malden, MA: Blackwell Pub.

Gripaldo, Rolando M. 2001. *Liberty and love: The Political and Ethical Philosophy of Emilio Jacinto*. Manila: De La Salle University Press.

Guerrero, Amado. 1970. Philippine Society and Revolution. http: http://www.bannedthought.net/Philippines/CPP/1970s/PhilippineSocietyAndRevolution-4ed.pdf.

Guevara, Sulpicio. 1972. *The Laws of the First Philippine Republic: The Laws of Malolos 1898–1899*. Manila: National Historical Commission.

Guillermo, Ramon. 2008. "In the name of Civil Society: From Free Election Movements to People Power in the Philippines (Review)." *Sojourn: Journal of Social Issues in Southeast Asia* 23 (1): 155–9.

Gutman, Herbert G. 1966. "Protestantism and the American Labor Movement: The Christian Spirit in Gilded Age America." *The American Historical Review* 72 (1): 74–101. doi: 10.2307/1848171.

Gutting, Gary, and Johanna Oksala. 2018. Michel Foucault. In *The Stanford Encyclopedia of Philosophy*, edited by Edward N. Zalta. California: Stanford University Press.

Harris, Susan K. 2011. *God's Arbiters: Americans and the Philippines, 1898–1902*. Oxford: Oxford University Press.

Hau, Caroline Sy. 2000. *Necessary Fictions: Philippine Literature and the Nation, 1946–1980*. Manila: Ateneo University Press.

Hedman, Eva-Lotta E. 2001. "The Spectre of Populism in Philippine Politics and Society: Artista, Masa, Eraption!" *South East Asia Research* 9 (1): 5–44. doi: 10.5367/000000001101297306.

Hedman, Eva-Lotta E. 2006. *In the Name of Civil Society: From Free Election Movements to People Power in the Philippines*. Honolulu: University of Hawaii Press.

Hedman, Eva-Lotta E. 2010. "The Politics of 'Public Opinion' in the Philippines." *Journal of Current Southeast Asian Affairs* 29 (4): 97–118.
doi: 10.1177/186810341002900405

Hedman, Eva-Lotta E, and John Thayer Sidel. 2000. *Philippine Politics and Society in the Twentieth Century: Colonial Legacies, Post-Colonial Trajectories*, Vol. 26. Psychology Press.

Heiman, Rachel, Mark Liechty, and Carla Freeman. 2012. "Introduction: Charting an Anthropology of the Middle Classes." In *The Global Middle Classes: Theorizing Through Ethnography*, edited by Rachel Heiman,

Mark Liechty, and Carla Freeman, 3–30. Sante Fe, New Mexico: SAR Press.

Hilario, Juan. 1947. "Praise, Wisdom, Warning." *Philippine Free Press*, February 8, 12.

Hilfrich, Fabian. 2012. *Debating American Exceptionalism: Empire and Democracy in The Wake of the Spanish–American War*. 1st ed. New York: Palgrave Macmillan.

Hogan, Trevor. 2006. "In but Not of Asia: Reflections on Philippine Nationalism as Discourse, Project and Evaluation." *Thesis Eleven* 84 (1): 115–32. doi: 10.1177/0725513606060527.

Hoganson, Kristin L. 2017. *American Empire at the Turn of the Twentieth Century: A Brief History with Documents*. Boston: Bedford/St. Martin's.

Huntington, Samuel P. 1965. "Political Development and Political Decay." *World Politics* 17: 386–430.

Huntington, Samuel P. 1996. "Democracy for the Long Haul." *Journal of Democracy* 7 (2): 3–13. doi: 10.1353/jod.1996.0028.

Ileto, Reynaldo Clemeña. 1979. *Pasyon and Revolution: Popular Movements in the Philippines, 1840–1910*. Quezon City: Ateneo de Manila University Press.

Ileto, Reynold Clemeña. 1993. "The 'Unfinished Revolution' in Philippine Political Discourse." *Japanese Journal of Southeast Asian Studies* 31 (1): 62–82.

Ileto, Reynaldo Clemeña. 1998. *Filipinos and Their Revolution: Event, Discourse, and Historiography*. Quezon City: Ateneo de Manila University Press.

Ileto, Reynaldo Clemeña. 2001a. "Colonial Wars in Southern Luzon: Remembering and Forgetting." *Hitotsubashi Journal of Social Studies* 33 (1): 103–18.

Ileto, Reynaldo Clemeña. 2001b. "Orientalism and the Study of Philippine Politics." *Philippine Political Science Journal* 22 (45): 1–32. doi: 10.1080/01154451.2001.9754223.

Inglehart, Ronald, and Christian Welzel. 2009. "How Development Leads to Democracy: What We Know about Modernization." 88 (2): 33–48.

Isaacs, Harold. 1950. "The Danger in the Philippines: The Chance for American Policy." *Philippine Free Press*, June 24, 39, 40.

Ivie, Robert L. 2005. "Savagery in Democracy's Empire." *Third World Quarterly* 26 (1): 55–65. doi: 10.1080/0143659042000322900.

Jenkins, Shirley. 1954. *American Economic Policy Toward the Philippines, Published under the Auspices of the American Institute of Pacific Relations*. California: Stanford University Press.

Kaplan, Amy. 2002. *The Anarchy of Empire in the Making of U.S. Culture*. Cambridge, Mass.: Harvard University Press.

Kaplan, Amy, and Donald E. Pease. 1993. *Cultures of United States Imperialism*. Durham: Duke University Press.

Karl, Rebecca E. 2002. *Staging the World: Chinese Nationalism at the Turn of the Twentieth Century*. Durham, NC: Duke University Press.

Karnow, Stanley. 1989. *In Our Image: America's Empire in the Philippines.* New York: Random House.

Keane, John. 2008. Hypocrisy and Democracy: The Gap Between Ideals and Perceived Reality Is Widening. *WZB-Mitteilungen.* Heft 120 Juni: 30–2.

Keane, John. 2009. *The Life and Death of Democracy.* New York: Simon & Schuster.

Keane, John. 2017. The Pathologies of Populism. *The Conversation.* September 28. https://theconversation.com/the-pathologies-of-populism-82593. Accessed November 29.

Keane, John. 2020. *New Despotism.* Harvard University Press: Cambridge.

Kerkvliet, Benedict J. 2014. *The Huk Rebellion: A Study of Peasant Revolt in the Philippines.* Quezon City: Ateneo de Manila University Press.

Kimura, Masataka. 2003. "The Emergence of the Middle Classes and Political Change in the Philippines." *The Developing Economies* 41 (2): 264–84. doi: 10.1111/j.1746-1049.2003.tb00941.x.

Kolakowski, L. 1964. "In Praise of Inconsistency." *Dissent* 11 (2): 201–9.

Koo, Hagen. 1991. "Middle Classes, Democratization, and Class Formation: The Case of South Korea." *Theory and Society* 20 (4): 485–509. doi: 10.1007/BF00157323.

Kramer, Paul A. 2006. "Race-Making and Colonial Violence in the U.S. Empire: The Philippine–American War as Race War." *Diplomatic History* 30 (2): 169–210. doi: 10.1111/j.1467-7709.2006.00546.x.

Krause, Kristine, and Katharina Schramm. 2011. "Thinking Through Political Subjectivity." *African Diaspora* 4 (2): 115–34.

Krauze, Enrique. 2011. *Redeemers: Ideas and Power in Latin America,* translated by Hank Heifetz and Natasha Wimmer. New York: Harper.

Kurihara, Kenneth Kenkichi. 1945. *Labor in the Philippine Economy.* California: Stanford University Press.

Kurlantzick, Joshua. 2013. *Democracy in Retreat: The Revolt of the Middle Class and the Worldwide Decline of Representative Government.* New Haven: Yale University Press.

Kusaka, Wataru. 2017a. "Bandit Grabbed the State: Duterte's Moral Politics." *Philippine Sociological Review* 65 (S1): 49–75.

Kusaka, Wataru. 2017b. *Moral Politics in the Philippines: Inequality, Democracy and the Urban Poor.* Singapore: NUS Press.

Laclau, Ernesto. 1990. *New Reflections on the Revolution of Our Time: Ernesto Laclau.* London: Verso.

Lande, Carl Herman. 1959. "Democracy in the Philippines." *Mirror,* 24 October, 9–11.

Lande, Carl Herman. 1965. *Leaders, Factions, and Parties: The Structure of Philippine Politics.* New Haven: Yale University.

Lande, Carl Herman. 2001. "The Return of 'People Power' in the Philippines." *Journal of Democracy* 12: 88–102. doi: 10.1353/jod.2001.0029.

Laplanche, Jean, and J. B. Pontalis. 1973. *The Language of Psycho-Analysis,* Volume 94. London: Hogarth Press.

Lavine, Howard. 2001. "The Electoral Consequences of Ambivalence toward Presidential Candidates." *American Journal of Political Science* 45 (4): 915–29. doi: 10.2307/2669332.

Le Roy, James A. 1908. "Philippine Problems After Ten Years' Experience." *Proceedings of the American Political Science Association* 5: 203–18. doi: 10.2307/3038526.

Lefort, Claude. 1991. "On the Genesis of Ideology in Modern Societies." *CTheory* 15 (1–3): 46–86.

Lewis, Anthony. 1986. "Abroad at Home; Why We Celebrate." *The New York Times*, 27 February. http://www.nytimes.com/1986/02/27/opinion/abroad-at-home-why-we-celebrate.html.

Lipset, Seymour Martin. 1959. "Some Social Requisites of Democracy: Economic Development and Political Legitimacy." *The American Political Science Review* 53 (1): 69–105. doi: 10.2307/1951731.

Lipset, Seymour Martin. 1988. "American Exceptionalism Reaffirmed." *International Review of Sociology Series* 1 2 (3): 25–69. doi: 10.1080/03906701.1988.9971374.

Locsin, Teodoro M. 1946a. "The Democratic Alliance." *Philippine Free Press*, April 6, 2,11.

Locsin, Teodoro M. 1946b. "The New Social Cancer." *Philippine Free Press*, July 13, 4.

Locsin, Teodoro M. 1949. "Utter, Incredible Stupidity." *Philippine Free Press*, October 8, 2, 70.

Locsin, Teodoro. 1950a. "Democracy: Made in the Philippines." *Philippine Free Press*, 18 March, 2, 63.

Locsin, Teodoro M. 1950b. "Fil-American: The Story of a Relationship." *Philippine Free Press*, June 24, 2–3.

Locsin, Teodoro. 1969. "The Masks of Filipinos." *Philippine Free Press*, 30 August, 22, 24, 170, 172, 174.

Lopez, A. Ricardo, and Barbara Weinstein, eds. 2012. *The Making of the Middle Class: Toward a Transnational History*. Durham, NC.: Duke University Press.

Lopez, Oscar Moreno. 1951. "A Brief History of the Communist Movement in the Philippines." Doctoral Dissertation, Harvard University.

Lyons, Norbert. 1924. *The Philippine Problem Presented from a New Angle*. With an appendix containing complete texts of the Philippine Organic Act known as the Jones Law, the Treaty of Paris, the Constitution of the United States. Manila: American Chamber of Commerce of the Philippine Islands.

Magadia S.J., Jose J. 2005. "The Political Landscape of the '70s and Some Jesuit Responses to the Changing Times." In *Down from the Hill: Ateneo de Manila in the First Ten Years Under Martial Law, 1972-1982*, edited by Cristina J. Montiel and Susan Evangelista, 205–50. Quezon City: Ateneo de Manila University Press.

Maggay, Melba Padilla. 2011a. *A Clash of Cultures: Early American*

Protestant Missions and Filipino Religious Consciousness. Manila: Anvil Publishing.

Maggay, Melba Padilla. 2011b. "Confronting EDSA Fictions: Renewing our Collective Memory " Melba Padilla Maggay, Ph.D. Articles on cultural, missiological and social development issues, 12 June. https://mpmaggay.blogspot.com/2011/03/confronting-edsa-fictions-renewing-our.html.

Maggay, Melba Padilla. 2011c. "Diary from the Barricades." Melba Padilla Maggay. Ph.D. Articles on Culural, Missiological and Social Development issues, 12 June. http://mpmaggay.blogspot.com.au/2011/02/diary-from-barricades.html

Mahajani, Usha. 1971. *Philippine Nationalism, External Challenges and Filipino Response, 1565–1947*. St Lucia: University of Queensland Press.

Mahoney, James, and Richard Snyder. 1999. "Rethinking Agency and Structure in the Study of Regime Change." *Studies in Comparative International Development* 34 (3): 3–32.

Majul, Cesar Adib 1957. *The Political and Constitutional Ideas of the Philippine Revolution*. Quezon City: University of the Philippines Press.

Malcolm, George A. 1925. *Philippine Civics*. 3rd ed. revised. New York: D. Appleton and Company.

Marcos, Ferdinand E. 1965. Inauguration Address, President Marcos, 30 December. Official Gazette, Manila: Government of the Republic of the Philippines.

Marcos, Ferdinand E. 1969. Second Inaugural Address of President Marcos, 30 December. Official Gazette, Manila: Government of the Republic of the Philippines. https://www.officialgazette.gov.ph/1969/12/30/second-inaugural-address-of-president-marcos/.

Marcos, Ferdinand E. 1974. *The Democratic Revolution in the Philippines*. Englewood Cliffs, N.J., Prentice-Hall International.

Marcos, Ferdinand E. 1973a. Eighth State of the Nation Address, 21 September. Official Gazette, Manila: Government of the Republic of the Philippines.

Marcos, Ferdinand E. 1973b. *Notes on the New Society of the Philippines*. Manila: Marcos Foundation.

Matic Jr, Tomas. 1949. "A Citizen Writes to his President." *Philippine Free Press*, December 3, 50, 51.

McCallus, Joseph P. 1989. "The Myths of the New Filipino: Philippine Government Propaganda during the early years of Martial Law." *Philippine Quarterly of Culture and Society* 17 (2): 129–48.

McCoy, Alfred W., and Francisco A. Scarano. 2009. *The Colonial Crucible: Empire in the Making of the Modern American State*. Madison, Wisconsin: University of Wisconsin Press.

McCoy, Alfred W., Francisco A. Scarano, and Courtney Johnson. 2009. "On the Tropic of Cancer: Transitions and Transformations in the U.S. Imperial State." In *Colonial Crucible: Empire in the Making of the Modern*

American State, edited by Alfred W. McCoy and Francisco A. Scarano, 3–33. Madison: University of Wisconsin Press.

McKinley, William. 1900a. "Speech at Dinner of the Home Market Club, Boston, February 16, 1899." In *Speeches and Addresses of William McKinley, from March 1, 1897 to May 30, 1900*. New York: Doubleday and McClure.

McKinley, William. 1900b. "Speech at Fargo, North Dakota, Octer 13, 1899." In *Speeches and Addresses of William McKinley, from March 1, 1897 to May 30, 1900*. New York: Doubleday and McClure.

McKinley, William. 1898. "Message to the Congress of the United States, April 11, 1898." *In Messages and Papers of the Presidents*, edited by J.D. Richardson. Washington DC. 10: 139–50.

Mojares, Resil. 2006. *Brains of the Nation: Pedro Paterno, T.H. Pardo de Tavera, Isabelo de los Reyes and the Production of Modern Knowledge*. Manila: Ateneo University Press.

Montes, Vanetin G. 1947. "Bibles for Huks?" *Philippine Free Press*, November 22, 28.

Montiel, Cristina J. 1994. "Filipino Culture, Religious Symbols and Liberation Politics." In *Values in Philippine Culture and Education*, edited by Manuel B. Dy Jr, 115–20. Washington: The Council for Research in Values and Philosophy.

Moore, Barrington. 1967. *Social Origins of Dictatorship and Democracy: Lord and Peasant in the Making of the Modern World*. London: Lane.

Morgan, Edmund S. 1975. *American Slavery-American Freedom: the Ordeal of Colonial Virginia*. New York: Norton.

Mydans, Seth. 1985. "Marcos Declares He'll Call a Vote Early Next Year." *New York Times*, 4 November.

Nai, Alessandro. 2013. "The Cadillac, the Mother-in-Law, and the Ballot: Individual and Contextual Roots of Ambivalence in Swiss Direct Democracy." *Electoral Studies* 33: 292–306. doi: 10.1016/j.electstud.2013.06.010.

Nery, John. 2011. *Revolutionary Spirit: José Rizal in Southeast Asia*. Singapore: Institute of Southeast Asian Studies.

Nietzsche, Friedrich. 1994. *Nietzsche: 'On the Genealogy of Morality' and Other Writings*. Cambridge: Cambridge University Press.

Nietzsche, Friedrich. 2001. *Nietzsche: Beyond Good and Evil: Prelude to a Philosophy of the Future*. Cambridge: Cambridge University Press.

Norris, Pippa. 2011. *Democratic Deficit: Critical Citizens Revisited*. Cambridge: Cambridge University Press.

Nuera, Mariono G. 1946. "Democracy in the Philippines." *Philippine Free Press*, October 19, 20.

Ota, Yasu. 2016. "Philippine 'middle-Class Revolution' Highlights Need for Inclusive Growth." *Nikkei Asian Review*, 10 May. http://asia.nikkei.com/Politics-Economy/Policy-Politics/Philippine-middle-class-revolution-highlights-need-for-inclusive-growth?page=1.

Paley, Julia. 2002. "Toward an Anthropology of Democracy." *Annual Review of Anthropology* 31 (1): 469–96. doi: 10.1146/annurev.anthro.31.040402.085453.

Pamor, Florentino. 1947. "Annul the Elections!" *Philippine Free Press*, December 20, 45–6.

Panizza, Francisco. 2005. "Introduction: Populism and the Mirror of Democracy." In *Populism and the Mirror of Democracy*, edited by Francisco Panizza, 1–31. London: Verso.

Pappas, Gregory Fernando. 2008. *John Dewey's Ethics: Democracy as Experience*. Bloomington: Indiana University Press.

Pascual, Ricardo R. 1952. *Partyless Democracy*. Quezon City: University of the Philippines.

Patanne, E.P. 1960. "The Liberation Era Lingers on." *Progress*, 110–14.

Pertierra, Anna Cristina. 2017. "Celebrity Politics and Televisual Melodrama in the Age of Duterte." In *A Duterte Reader: Critical Essays on Rodrigo Duterte's Early Presidency*, edited by Nicole Curato, 21923. Quezon City: Ateneo de Manila University Press.

Pinches, Michael. 1996. "The Philippines' New Rich: Capitalist Transformation Amidst Economic Gloom." In *The New Rich In Asia: Mobile Phones, Mcdonalds and Middle-Class Revolution*, edited by Richard Robinson and David S.G. Goodman, 105–36. London: Routledge.

Pinches, Michael. 1997. "Elite Democracy, Development and People Power: Contending Ideologies and Changing Practices in Philippine Politics." *Asian Studies Review* 21 (2–3): 104–20. doi: 10.1080/03147539708713166.

Pinches, Michael. 2010. "The Making of Middle Class Civil Society in the Philippines." In *The Politics of Change in the Philippines*, edited by Yuko Kasuya and Nathan G. Quimpo, 284–312. Manila: Anvil Publishing.

Pye, Lucian W. 1985. *Asian Power and Politics: The Cultural Dimensions of Authority*. Cambridge, Mass.: Belknap Press.

Quezon, Manuel Luis. 1924. Quezon's Addresses: Extracts from the Speeches of Manuel L. Quezon, President of the Philippine Senate, in the United States and Philippines / published by the Philippine Commission of Independence. Manila: Bureau of Printing (Philippine information pamphlets vol. 1, no. 1).

Quezon, Manuel Luis. 1936. Message to the National Assembly, at the Opening of the First Session, National Assembly Hall, Legislative Building, edited by Manila Bureau of Printing. Manila: [American Historical Collection, ADMU].

Quezon, Manuel Luis. 1937. Third State of the Nation Address, Delivered at the Opening of the Second Session of the National Assembly, in the Assembly Hall, Legislative Building. Manila: https://www.officialgazette.gov.ph/1937/10/18/manuel-l-quezon-third-state-of-the-nation-address-october-18-1937/.

Quimpan, Esolastico S. 1950. "Texts of Democracy in the Philipines." *Philippine Free Press*, May 6.

Quimpo, Nathan Gilbert. 2008. *Contested Democracy and the Left in the Philippines after Marcos*. Manila: Ateneo de Manila University Press.

Rafael, Vicente L. 2000. *White Love and Other Events in Filipino History*. Durham: Duke University Press.

Rafael, Vicente L. 2003. "The Cell Phone and the Crowd: Messianic Politics in the Contemporary Philippines." *Philippine Political Science Journal* 24 (47): 3–36.

Rappler.com. 2016. "Transcript: Duterte on Obama." *Rappler*, 6 September. https://www.rappler.com/nation/145337-transcript-duterte-obama-human-rights.

Richardson, Jim June. 2013. *The Light of Liberty : Documents and Studies on the Katipunan, 1892–1897*. Quezon City, Philippines: Ateneo de Manila University Press.

Rivera, Temario C. 2001. "The Middle Classes and Democratisation in the Philippines: From the Asian Crisis to the Ouster of Estrada." In *Southeast Asian Middle Classes: Prospects for Social Change and Democratisation*, edited by Abdul Rahman Embond, 230–60. Bangi: Penerbit Universiti Kebangsaan Malaysia.

Rivera, Temario C. 2006. "The Crisis of Philippine Democracy." In *Asian New Democracies: The Philippines, South Korea and Taiwan Compared*, edited by Hsin-Huang Michael Hsiao, 17–38. Taipei: Taiwan Foundation for Democracy.

Roxas, Manuel. 1946. "Independence Day (Reprinted Speech)." *Philippine Free Press*, 13 July, 11–12.

Rueschemeyer, Dietrich, Evelyn Huber Stephens, and John D. Stephens. 1992. *Capitalist Development and Democracy*. Cambridge: Polity Press.

Russell, Charles Edward. 1923. "Filipinos Understand Democracy." *The Independent*, March 3, 9.

Saar, Martin. 2008. "Understanding Genealogy: History, Power, and the Self." *Journal of the Philosophy of History* 2 (3): 295–314. doi: 10.1163/187226308X335976.

Said, Edward W. 2003. *Orientalism*. Reprint with a new preface. ed. Harmondsworth: Penguin.

Salamanca, Bonifacio S. 1984. *The Filipino Reaction to American Rule, 1901–1913*: Quezon City: New Day Publishers.

Salonga, Jovito R. 2001. *A Journey of Struggle and Hope: The Memoir of Jovito R Salonga*. Quezon City: UP Center for Leadership, Citizenship and Democracy & Regina Publishing.

San Juan Jr, E. 2011. *Rizal in Our Time (Revised Edition): Essays in Interpretation*. Mandaluyong City: Anvil Publishing.

Sanchez, Leopoldo. 1950. "An Open Letter to Uncle Sam." *Philippine Free Press*, July 1, 62.

Satoshi, Nakano. 2004. "Gabriel L. Kaplan and US Involvement in Philippine

Electoral Democracy: A Tale of Two Democracies." *Philippine Studies* 52 (2): 149–78.
Schaffer, Frederic Charles. 1998. *Democracy in Translation: Understanding Politics in an Unfamiliar Culture*. Ithaca: Cornell University Press.
Schaffer, Frederic Charles. 2014. "Thin Descriptions: The Limits of Survey Research on the Meaning of Democracy." *Polity* 46 (3): 303–30. doi: 10.1057/pol.2014.14.
Scott, James C. 1985. *Weapons of the Weak: Everyday Forms of Peasant Resistance*. New Haven: Yale University Press.
Segovia, Raul E. 2008. *Inside the Mass Movement: A Political Memoir*. Pasig City: Anvil Publishing.
Shin, Doh Chull. 2006. Democratization: Perspectives from Global Citizenries. CSD Working Papers. UC Irvine: Center for the Study of Democracy.
Shin, Doh Chull, and Hannah June Kim. 2017. "Liberal Democracy as the End of History: Western Theories versus Eastern Asian Realities." *Asian Journal of Comparative Politics* 2 (2): 133–53. doi: 10.1177/2057891116673745.
Shiraishi, Takashi. 2008. "The Rise of Middle Classes in Southeast Asia." In *The Rise of Middle Classes in Southeast Asia*, edited by Takashi Shiraishi and Pasuk Phongpaichit. Kyoto: Kyoto University Press.
Silen, Ramon. 1946. "Why Ilocandia is Huk-Proof." *Philippine Free Press*, October 19, 14–15.
Simbulan, Roland. 2018. "The Historic Senate Vote of 16 September 1991: Looking Back and Looking Forward Twenty-Five Years After." *Philippine Studies: Historical and Ethnographic Viewpoints* 66 (1): 3–18. doi:10.1353/phs.2018.0001.
Singh, Amritjit, and Peter Schmidt. 2000. "On the Borders Between U. S. Studies and Postcolonial Theory." In *Postcolonial Theory and the United States: Race, Ethnicity, and Literature*, edited by Amritjit Singh and Peter Schmidt, 471. Jackson: University Press of Mississippi.
Slater, David. 2006. "Imperial Powers and Democratic Imaginations." *Third World Quarterly* 27 (8): 1369–86. doi: 10.1080/01436590601027230.
Southall, Roger. 2016. *The New Black Middle Class in South Africa*. Rochester, NY: Boydell & Brewer.
Spivak, Gayatri Chakravorty. 1988. "Can the Subaltern Speak? Speculations on Widow Sacrifice." In *Marxism and the Interpretation of Culture*, edited by Cary Nelson and Lawrence Crossberg, 271–313. London: Macmillan Education.
Stauffer, Robert B. 1990. "Philippine Democracy: Contradictions of Third World Democratization." *Kasarinlan* 3rd & 4th Quarters: 7–22.
Stobbe, Lineke. 2005. "Doing Machismo: Legitimating Speech Acts as a Selection Discourse." *Gender, Work & Organization* 12 (2): 105–23. doi: 10.1111/j.1468-0432.2005.00265.x.
Stoler, Ann Laura. 2006. *Haunted by Empire: Geographies of Intimacy in North American History*. Durham: Duke University Press.

Stoler, Ann Laura. 2016. *Duress: Imperial Durabilities in Our Times*. Durham: Duke University Press.
Stovall, Tyler. 2013. "Empires of Democracy." In *The Oxford Handbook of Postcolonial Studies*, edited by Graham Huggan, 67–90. Oxford: Oxford University Press.
Strobel, Elenita Mendoza. 1993. "On Becoming a Split Subject: A Personal Story." *PATMOS*, 8–11.
Suri, Jeremi. 2009. "The Limits of American Empire: Democracy and Militarism in the Twentieth and Twenty-first Centuries." In *Colonial Crucible: Empire in the Making of the Modern American State*, edited by Alfred W. McCoy and Francisco A. Scarano, 523–31. Madison, Wisconsin: The University of Wisconsin Press.
Suyko, Damasco. 1949. "Readers Comments." *Philippine Free Press*, December 17, 21.
SWS (Social Weather Stations). 2016. "2016 Exit Poll."
SWS (Social Weather Stations). 2019. "Voter Preference for Rodrigo Duterte, SWS Face-to-Face Surveys, National Capital Region by Class, Jan 8–10 to May 1–3, 2016." Quezon City.
Tan, Antonio S. 1981. "The Ideology of Pedro Abad Santos' Socialist Party." Asian Center, University of the Philippines Occasional Papers Series II (3).
Tan, Dominador M. 1941. "From a Speech in the National Assembly." *Philippine Magazine*, February, 59–61.
Terami-Wada, Motoe. 2014. *Sakdalistas' Struggle for Philippine Independence 1930–1945*. Quezon City: Ateneo de Manila University Press.
Thompson, Mark. 2002. "Female Leadership of Democratic Transitions in Asia." *Pacific Affairs* 75 (4): 535–55.
Thompson, Mark. 2010. "Populism and the Revival of Reform." *Contemporary Southeast Asia* 32 (1): 1–28.
Tocqueville, Alexis de. 2007. *Democracy in America (Abridged Edition)*. HarperCollins Publishers. New York.
Tormey, Simon. 2018. "Populism: Democracy's Pharmakon?" *Policy Studies* 39 (3): 260–73.
Totanes, Stephen Henry S. 2005. "Student Activism in the Pre-Martial Law Era: An Historical Overview." In *Down from the Hill: Ateneo de Manila in the First Ten Years Under Martial Law, 1972–1982*, edited by Cristina J. Montiel and Susan Evangelista, 1–54. Quezon City: Ateneo de Manila University Press.
Treyes, Artemio A. 1948. "We Will Not Forget." *Philippine Free Press*, July 3, 32.
Turner, Mark. 1995. "Imagining the Middle Class in the Philippines." *Pilipinas* 25: 87–101.
Tutay, Filemon V. 1946. "Why They Revolt". *Philippine Free Press*, March 30, 5.
Twain, Mark. 1901. "To the Person Sitting in Darkness." *North American Review* CLXXIL: 161–76.

Twain, Mark, and Jim Zwick. 1992. *Mark Twain's Weapons of Satire: Anti-Imperialist Writings on the Philippine–American War*. Syracuse: Syracuse University Press.

Ty, Leon. 1947. "More Ticklish than the Huk Problem." *Philippine Free Press*, January 16, 2.

Urbinati, Nadia. 2014. *Democracy Disfigured: Opinion, Truth, and the People*. Cambridge, Mass.: Harvard University Press.

Usul, Ali Resul. 2011. "Academia and the Legitimising of International Politics: Studies of Democratisation and World Politics." *Third World Quarterly* 32 (9): 1691–702. doi: 10.1080/01436597.2011.618655.

Valencia, Teodoro F. 1973. "Discipline Can Be Fun." *Expressweek*, 25 January, 7.

Van Meter, H. H. 1900. *The Truth About the Philippines from Official Records and Official Sources*. Chicago: Liberty League.

Velarde Jr, Herminio. 1947. "The Greatness of America." *Philippine Free Press*, March 22, 27.

Velasco, Renato S. 1997. "Philippine Democracy: Promise and Performance." In *Democratization in Southeast and East Asia*, edited by Anek Laothamatas, 77–112. Singapore: Institute of Southeast Asian Studies.

Vilamin, Vincente. 1948. "Bulwark against Communism." *Philippine Free Press*, February 7, 18–19.

Villa Jr, Julio. 1950. "What US Filipinos Think of the Philippine Government." *Philippine Free Press*, July 22, 45.

Villegas, Celso M., and Myung-Ji Yang. 2013. "Making Narratives of Revolution: Democratic Transition and the Language of Middle-Class Identity in the Philippines and South Korea, 1970s–1987." *Critical Asian Studies* 45 (3): 335–64. doi: 10.1080/14672715.2013.829308.

Webb, Adele, and Nicole Curato. 2019. "Populism in the Philippines." In *Populism Around the World: A Comparative Perspective*, edited by Daniel Stockemer, 49–65. Cham: Springer.

Weisbrode, Kenneth. 2012. *On Ambivalence: The Problems and Pleasures of Having it Both Ways*. Cambridge, Mass.: MIT Press.

Werbner, Richard. 2002. "Introduction. Postcolonial Subjectivities: The Personal, the Political and the Moral." In *Postcolonial Subjectivities in Africa*, 1–21. London: Zed Books.

Whitehead, Laurence. 2002. *Democratization: Theory and Experience*. Oxford: Oxford University Press.

Williams, Eugene. 1949. "A Government Run Like Hell." *Philippine Free Press*, September 17, 25.

Wurfel, David. 1990. "Transition to Political Democracy in the Philippines: 1978-1988." In *Democratic Transition and Consolidation in Southern Europe, Latin America and Southeast Asia*, edited by Diane Ethier, 110–35. London: Palgrave.

Ziforun, Dariuš. 2015. "The Diversity of Milieu in Diversity Studies." In *Routledge International Handbook of Diversity Studies*, edited by Steven Vertovec, 98–105. New York: Routledge.

Index

A
Abueva, J. V., 46, 47
Africa, 40
Agoncillo, T., 97, 148, 152
agriculture, xi, 56, 83–4, 89
Aguinaldo, E., 34, 45, 60, 64, 78, 97
Alcid, V., 138
Althusser, L., 17
altruism, 35, 128, 148, 170
ambivalence:
  case for, 194–6
  causes, 194
  definition, 5–6
  and democracy, xiii, 5–11, 15, 23, 24, 27–30, 70, 75, 98, 103, 131–43, 146, 157, 163, 167, 178, 182, 185, 188, 191–2, 193, 194–7
  and populist leadership, 177–89, 196, 197
  see also middle class and ambivalence
America *see* US
American Federation of Labor, 89
Amsterdam, xiii
Andersen, H. C., 107
Anderson, B., 19, 20, 175, 191
Anderson, T. M., 57
Angeles, J. D., 139
Angeles David, P., 205(*n*10)
anti-colonialism, 35, 37, 38, 74, 148
anti-democratic politics, 28, 29, 103, 131, 133, 139, 149
anti-imperialism, 28, 148
anxiety, xii, 24, 27, 28, 108, 121–4, 143, 155, 168, 185, 187, 193
Apilado, M. C., 46
Appleman Williams, W., 41
Aquino, B. (Nonoy), xi, 157, 161, 162, 172, 184, 199(*n*1)
Aquino, C. (Cory), x, 142, 162, 164, 165, 169, 174–6, 177, 178, 180, 181, 184, 199(*n*1), 207(*n*5)
Aquino, M., 121, 122

Aquino III, B. (Noynoy), xi, 161, 172, 184, 185, 186, 199(*n*1)
Arcellana, E ., 158, 159
Argentina, 165
Aristotle, 1, 11
Arlington Cemetery, 53–54
Armitage, R., 169, 207(*n*7)
Asia, 5, 33, 40, 104, 107, 112, 142, 201(*n*3)
Asia Raya, 201(*n*3)
Asian financial crisis, 180
Astorga, C. A., 174
Ateneo de Manila University, xiv, 24, 155, 173, 206(*n*8)
authoritarian:
  governance, 6, 9
  manoeuvring, 101
  nostalgia, 4, 193
  regime, 28
  rule, 165
  rulers, 194
  system, 28
authoritarianism, 4, 29, 167, 188, 193
  limits, 161–3
  middle class acquiescence, 155–9
authority, 3, 17, 20, 26, 33, 36, 49, 55, 61, 65, 70, 74, 80, 97, 101, 106, 111, 143, 150, 156, 158, 159, 163, 167, 176, 187, 188, 195, 196, 187, 196
autocratic leadership, 4
autonomy, 28, 65, 87, 94, 103, 149

B
Bacolod City, 118
balance of power, 45, 86, 203(*n*4)
bandolerismo (banditry), 85, 86
Bantayan, 124
barrios (neighbourhoods), 109
Barrows, D., 60–1
Bataan, 104, 182
Batangas (Western), 138
Baum, B. D., 42

Bauman, Z., 196
Bayan, ix, x
Beers, B. F., 40, 45, 51, 201(*n*6)
Bell, D., 140
Bell Trade Act, 125, 126, 127, 129, 135, 204–5(*n*5), 205(*n*6)
beliefs, 2, 6, 11, 14, 17, 24, 39, 180, 192, 195
Bellin, E., 14
Bello, W., 185
benevolence, 5, 59, 79, 123, 128, 148
Berlin, I., 107
Berlin Conference, 40
Beveridge, A. J., 40, 55–6
Birdsall, N., 1
Blair, E., 60
Bohannan, C. T. R., 63
Bohlen, C., 61
Bolsonaro, J., 1
Bonifacio, A., 149, 172, 179, 182, 205(*n*2)
Bonner, R., 160
Borromeo, D. P., 121
Boston, 47, 49, 52
Bourdieu, P., 15
Brauer, J. C., 43
Brazil, 1, 165
Britain *see* United Kingdom
Brummit, M., 91
Bryan, W. J., 47–8, 57, 202(*n*11)
Bulacan, 45, 205(*n*8)
Bush, G., 161, 170, 207(*n*5)
Buss, C. A., 106–7, 204(*n*2)
Butler, J., 17

C
caciques, 80, 205(*n*10)
caciquism, 80
Calabang, C. T., 138
Calhoun, C., 16, 18, 19, 20
California, 90
Cammack, P., 159
Canberra, xiii
Capen, N., 52
Capistrano, S. R., 130–1
capital (economics), 84, 101, 102, 115, 126, 127, 129, 156
capitalism, 151, 165
Cardinal Sin, 177, 180, 181
Carmack, E. W., 51
Carnegie, A., 42
Castoriadis, C., 18–19

Catholic Church, 36, 45, 163, 173, 183, 185, 199(*n*6)
Cebu City, 25, 78, 129, 139, 203(*n*1)
censorship, 56–8, 161, 176
Chang, Y., 4, 199(*n*4)
charisma, 176
Chavarria, D., 121
Chen, X., 21-2
Chicago, 47, 55, 57
chicanery, 89, 191
China, ix, 21, 40, 90, 133, 193
Christianity, 38, 42, 50, 51
Citizens League (Makati), 146
citizenship, 13, 43, 44, 47, 89, 121
civic:
    culture argument, 147
    Education Program, 62
    sphere, xi, 27, 108, 131, 137, 143
    virtue(s), 54, 61, 121
civil:
    rights, 153, 185
    society, x, xii, 42, 165, 167, 176, 181, 195, 199(*n*6), 200(*n*6)
civilization, 33, 36, 40, 51, 53, 54, 55, 75, 82
Clark Air Field, 104, 107, 166, 169, 207(*n*5)
Claudio, L., 146, 167, 173, 174, 177
Cleveland, G., 98
Clyde, P. H., 40, 45, 51, 201–2(*n*6)
Code, L., 12
Cold War, 105, 131, 136, 139, 142, 144, 147, 159, 165, 172
Collective Bargaining Law, 101
Colmenares, N. J., ix
colonial:
    authority/ies, 35, 61, 65, 195
    bureaucracy, 74, 89
    democracy, xiii, 4, 27, 58–70, 75, 95, 103, 165
    discourses/narrative, 21, 23, 52, 55, 60, 74, 149, 204(*n*1)
    government, 36, 75, 87, 88
    history(ies), 13, 24, 168
    order, 27, 103
    "Other", 13, 37
    politics, 97
    power, 34, 37, 63, 82
    rule, viii, 21, 33, 52, 59, 65, 75, 108, 193
    subject(s), 13, 37
    subjugation, 39, 61, 67, 89, 186
    tutelage, 93

colonialism, 4, 13, 16, 21, 22, 24, 26, 29, 39, 40, 41, 52, 63, 105, 106, 146, 147, 153, 175, 196
commerce, 35, 40, 42, 90, 93
communism, 100, 112, 132, 134, 136, 139, 141, 165, 176
communist movement, 133, 176, 203(*n*4)
Communist Party of the Philippines (CPP), ix, xii, 93, 131, 151, 154, 155, 163, 164, 203(*n*2), 206(*n*4)
Connell, R. W., 13, 22
conquest, xiii, 5, 22, 34, 45, 46, 47, 50, 58, 97
Constantino, R., 61, 147, 148, 176, 177
Coolidge, C., 67, 68
Cornelio, J. S., xiii
Coronel, S., 184
corruption, xii, 36, 47, 49, 89, 94, 112, 113, 122, 140, 150, 151, 157, 174, 180, 181, 194
Cotterell, A., 45, 64
Cuba, 41, 44, 48, 57, 58, 202(*n*8)
Cullinane, M., 11, 74, 192
Curaming, R., 146
Curato, N., 196

D
DA (Democratic Alliance), 206(*n*4)
 and the Hukbalahap, 132–40
Daily Bulletin, 129
Daniels, J. W., 54
Davao, 3, 186, 187–188
David, S., 109
Dejung, C., 13, 36
Del Pilar, M. H., 39
Delmendo, S., 62, 63
democracy:
 and US, xiii, 41–42, 44, 118, 139, 142, 144, 147
 challenges, 2, 42, 139, 184
 colonial, xiii, 4, 27, 75, 95, 103, 165
 colonial school, 58–70
 concept, 7, 18, 41, 101, 128, 139, 144, 192
 critique, 18, 20
 cynicism/ loss of faith, 130, 140, 184, 185
 discursive tool, 201(*n*12)
 Eurocentric theory, 21
 evaluative frames, 9, 18, 194
 failure, 14, 29, 30, 185, 188

 ideal, 106, 144, 192
 and imperialism, 23, 56, 163
 institutions, 1, 18, 51, 63, 186, 206(*n*7)
 liberal, 13, 159, 165, 190, 196, 199(*n*4), 206(*n*7)
 literature, 190
 normative theories, 11–14
 paradox, 27, 75, 103, 193
 in Philippines, 2, 3, 7, 29, 101, 102, 123, 124, 130–1, 134, 135, 136, 137, 139, 140, 144, 145, 148, 149, 153, 155, 156, 162, 165, 168, 174, 176, 178, 180, 181, 185, 188, 193–4, 198, 204(*n*4)
 and political parties, 102, 103
 and populism, 150, 166, 196–8
 representative, 7, 42
 theories, 12
 Third Wave, 165
 Western, 157, 159, 165, 178, 201(*n*12)
 see also ambivalence; freedom; middle class
democratic:
 agency, xi, 14, 17, 21, 24, 30, 89–96, 125, 188, 191
 ambivalence, viii, xiii, 5–11, 15, 24, 28, 29, 75, 103, 143, 167, 178, 188, 191, 193, 194, 195, 197
 aspiration(s), 2, 27, 83, 103, 108, 119, 132, 143, 153, 156, 163, 174, 186, 194, 195
 deficit, 6
 discourses, viii, 34–9, 75, 83, 102, 103, 143, 159, 199(*n*6)
 empire, 5, 33–70
 freedom(s), xiii, 4, 89, 143, 193
 governance, 7, 176, 192
 ideal(s), xiii, 1, 4, 6, 12, 46, 178, 191
 idealism, 5, 46, 194
 imaginary, xii, xiii, 11, 15, 16, 17–20, 25, 27, 28, 29, 39, 42, 108, 143, 163, 177, 188, 191, 192
 imperialism, 5, 13
 politics, 1, 3, 10, 11, 29, 30, 123–4, 132, 143, 177–8, 182, 191, 193, 198
 power, 4, 30
 principle(s), 87, 98, 132, 157, 161, 188
 processes, 131, 161, 181

discourses *(continued)*
  reform(s), 156, 186
  regime(s), xii, 30, 156, 194
  renewal, 3, 188
  representation, 82
  revolution, 41, 149, 156
  right(s), 3, 132, 135, 160, 162
  transition, 165
  tutelage, viii, 4, 11, 27, 63–9, 97, 192
  values, 49, 184
  see also middle class
democratization, 7, 9, 11, 12, 14, 18, 20, 28, 159, 165, 176, 177, 190, 200(*n*6), 206(*n*7)
Dewey, G., 45, 51
Dewey, J., xiii, 32
Dian, B., 124
Dickinson, J. M., 77, 78, 80, 81, 82, 83, 84, 85–6, 87, 88, 98
dictatorship, ix, x, xi, 7, 99, 160, 164, 165, 168, 171, 187, 200(*n*7)
differential knowledge, 108
dignity, 28, 29, 43, 62, 63, 67, 73, 80, 87, 93, 129, 143, 146, 148, 150, 168, 170, 171, 173, 179, 180, 184, 185, 186, 187
Diliman Commune, 205(*n*3)
discipline, 2, 4, 5, 17, 26, 66, 69, 154, 155, 156, 157, 158, 159, 186, 187, 188
dissent, 74, 99, 100, 143, 163, 182–3, 187
domination, 17, 23, 26, 39, 67, 69, 92, 104, 127, 147, 154
Doty, R. L., 22, 23, 34, 52, 53, 109, 140, 200(*n*12)
Duterte, R., viii, 1–4, 29, 173, 177–89, 193, 197
Dy Jr, M. B., 173, 174

E
East Asia, 10, 33, 40
economic:
  activity, 43, 176
  development, 14, 56, 101
  growth, 12, 175
  independence, 93, 127
  interests, 82, 90
  prosperity, 1, 184
economy, 13, 36, 37, 44, 90, 99, 127, 135, 146, 149, 157, 161, 175, 176, 179, 180, 194, 205(*n*6)

EDSA revolution, x, 28, 125, 164, 165, 166–168, 173, 174, 176, 178, 181, 182, 183, 184, 186, 201(*n*15), 207(*n*10)
  post-EDSA, 167, 168, 174, 175, 177, 184, 186, 191
EDSA Shrine, 173, 181, 182, 183, 207(*n*10)
education, 8, 12, 25, 35, 38, 51, 56, 61, 62, 63, 89, 93, 103, 106, 108, 145, 203(*n*1), 207(*n*3)
egalitarianism, 41, 44
Egypt, 57
Eight-Hour Labor Law, 101
Eisenhower, D. D., 142
electoral politics, 188, 191, 203(*n*4)
elite(s), 10, 14, 22, 27, 44, 52, 61, 64, 65, 74, 89, 92, 93–103, 106, 108, 120, 131, 132, 133, 135, 137, 141, 147, 148, 149, 150, 155, 162, 165, 166, 168, 174, 175, 178, 179, 184, 185, 186, 191, 195, 196, 203(*n*14), 205(*n*9)
empire, 4, 5, 12, 13, 26, 33, 34, 36, 40–9, 50, 59, 63, 104, 202(*n*8)
England *see* United Kingdom
Enlightenment, 38, 39
Enrile, J., 170, 176
epistemic violence, 13, 21
equality, 3, 36, 37, 38–9, 41, 84, 101, 143, 183
Estabaya, I. R., 139
esteem, 29, 122, 188
Estrada, J., 28–9, 171, 177–183, 184, 186
Europe, 12, 13, 21, 32, 35, 36, 37, 38, 41, 42, 43, 48, 106, 165
exceptionalism, 5, 50 *see also* US exceptionalism
exploitation, 13, 26, 34, 36, 126, 162
Ezrahi, Y., 18, 19

F
Far Eastern University, 139
Feleo, J., 135
Fergusson, R. D., 83
Fernandez, A. M., 139
Filipino:
  agency, 34, 111, 114, 125, 127, 148
  character defence, 78–82
  culture, 93, 107
  defamation(s) of personhood, 4, 52–3, 59, 74, 79, 81, 82, 83, 91,

111, 112, 113, 114, 115, 116, 122, 168, 173
intellectuals, 36, 37, 38, 45, 147, 149
moral bankruptcy, 121–2
moral reconstruction/restoration, xii, 173–7
native 22, 34, 36, 187
people, xi, 60, 62, 68, 69, 75, 79, 81, 82, 87, 106, 112, 122, 128, 129, 145, 146, 152, 156, 158, 159, 162, 170, 181, 187, 191, 204(*n*1)
self-government, 26, 43, 49, 53, 56, 57, 59, 65, 66, 80, 82, 86, 88, 100, 112, 116, 121, 122, 143, 191, 193
subject(s) 23, 27, 28, 29, 37, 108, 111, 116, 119, 121, 122, 143, 150, 156, 168, 173, 174
subjectivity, 70, 83, 111, 120–1
Filipino-American War, 62
First World War, 40, 79
Fishkin, S. F., 69
Flores, A., 100
Forbes, W. C., 67, 78–9, 81
foreign policy, 22, 33, 44, 47, 54
Foucault, M., 17, 21, 24, 201(*n*14)
France, 13, 41, 45, 202(*n*7)
free trade, 90, 93
freedom:
  abuse, 2, 4, 3, 184
  and America, 5, 32, 42, 44, 47, 52, 54–6, 64, 67, 69, 70, 87, 98
  concept, ix, xiii, 2, 13, 17, 37, 39, 52, 54, 70
  and democracy, xii, xiii, 2–3, 4, 23, 27, 29, 52, 54, 69, 70, 89, 98, 101, 102, 108, 143, 163, 165, 180, 184
  discursive contradictions, xii, 39
  ideal, xiii, 128, 190
  imaginaries, 39
  Philippines, ix, 2, 3, 45, 47, 54–6, 64, 67, 69, 87, 93, 94, 98, 101, 106, 116, 119, 121, 128–9, 135, 136, 139, 140, 143, 153, 163, 165, 167, 171, 172, 174, 175, 180, 184, 187, 188, 190, 193, 207(*n*4)
  political, 29, 39, 93
  pursuit, xii, 27, 28, 93, 116, 121, 139, 143, 163, 193

Tagalog meanings, 39, 201(*n*5)
Freeman, C., 199(*n*2)
French Revolution, 38
Friend, T., 103
Frohnen, B. P., 41
Fukuyama, F., 165

G
Gardner, W. H., 66
genealogical narrative, 15
genealogy, 23–4, 192, 201(*n*13), 201(*n*14)
geopolitics, 131, 202(*n*7)
Germany, xiv, 51, 202(*n*7)
GDP, 180, 185
Gilded Age, 42
globalization 15, 20
Go, J., 22, 50, 63, 65
Gramsci, A., 21
Grant, J., 18
Great Depression, 89, 90
Greece, 57, 106
Gregory, D., 21, 22
Gripaldo, R. M., 38, 39
Guerrero, A., 151, 206(*n*4)
Guillermo, R., 200(*n*6)
Gutman, H. G., 43
Gutting, G., 17

H
Harding, W., 67
Harris, D., 42
Harris, S. K., 26, 41, 43, 50, 51, 53, 54, 59
Hau, C. S., 10, 66, 108, 146, 147, 149
Hawaii, 94, 161, 164, 166, 201(*n*6)
Hawes, H. B., 93
Hayden, J. R., 59
Health Alliance for Democracy (HEAD), x
Hedman, E-L. E., 4, 154, 165, 178, 180, 181, 199–200(*n*6)
hegemony, 10, 21, 59, 96, 165, 191, 200(*n*6)
Heiman, R., 199(*n*2)
hierarchy/ies, xii, xiii, 3, 12, 22, 39, 52, 93, 178, 183, 201(*n*12)
Hilario, J., 129
Hilfrich, F., 44, 46, 47, 49, 54, 55, 56, 202(*n*9)
Hogan, T., xiv, 146
Hoganson, K. L., 42, 44
Holland, 202(*n*7)

Homma, M. (General), 104
honesty, 43, 51
Hong Kong, 38, 45
honour, 54, 170, 202(*n*10)
Hukbalahap (Huks), 105, 110, 132–40, 142, 149, 205(*n*7), 205(*n*8), 205(*n*10)
Hukbong Bayan Laban sa mga Hapon (People's Army Against the Japanese), 132–140
human rights, 3, 25, 160–1, 179, 187, 197
humanity, 20, 38, 49, 53, 55
humiliation, xii, 24, 70, 89–91, 103, 122, 152, 176
Hungary, 1
Huntington, S., 9, 206(*n*7)

I
ideology, 11, 13, 18, 41, 94, 139, 155, 156, 167
Ileto, R. C., 35, 37, 39, 59, 61, 64, 69, 100, 147, 148, 150, 153, 156, 157, 201(*n*5), 205(*n*2), 206(*n*3)
ilustrados (educated class), 26, 36, 37, 38, 39, 61, 64, 74, 148, 205(*n*2)
imperial power, 4, 42, 47, 59, 108
imperialism, xiii, 4–5, 13, 28, 40, 46–9, 68, 69, 112, 151, 165, 173, 192, 193, 202(*n*9), 202(*n*12)
India, 90
indignation, xii, 27, 75–88, 89, 94, 103, 204(*n*1)
indignity/ies, xi, 24, 38, 75–88, 92–3, 108, 121–4, 141, 143, 156, 167, 198
indio (native subject), 63
individual rights, 158, 196
Indonesia, 180, 201(*n*3)
Indonesian Revolution, 201(*n*3)
industrialization, 43
inequality, 23, 36, 179, 185, 196
Inglehart, R., 200(*n*10)
interpellation(s), 17, 20, 146, 174, 186
intimidation, 34, 129, 134, 136
intolerance, 33, 43
Iran, 160
Isaacs, H., 140
Isang Bansa, Isang Diwa (One Nation, One Spirit), 156
Ivie, R. L., 52

J
Jacinto, E., 38, 39, 201(*n*4)
Jakarta, 201(*n*3)
Japan, 57, 105, 172, 204(*n*2)
Japanese occupation, 104, 105, 109, 131, 132, 133, 139, 204(*n*1), 204(*n*2)
Jenkins, S., 90, 94, 126, 127, 204–5(*n*5)
Joaquin, L., 83–84
Johnson, C., 41, 59, 60
Johnson, L., 151
Jones Law, 66, 97, 203(*n*14)
justice, 32, 36, 55, 62, 101, 113, 170, 176, 195
  social, 102, 103, 179, 203(*n*4)

K
kabayan (countrymen), 179
Kaczyński, J., 1
Kalayaan (freedom), ix, 39, 64
Kalayaan (newspaper), 38
Kaplan, A., 26, 41
Karl, R. E., 33
Karnow, S., 89, 104, 134, 136, 140, 142, 166, 169, 207(*n*5)
Katipunan:
  Revolution, 61, 182
  revolutionary society, 38, 39, 64, 149, 200(*n*9)
Keane, J., xiii, 7, 42, 52, 193, 194, 197, 202(*n*12), 208(*n*1)
Kerkvliet, B. J., 99, 132, 133, 134, 135, 136, 205(*n*8)
Kim, H. J., 199(*n*4)
Kimura, M. 10, 108, 167
King, C., 57
Kolakowski, L., 195–6
Koo, H., 14
Korea, 160
Kramer, P. A., 33, 47, 52, 53, 54, 63, 64, 201(*n*1)
Krause, K., 17
Krauze, E., 208(*n*1)
Kurihara, K., 203(*n*4)
Kurlantzick, J., 1
Kusaka, W., 10, 161, 167, 174, 177, 178, 179, 180, 181, 182, 183, 188, 192, 196, 207(*n*10)

L
La Solidaridad, 36
La Vanguardia, 84

labour, 13, 86, 91, 100, 101, 102, 156, 203(*n*4)
Laclau, E., 196
Lacson, A., 145
Lande, C.H., 4, 178, 179, 180, 199(*n*3)
landowner(s), 64, 84, 108, 140
Lansdale, E., 141, 142
Laplanche, J. 6
Laurel–Langley Treaty, 205(*n*6)
Le Roy, J., 65
leadership, xi, xii, 3, 4, 75, 77, 92, 132, 140, 141, 142, 156, 162, 163, 164, 168, 176–89, 194
Lagardo, B., 76
Lefort, C., 195
legitimacy, xii, 6, 21, 59, 64, 103, 150, 155, 156, 163, 166, 179, 182, 188
Lenin, 153
Lewis, A., 206(*n*2)
Libel Law, 73, 87
liberal
 democracy, 13, 159, 165, 190, 196, 199(*n*4), 206(n7)
 democratic discourse, 199(*n*6)
 democratic theory, 12
 democratic values, 184
Liberal Party, xi, 150, 161, 164, 204(*n*1)
liberalism, 167
liberation, 22, 35, 47, 54, 55, 105, 128, 167, 168, 172
liberty, 2, 26, 39, 40, 41, 45, 50, 54–6, 62, 65, 67, 87, 90, 97, 98, 99, 100, 101, 102, 111–21, 158, 166, 175, 188, 197
Liechty, M., 199(*n*2)
Lincoln, A., 55, 119
Lipset, S. M., 11, 43
Locsin, T., 109, 123, 124, 134, 145, 146, 204(*n*4), 205(*n*10)
Lopez, A. R., 14, 16
Lopez, O. M., 101, 133, 205(*n*7)
Lopez, S. P., 160
Luzon, 55, 57, 58, 78, 90, 92, 99, 104, 110, 131, 132, 133, 134, 135, 136, 138, 162, 203(*n*4), 205(*n*2)
Lyons, N., 66, 68, 69

M
Mabini, A., 37, 73
Macapagal, D., 150, 160
Macapagal-Arroyo, G., 181, 182, 207(*n*9)

MacArthur, D., 104, 105
Mactan, 182
Madrid, 36
Magadia S. J., J. J., 152
Magellan, F., 34
Maggay, M., xii, xiii, 43, 44, 50, 51, 164, 167
Magsaysay, R. 141–2, 146, 149–50, 155
Mahajani, U., 63, 65, 67
Mahoney, J., 15
Majul, C. A., 61, 73
Makati, ix, x, 146, 157, 162, 163
Malacañan, 123
Malacanang Palace, 183, 207(*n*5)
Malaysia, 10
Malcolm, G. A. 62
Malolos, 45, 64, 100, 203(*n*1), 205(*n*8)
Manglapus, R., 169
Manifesto of Freedom, Democracy, and Sovereignty, 162, 206(*n*8)
Manila, ix, x, xi, xiii, xiv, 2, 7, 24, 25, 33, 35, 38, 45, 49, 51, 56, 60, 62, 65, 73, 77, 78, 82, 90, 91, 97, 99, 100, 102, 104, 105, 108, 127, 129, 133, 134, 151, 156, 160, 161, 162, 164, 177, 178, 185, 188, 201(*n*15), 203(*n*1), 204(*n*2), 205(*n*10)
Manila Bay, x, xiii, 33, 45, 49, 55, 60, 77, 99, 106, 142
Mao Zedong, 151, 153
Marcos, F., ix, x, xi, xii, 1, 2, 3, 4, 28, 109, 142, 145, 149–64, 166, 167, 166, 167, 168, 170, 171, 174, 175, 176, 178, 179, 180, 184, 186, 188, 193, 197, 200(*n*7), 201(*n*15), 206(*n*3), 206(*n*4), 206(*n*6), 206(*n*1) *see also* martial law
 "New Society", 153, 155, 156, 157, 159
 populist nationalism, 149–52
Marcos, I., 160, 179
martial law, 109, 151, 152–63, 172, 178, 184
Marx, K., 15, 16, 153
masa (masses), 179
Matic Jr, T., 139, 140
McBride, W. L., 38
McCallus, J. P., 156
McCosham, H. D. (Sergeant), 58
McCoy, A. W., 26, 41, 59, 60

McKinley, W., 34, 44, 45, 46, 47, 48, 49, 51, 52, 54, 55, 56, 57, 58, 63, 88, 123, 203(n14)
McNamara, R., 160
McNutt, P. V., 104, 125, 127
Melchor, A., 160
Mendoza Strobel, E., 107, 108
Merrit, W., 82
Mexican-American War, 42
Mexico, 52
middle class (Philippines):
  acknowledgment, 200(n7)
  actors, 11, 25, 27, 103, 200(n6)
  agency, 9, 10, 11, 14, 197
  ambivalence, 5–11, 15, 24, 28, 29, 70, 75, 108, 132, 143, 157, 163, 167, 178, 182, 188, 191–2, 193, 195, 197–8
  Americanization, 108, 143
  and authoritarianism, 1, 155–9, 161–2, 193
  and colonial rule, 21, 27, 74, 77, 89, 97, 101, 103
  commitment to democracy, 6, 14
  concept, 15–16
  consciousness, 16, 23
  debates, 15–16
  and democracy, xi, xii, xiii, 1–2, 4, 6, 9, 10, 11, 12, 15, 27, 74–5, 132, 165, 166, 176–7, 181, 185, 193–4, 197
  democratic change, 1, 165, 166, 174, 177, 199(n6)
  democratic imaginary see democratic (imaginary)
  democratic normative theories, 11–14
  democratic orientations, 10, 15
  discourses/narratives, 16, 137, 143, 149, 167, 192
  and dominant powers, 199(n6)
  ethnography, 3, 199(n2)
  growth, 108, 145–6
  and imperialism, 97, 193
  and independent nation-state, 11, 89
  intelligentsia, 26, 36
  lack of analysis, 13–14
  moral leadership, xii, 93
  narratives, xii, 1, 2, 9, 10, 11, 14, 15, 16, 25, 27, 75, 149, 166, 167, 173, 182, 183, 186, 192
  norms, 16, 93
  and otherness, 12
  and People Power, 183, 185
  political beliefs, 2, 6, 11, 14, 192
  political consciousness, 10, 167, 194
  political subjectivity see political (subjectivity)
  postcolonial, 15, 27
  role in socio-political change, 10–11, 12, 14, 92, 193
  values, 12, 93, 200(n7)
middle classness, 12, 14, 15, 16
Military Bases Agreement, 125, 151
Mindanao, 38, 52, 67, 131
modernization, 9, 11, 12, 37, 56, 145
  theory, 1, 11–12, 147
Modi, N., 197
Mojares, R., 11, 34, 35, 36, 38, 59, 192
Mondale, W., 160
Montes, V., 205(n10)
Montiel, C., 173
Moody, D., 42
Moore, B., 14
Moorer, T., 160
morality, 93, 152, 168, 173, 178, 181
Morgan, E. S., 42
Moro province, 81
Morton, S. G., 42
Motadel, D., 13, 36
Mouffe, C., 208(n1)
Movement for the Advancement of Nationalism (MAN), 151
Movement for Good Governance, x
Mutual Defense Treaty, 151
Mydans, S., 206(n1)
mythology/ies, 35, 39, 167

N
National Democratic Front, ix
National Democrats (Natdems), 154, 155, 162, 164, 177, 206(n8), 206–7(n3)
National Humiliation Day, 89–91
National Peasants Union, 136, 137
nationalism, 19, 61, 63, 93, 131, 146–52, 168, 186, 205(n6)
nationhood, 33, 41, 110, 206(n6)
neoliberalism, 192
Nery, J., 201(n3)
New Deal, 101
New People's Army (NPA), 151, 154
New York, 48, 98, 122
New York Times, 206(n1)
Newsweek, 151, 206(n5)

Ngo Dinh Diem, 142
Nicaragua, 160
Nietzsche, F., 24, 201(*n*13), 201(*n*14)
Non-Government Organizations (NGOs), 169, 177, 179, 183
Norris, P., 6
Nuera, M. G., 121

O
Obama, B., 186, 187
occidentalism, 22
Oksala, J., 17
oligarchy, 10, 108, 143, 175, 191, 197
Olongapo, 170, 207(*n*6)
oppression, 22, 28, 40, 44, 48, 55, 80, 128, 133, 139, 173, 191, 201(*n*3)
Orbán, V., 1, 197
orderliness, 43, 51
Organic Act *see* Jones Law
orientalism, 21, 52
Osmeña, S., 78, 82, 89, 93, 97, 132, 134, 204(*n*1)
Osterhammel, J., 13, 36
Ota, Y., 185
Otis, E., 57, 58
Ou Jujia, 33

P
Pace, E. J., 50
Pacific, xiii, 34, 40, 48, 51, 89, 142, 171, 192, 202(*n*6), 202(*n*7)
Paley, J., 18
Pamalakaya-Pilipinas, x
Pamor, F., 122
Pampanga, 107, 135, 137, 205(*n*10)
Panizza, F., 146, 179, 196
Pappas, G. F., xiii
Pardo de Tavera, T. H., 75, 76, 77, 203(*n*1)
parity provision, 124–31, 205(*n*6)
Park, C., 4, 199(*n*4)
Park, C. H., 159
Partido Federalista (Federal Party), 75–6, 78
Partido Nacional Progresista (National Progressive Party), 76, 77, 78
Partido Nacionalista (National party), 76, 77, 78, 79, 89, 91, 92, 134, 150, 178, 203(*n*4), 204(*n*1)
Pascual, R. R., 102
pasyon (religious epic), 35
Patanne, E. P., 105

patriotism, 49, 102
peace, 55, 62, 75, 85, 86, 100, 123, 135, 139, 156, 188
Pearl Habour, 104, 201(*n*6)
peasant(s), 37, 60, 138, 154
  agitation, 139, 203(*n*4)
  class, 99, 101, 205(*n*9)
  landlessness, 154
  movement, 92, 110, 133, 134, 135, 136, 137, 205(*n*10), 205(*n*2)
  rebellion/unrest/uprising, 99, 131, 132, 135, 142, 205(*n*9)
Pease, D. E., 26, 41
Pentecost, G. F., 50
People Power, 178–83, 184
  ambivalence, 28, 167
  discourse/narrative, 28, 167, 170, 174, 175, 182, 183
  and middle class, xii, 166–7, 173, 177, 181, 182, 183
  notion, 177
  revolutions, viii, x, 28, 125, 150, 152, 165, 166, 167, 172, 173, 174, 175, 176, 177, 182, 185, 200(*n*6)
People Power 1, 180, 181, 193
People Power 2, 177, 181, 182–3, 193, 207(*n*10)
People Power 3, 183, 193, 207(*n*10)
Pertierra, A. C., 207(*n*8)
Philippine Civic Organization, 145
Philippine Rehabilitation Act, 127
Philippine Trade Act *see* Bell Trade Act
Philippine–American War, 34, 48, 69, 89, 140
Philippines:
  agrarian issue, 92, 99, 101, 131, 137–8
  American colonialism, 21, 26, 33, 34, 40, 50, 56, 58–9, 105, 116
  anti-American sentiment, 74, 90, 91, 96, 140, 147–8, 149, 151, 168
  anti-nuclear position, 169, 207(*n*4)
  Assembly, 65, 66, 67, 74, 76, 77, 78, 81, 87, 88, 89, 95, 98, 99, 101, 106, 202–3(*n*14)
  Chamber of Commerce, 90, 145
  Commission(s), 51, 52, 53, 60, 61, 63, 64, 66, 67, 97, 203(*n*14)
  Committee on Education, Arts, and Culture, 174
  Congress, ix, 7, 8, 45, 55, 59, 64, 85, 88, 95, 125, 127, 128, 129,

234 | Index

Philippines: Congress *(continued)*
  134, 141, 150, 152, 154, 181, 187, 203(*n*1), 206(*n*4)
 Constitution, 59, 125–6, 128, 129, 135, 144, 153, 158, 161, 166, 169, 175, 186, 203(*n*1), 207(*n*4), 207(*n*7)
 Declaration of Independence, 26
 Department of Education, Culture and Sports (DECS), 174
 elections, xi, 1, 2, 74, 76, 78, 94, 95, 110, 115, 120, 121, 123, 124, 125, 130, 134, 139, 142, 151–2, 160, 161, 162, 164, 175, 176, 177, 178, 181, 184, 185, 186, 188, 191, 193, 199(*n*1), 199(*n*6), 203(*n*14), 204(*n*1), 205(*n*9), 206(*n*4), 206–7(*n*3)
 House of Representatives, 134, 166, 181
 Independence Act, 203(*n*3)
 Independence Day, ix, 117, 118, 170
 Independence Day Rally, ix, x
 independence struggle, 73, 75–94, 100, 116–9
 "Magnificent 12", 172, 179
 military casualties, 201(*n*1)
 moral restoration project, 173–7
 nation, 20, 29, 33, 63, 116, 146, 147, 159, 174
 national democratic movement, xii, 154
 national identity, 63, 82, 146, 147, 151, 168, 186
 National Information Board, 99
 National Referendum, 127
 National Treasury, 151
 nationalist project, 147–52
 new Republic, 114, 122, 126, 131, 143 *see also* republic
 oligarchy, 10, 108, 143, 175, 191, 197
 plebiscites, 128, 129, 130, 161
 post-independence, 105, 118, 119, 122, 123, 131, 139, 143, 149
 pro-American sentiment, 127–9, 139, 170, 203(*n*1)
 public discourse, 3, 111, 120, 132
 republic, viii, 33, 45, 47, 48, 53, 64, 79, 100, 106, 114, 122, 126, 131, 136, 143, 150, 153, 156, 181, 203(*n*1), 204(*n*1) *see also* New Republic
 revolution, 26, 33, 37, 38, 60, 61, 64, 74, 83, 99, 119, 136, 145, 148, 149, 155, 156, 157, 179, 201(*n*4), 205(*n*2), 206(*n*4), 207(*n*3) *see also* People Power revolution
 revolution (unfinished), xi, 146, 150, 171, 179, 182, 205(*n*2), 206(*n*3)
 Senate, xi, 66, 91, 93, 97, 125, 127, 129, 151, 162, 169, 170, 171, 172, 174, 175, 178, 203(*n*14), 207(*n*7)
 society, 9, 10, 20, 27, 35, 36, 60, 78, 107, 133, 149, 153, 155, 157, 200(*n*7)
 and US, xiii, 5, 26, 28, 60, 74, 100, 140–3, 165–6, 168, 172, 186, 193, 202(*n*8), 202(*n*9), 207(*n*5), 207(*n*6)
 US military bases agreement fallout, 169–72, 179
 violence (state), 135, 136, 137, 178, 185
Philippines Free Press, 25, 27, 99, 109, 110, 111, 112, 115, 117, 120, 122, 123, 124, 127, 128, 129, 130, 132, 136, 137, 138, 139, 141, 204(*n*3), 204(*n*4)
Philippines Sugar Estates Development Company, 85
Pinches, M., xii, 108, 145, 155, 161, 163, 166, 167, 168, 172, 200(*n*8)
Poland, 1
political:
 agency, 43, 148, 166
 authority, 150, 188
 beliefs, 6, 11, 14, 192
 elite(s), 27, 74, 89, 97, 103, 108, 120, 131, 150, 155, 166, 168, 174, 191, 195
 freedom, 29, 39, 93
 imaginary/ies, 18, 19, 35
 independence, xiii, 39, 62
 orientation(s), 15, 17, 25
 subject(s), xiii, 17, 59, 111
 subjectivity/ies, 11, 15, 16–17, 23, 190, 194
 system, 7, 8, 12, 64, 132, 145, 152, 166, 175, 205(*n*2)
Pontalis, J. B. 6
Popular Front, 205(*n*9)
populism, 186, 196–8, 208(*n*1)

populist:
    and ambivalence, 177–8, 196
    discourse, 178, 179
    leaders, 1, 196, 197
    narrative(s), 146, 196, 197
    nationalism, 149–52, 186
Porter, C., 107
postcolonial:
    democratic imaginings, 192
    history of the present, 20–3
    and middle class, 15, 27, 192
    perceptions of self, 193
    scholarship, 21, 23
    society/ies, 3, 20, 193
poverty, xii, 43, 93, 101, 157, 175, 176, 177, 179, 185, 205(*n*10)
power abuse, xiii, 23, 188, 194
progress, xii, 1, 11, 13, 22, 36, 37, 38, 50, 53, 56, 80, 81, 101, 102, 112, 114, 115, 116, 121, 129, 139, 149, 181, 203(*n*1)
Propaganda Movement, 37–8, 61
Protestant Church, 43
public sphere, 16, 19, 108, 141, 174, 178, 188
    post-war, 108–31
Puerto Rico, 41, 202(*n*8), 202(*n*9)

Q
Quezon, M., 78, 79, 89, 91, 92, 95, 96, 97–103, 140, 149, 155–6, 175, 186, 203(*n*4), 204(*n*1)
Quimpan, 204(*n*4)
Quimpo, N. G., 164, 206(*n*4), 207(*n*3)
Quirino, E. (President), 140, 141, 142

R
racism/racist/racial, 16, 33, 36, 42, 44, 47, 49, 50, 52, 53, 63, 80, 90, 91, 93
Rafael, V. L., 39, 59, 60, 61, 63, 166, 181, 183
Ramos, B., 91–2, 94, 95, 96
rationality, 25, 30, 47, 52
Reagan, R., 161, 164, 166
rebellion, 38, 74, 86, 132, 135, 136, 142, 149, 151, 152, 183
Recto, C., 147, 150
reform(s) (noun), xi, 25, 37, 95, 96, 136, 139, 140, 141, 142, 147, 156, 177, 179, 184, 186, 191
religion, 29, 37, 39, 42, 44, 155

representation(s), 16, 19, 21, 22, 34, 37, 82–8, 116, 137, 193
repression, 38, 134, 136, 186
republicanism, 42, 43
resources, 14, 16, 73, 125, 126, 127, 162
responsibility/ies, 51, 54, 55, 66, 68, 79, 88, 116, 121, 140, 184
Revolutionary Society, 38, 39
Reyes Jr, R., ix–x
Richardson, J. J. 11, 192, 200(*n*9)
Rivera, T. C., 10, 200(*n*8)
Rizal, J., 36, 37, 38, 39, 61, 62, 63, 90, 92, 113, 119, 121, 149, 172, 201(*n*3), 202(*n*7)
Robertson, J., 60
Rockefeller, J. D., 42
Roosevelt, T., 53, 54, 61, 65, 77, 88, 101, 207(*n*6)
Roxas, G., 160
Roxas, M., 89, 93, 104, 106, 127, 134, 135, 136, 137, 204(*n*1)
Rueschemeyer, D., 14
rule of law, 188, 206(*n*7)
Russell, C. E., 69
Russia, 57, 139, 144, 193

S
Saar, M., 23, 24
Said, E. W., 5, 21, 52, 108
Saigon, 142
Sakay, M., 64
Sakdal, 92, 95
Sakdalista Party, 94, 95–6
Sakdalistas, 91–6, 97, 98–9, 100, 134, 197
Salamanca, B. S., 67, 75, 76, 77, 78, 79, 98, 202(*n*13)
Salonga, J. R., 96, 104, 105, 125, 127, 151, 152, 153, 154, 155, 156–7, 160–1, 168, 170–2, 207(*n*6), 207(*n*7)
salvation, 34, 51, 115, 195
Samoan Islands, 202(*n*6)
San Fernando, 107, 139
San Francisco, 77, 82
San Juan, 36–7, 178, 202(*n*7)
San Juan (location), 178
Sanchez, L. 118
Satoshi, N. 108, 142, 147
savagery, 52, 53, 54, 63
Scarano, F. A., 26, 41, 59, 60
Schaffer, F. C., 9, 18

Schmidt, P., 21
Schramm, K., 17
Scott, J., 29
Second World War, 13, 26, 40, 103, 106, 131, 159, 204(*n*2), 207(*n*6)
sedition, 86, 88, 96
Sedition Law, 73–4, 87, 99
Segovia, R. E., 162, 177
self-control, 43, 51
self-determination, 70, 153
shame, 121, 122, 143, 152, 156
Shin, D. C., 9, 199(*n*4)
Shiraishi, T., xii
Sidel, J. T., 4
Silen, R., 138
Singapore, 10
Singh, A., 21
Singson, L., 180
Sison, J. M., 151, 206(*n*4)
Slater, D., 12, 200–1(*n*12)
Snyder, R., 15
Social Democrats (Socdems), 154, 155, 162, 206(*n*8)
Social Weather Station (SWS), 200(*n*7)
socialism, 206(*n*7)
Socialist Party, 203(*n*4)
solidarity, 20, 179, 185, 193
South Korea, 159
South Vietnam, 142, 150
Southall, R., 15
Southeast Asia, 37, 40, 204(*n*2), 207(*n*6)
sovereignty, ix, xii, 5, 20, 49, 54, 55, 64, 68, 73, 75, 81, 87, 89, 93, 94, 97, 104, 105, 106, 125, 127, 128, 129, 143, 147, 150, 162, 168, 169, 170, 172, 187, 192, 193, 197
Spain:
  authority/ies 38, 45, 80
  Catholicism, xiii, 34–5
  colonialism, 26, 29, 33, 34–5, 37, 38, 44, 45, 52, 54, 58, 60, 61, 83, 84, 90, 101, 139, 202(*n*7)
  revolution against, 37, 38, 62, 201(*n*4), 203(*n*1)
  and US, 46, 47, 48, 55, 56, 61, 80, 202(*n*8)
Spanish–American War, 42, 44, 45, 47
Spivak, G. C., 13, 21
Spooner, J. C., 54
Stalin, 153
Stanford University, 106
Stauffer, R. B., 165

Stephens, J. D., 14
Stephens Huber, E., 14
Stobbe, L., 21, 108
Stoler, A-L., 5, 21, 23, 24, 26, 72, 89, 108, 190
Stone, M. E., 56
Stovall, T., 13
Subic Bay, 169, 207(*n*6)
subjugation, xi, xiii, 11, 26, 37, 39, 55, 61, 66, 67, 70, 81, 89, 92, 98, 103, 136, 186
Suez Canal, 35
Suri, J., 5
Suyko, D., 124

T
Taft, W. H., 61, 63, 65, 67, 74, 75, 76, 77, 79, 82, 88, 203(*n*1)
Tagalog, 38, 39, 179, 201(*n*5)
Tan, D. M. 106, 205(*n*9)
Taruc, L., 134, 135, 136, 137, 140
Taruc, P., 132
Tayabas, 78, 99
Terami-Wada, M., 74, 90, 91, 92, 93, 94, 95, 96
Thailand, 180
The Financial Times, 180
The Tribune, 92
theory of democratic culture, 200(*n*10)
theory of Partyless Democracy, 102, 103, 155–6
Thompson, M., 174, 184
Time, 142, 206(*n*5)
Tobera, F., 90, 91
Tocqueville, A., 41, 42, 194
Tokyo, 104
Tormey, S., 197
torture, 34, 53, 162
Totanes, S. H. S., 151, 152
trade, 34, 35, 56, 93, 105, 125, 126, 151, 155, 161, 170
tradition(s), 19, 38, 41, 119, 148, 165, 202(*n*7)
Treaty of Paris, 46, 48, 55, 202(*n*8), 202(*n*11)
Treyes, A. A., 118
Truman, H., 136, 140
Trump, D., 1, 197
Turin Santiago, J., 86–7, 88
Turkey, 57
Turner, M., 10, 200(*n*7)
Tutay, F. V., 205(*n*10)
Ty, L., 139

Tydings-McDuffie Act, 95, 203(*n*3)
Twain, M., 32, 48, 49, 69
tyranny, 28, 54, 58, 148, 176

U
union movement, 44, 203(*n*4)
United Front, 134, 205(*n*9)
United Kingdom, 12, 13, 45, 90, 51, 202(*n*7)
University of Michigan, 60
University of Paris, 203(*n*1)
University of the Philippines, x, 62, 90, 145, 151, 157, 179, 205–6(*n*3)
University of Santo Tomas, 38
University of Sydney, xiv
Urbinati, N., 30
US (United States):
  Anti-Imperialist League, 47, 48, 56
  Bacon Amendment, 47, 48
  benevolent assimilation, 55, 59, 63, 69, 97
  benevolent empire narrative, 26, 33
  Chamber of Commerce, 66, 90, 160
  colonial project, 5, 22, 39, 58, 59, 60, 62, 63, 75, 83, 114, 121, 150, 165, 188, 192
  Congress, 44, 45, 55, 66, 77, 78, 82, 85, 87, 88, 89, 94, 95, 97, 125, 128
  Constitution, 48, 106
  Declaration of Independence, 42, 54, 98, 106
  democratic discourse, viii, 75, 83, 103, 106, 165
  Divine mandate, 50–1
  economic concessions, 125, 128
  exceptionalism, 26, 41–2, 44, 46, 50
  foreign policy, 22, 33, 44, 47, 54
  House of Representatives, 78
  imperial rule (Philippines), 4–5, 20–1, 26–7, 33, 41
  imperialism debate, 46–9, 202(*n*9)
  Independence Day, 98
  Indian Wars, 42
  influence over Philippines, 124–5, 172, 190
  intervention, xiii, 5, 26, 28, 60, 74, 100, 140–3, 165–6, 168, 186, 193, 207(*n*5), 207(*n*6)
  knowledge production, 12, 22, 34, 51–2, 59, 60, 63
  manifest destiny, 41–4
  military, ix, 59, 172

  national identity, 41, 43, 44
  Philippine annexation, 22, 34, 46–7, 49, 50, 54, 123, 202(*n*10)
  policy towards Philippines, 26, 50, 58, 63–70, 80–3, 89, 97, 192, 202(*n*9)
  Senate, 46, 51, 65, 66, 201(*n*6)
  strategies to control independence, 63–70
  violence, 5, 22, 26, 34, 51, 53, 55, 90, 137
  white man's burden, 26, 51
United States Army Forces in the Far East (USAFFE), 104, 133, 205(*n*8)
Usul, A. R., 147, 159, 206(*n*7)

V
Van Meter, H. H., 46, 56, 57, 58, 69
Vance, C., 160
Vancouver, 48
Velarde Jr, H., 122
Velasco, R. S., 9, 10
Vietnam, 142, 151
Vietnam War, 151
Vilamin, V., 139
Villa Jr, J., 122
Villegas, C. M., 162, 167
Virata, L., 145
Virginia, 54
Visayas, 78, 134

W
Wall Street crash, 89
Warsaw, 105
Washington DC, 34, 46, 47, 48, 64, 66, 78, 79, 91, 93, 94, 119, 122, 124, 126, 136, 140, 141, 159, 164, 169, 207(*n*5)
Watsonville, 90, 91
wealth, 42, 43, 44, 45, 102, 114, 180, 205(*n*9)
Webb, A., 196
Weber, M., 16
Weyler regime, 57
Weinstein, B., 14, 16
Welzel, C., 200(*n*10)
Werbner, R., 17
White House, 151, 159
Whitehead, L., 19
Williams, E., 122–3
Wilson, W., 66, 98
Wood, L., 67
Worcester, D. C., 53, 60

working class, 14, 74, 145, 205(*n*9)
World Bank, 160
Wurfel, D., 173

Y
Yang, M., 162, 167

Z
Zhu, Y., 4, 199(*n*4)
Ziforun, D., 200(*n*11)
Zwick, J., 48, 49

9781789760439